DID YOU KNOW?

- Hundreds of plant-based flavonoids have been identified and many can be used as natural estrogens and antioxidants

- No-fat foods can make you gain weight

- The phytochemical lutein has been shown in studies to be a more powerful antioxidant than beta-carotene

- Studies show that some soybean products are effective in inhibiting the growth of breast and prostate cancers as well as alleviating the discomfort of menopause

- Low potassium levels can cause caffeine cravings and a "sweet tooth"

- Magnesium is an aide in fighting depression and preventing heart attacks

- Not only are antioxidants good for humans, but many are essential to your pets' good health

- Vitamin B6, folic acid, and vitamin B12 can save your life.

UP-TO-DATE AND COMPREHENSIVE, EVERYTHING
YOU'VE EVER WANTED TO KNOW ABOUT
VITAMINS, HEALTH AIDES, THERAPIES, AND
SUPPLEMENTS IS IN

EARL MINDELL'S VITAMIN BIBLE
FOR THE TWENTY-FIRST CENTURY

Also by Earl Mindell

Earl Mindell's Shaping Up With Vitamins
Safe Eating

Published by
WARNER BOOKS

EARL MINDELL'S

VITAMIN BIBLE

FOR THE 21ST

CENTURY

WARNER BOOKS

A Time Warner Company

WARNER BOOKS EDITION

Cover photo by Don Banks
Cover design by Anne Twomey

Warner Books, Inc.
1271 Avenue of the Americas
New York, N.Y. 10020

Visit our Web site at
www.warnerbooks.com

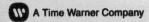 A Time Warner Company

Printed in the United States of America

First Printing: May, 1999

10 9 8 7 6 5 4 3 2 1

This book is dedicated to
GAIL, ALANNA, EVAN,
our parents, families, and friends
and to
the future

The first wealth is health.

Ralph Waldo Emerson
"The Conduct of Life"

Acknowledgments

I wish to express my deep and lasting appreciation to my friends and associates who have assisted me in the preparation of this book since its first publication, especially J. Kenney, Ph.D.; Linus Pauling, Ph.D.; Harold Segal, Ph.D.; Bernard Bubman, R.Ph.; Mel Rich, R.Ph.; Sal Messineo, Pharm. D.; Arnold Fox, M.D.; Dennis Huddleson, M.D.; Stuart Fisher, M.D.; Robert Mendelson, M.D.; Gershon Lesser, M.D.; David Velkoff, M.D.; Rory Jaffee, M.D.; Vickie Hufnagel, M.D.; Donald Cruden, O.D.; Joel Strom, D.D.S.; Nathan Sperling, D.D.S.; Ray Faltinsky; Kevin Fournier; Rick Handel; Linda Chae; Finn Jegard; Morten Weidner, Ph.D.; Peter Mallory; Teri Cox; Carol Coleman Gerber; and Hester Mundis.

I would also like to thank the Nutrition Foundation; the International College of Applied Nutrition; the American Medical Association; the American Pharmaceutical Association; the New York Blood Center; the American Academy of Pediatrics; the American Dietetic Association; the National Academy of Sciences; the National Dairy Council; the Society for Nutrition Education; the United Fresh Fruit and Vegetable Association; the Albany College of Pharmacy; Edward Leavitt, D.V.M.; Jane Bicks, D.V.M.; Betty Haskins; Shelby Zoad; Jim Zeeperman; Stephanie Marco; Susan Towlson; Ronald Borenstein; Laura Borenstein; Glenn Williams; Eleanor Rawson; and Richard Curtis, without whom a project of this scope could never have been completed.

Contents

(1) Why I did—(2) What vitamins are—(3) What
vitamins are not—(4) How they work—(5) Should you
take supplements?—(6) What are nutrients?—(7) The
difference between micronutrients and macronutrients—
(8) How nutrients get to work—(9) Understanding your
digestive system—(10) Name that vitamin—(11) Name
that mineral—(12) Your body needs togetherness—(13)
Name that antioxidant—(14) Name that alternative
therapy—(15) Eye-opening nutrition facts—(16) Any
questions about chapter I?

(17) Where vitamins come from—(18) Why vitamins
come in different forms—(19) Oil vs. dry or water
soluble—(20) Synthetic vs. natural and inorganic vs.
organic—(21) Chelation, and what it means—(22) Time
release—(23) Fillers, binders, or what else am I
getting?—(24) Storage and staying power—(25) When
and how to take supplements—(26) What's right for
you—(27) Any questions about chapter II?

sources of primary antioxidant vitamins and minerals—
(340) Big-time immune system boosters—(341) Quick
reference cancer defense guide

A Note to the Reader About This Revised Millennium Edition

There is no longer any doubt that numerous life-threatening diseases can be prevented and chronic illnesses alleviated, possibly cured, through optimal nutrition. There is also no longer any doubt that it is easier, cheaper, quicker, and smarter to prevent an illness than to treat it—and that the person who can do the most for your health is you!

For two decades, *The Vitamin Bible*—with its now well-known numbered sections for instant cross-reference—has been relied on by millions of people around the world as the easily accessed source of clear, uncomplicated nutritional information. Since its last revision, the world of vitamins and supplements has mushroomed, making hundreds of new products available and opening up exciting nutritional options for self-health. My goal in this fully revised millennium edition is to empower *you* to make the most of them!

I've added new personalized regimens and updated others with the latest available supplements—including nutraceuticals, which have been shown to provide effective medical health benefits in the treatment of a wide variety of common ailments and diseases. (There is also an at-a-glance reference chapter to simplify your selection of these new supplements.) Along with bringing the guidelines and cautions for all vitamins and minerals up to date, based on recent nutritional and medical studies, I've added more than three dozen sections to the book to cover phytochemicals, plant hormones, necessary antioxidants, the soy phenomenon, and the latest in natural alternatives to prescription drugs. I've greatly expanded the herb sections and added homeopathic remedies as well as a guide to aromatherapy and essential oils. In addition, the chapter on locating alternative and nutritionally oriented health practitioners now includes web sites, enabling readers worldwide to benefit from it.

Because this is not the sort of book that is generally read cover-to-cover, I suggest that you make it a point to check out the "questions" section at the end of the chapters. Much new information appears there—including the latest on preventing osteoporosis, treating carpal tunnel syndrome, protecting yourself against cancer, invigorating your sex life, and more.

ONE IMPORTANT REMINDER

The regimens throughout this book are recommendations, not prescriptions, and are not intended as medical advice. Before starting any new program, check with your physician or a nutritionally oriented doctor (see section 342), especially if you have a specific physical problem or are taking any medication.

Preface

This book is written for *you*—the untold legions of men and women who are forever trying to fit yourselves into statistical norms only to find that the charts are designed for some mythical average person who is taller, shorter, fatter, skinnier, less or more active than you'll ever be. It is a guide to healthy living for individuals, not statistics. Wherever feasible I have given personal advice. For this, I believe, is the only way to lead anyone to optimal health, which is the purpose of this book.

In these pages I have combined my knowledge of pharmacy with that of nutrition to best explain the confusing, often dangerous, interrelation of drugs and vitamins. I've attempted to personalize and be specific so as to eliminate much of the confusion abut vitamins that has arisen with generalizations.

In using the book you will occasionally find that your vitamin needs fall into several different categories. In this case, let common sense dictate the necessary adjustment. (If you are already taking B6, for example, there's no need to double up on it unless a higher dosage is called for.)

The recommendations I've made are not meant to be prescriptive but can easily be used as flexible programs when working with your doctor. No book can substitute for professional care.

It is my sincere hope that I have provided you with information that will help you attain the longest, happiest, and healthiest of lives.

EARL L. MINDELL, R.PH., PH.D.

I

Getting into Vitamins

1. Why I Did

My professional education was strictly establishment when it came to vitamins. My courses in pharmacology, biochemistry, organic and inorganic chemistry, and public health hardly dealt with vitamins at all—except in relation to deficiency diseases. Lack of vitamin C? Scurvy. Out of B1? Beriberi. Not enough vitamin D? Rickets. My courses were the standard fare, with the usual references to a balanced diet and eating the "right foods" (all unappetizingly illustrated on semiglossy charts).

There were no references to vitamins being used for disease prevention or as ways to optimum health.

> Both of us were working fifteen hours a day,
> but only *I* looked and felt it.

In 1965 I opened my first pharmacy. Until then I never realized just how many drugs people were taking, not for illness but simply to get through the day. (I had one regular patron who had prescriptions for pills to supplant virtually all his bodily functions—and he wasn't even sick!) My partner at the time was very vitamin-oriented. Both of us were working fifteen hours a day, but only *I* looked and felt it. When I asked him what his secret was, he said it was not secret at

1

all. It was vitamins. I realized what he was talking about had very little to do with scurvy and beriberi and a lot to do with me. I instantly became an eager pupil, and have never since regretted it. He taught me the benefits that could be reaped from nature's own foods in the form of vitamins, how B complex and C could alleviate stress, how vitamin E would increase my endurance and stamina, and how B12 could eliminate fatigue. After embarking on the most elementary vitamin regimens I was not only convinced. I was converted.

Suddenly nutrition became the most important thing in my life. I read every book I could find on the subject, clipped articles and tracked down their sources, dug out my pharmacy school texts and discovered the amazingly close relationship that did indeed exist between biochemistry and nutrition. I attended any health lecture I could. In fact, it was at one such lecture that I learned of the RNA-DNA nucleic complex and its age-reversing properties. (I have been taking RNA-DNA supplements since then, as well as SOD—superoxide dismutase. Today, because of these, most people guess me to be five to ten years younger than I am.) I was excited about each new discovery in the field, and it showed.

A whole new world had opened up for me and I wanted others to share it. My partner understood completely. We began giving out samples of B complex and B12 tablets to patrons, suggesting they try decreasing their dependency on tranquilizers, pep pills, and sedatives with the vitamins and vitamin-rich foods.

The results were remarkable! People kept coming back to tell us how much better and more energetic they felt. Instead of the negativity and resignation that often accompanies drug therapies, we received overwhelming positiveness. I saw a woman who had spent nearly all her young adult life on Librium, running from doctor to therapist and back again, become a healthy, happy, drug-free human being; a sixty-year-old architect, on the brink of retirement because of ill health, regain his well-being and accept a commission for what is now one of the foremost office buildings in Los Angeles; a middle-aged pill-dependent actor kick his habit and land a sought-after supporting role in a TV series that still nets him handsome residuals.

By 1970 I was totally committed to nutrition and preventive medicine. Seeing the paucity of knowledge in the area, I went into partnership with another pharmacist for the prime purpose of making natural vitamins and accurate nutrition information available to the public.

Today, as a nutritionist, lecturer, and author, I'm still excited about that world that opened up to me over thirty years ago—a world that continues to grow with new discoveries daily—and I'm eager to share it.

2. What Vitamins Are

> We must obtain vitamins from natural foods, or dietary supplements in order to sustain life.

When I mention the word *vitamin*, most people think *pill*. Thinking *pill* brings to mind confusing images of medicine and drugs. Though vitamins can and certainly often do the work of both medicine and drugs, they are neither.

• Quite simply, vitamins are organic substances necessary for life. Vitamins are essential to the normal functioning of our bodies and, save for a few exceptions, cannot be manufactured or synthesized internally. Necessary for our growth, vitality, and general well-being, they are found in minute quantities in all natural food. We must obtain vitamins from these foods or from dietary supplements.

What you have to keep in mind is that supplements, which are available in tablet, capsule, liquid, powder, spray, patch, and injection forms, are still just food substances, and, unless synthetic, are also derived from living plants and animals.

• It is impossible to sustain life without *all* the essential vitamins.

3. What Vitamins Are Not

> Vitamins are neither pep pills nor
> substitutes for food.

A lot of people think vitamins can replace food. They cannot. In fact, vitamins cannot be assimilated without ingesting food. There are a lot of erroneous beliefs about vitamins, and I hope this book can clear up most of them.

• Vitamins are not pep pills and have no caloric or energy value of their own.
• Vitamins are not substitutes for protein or for any other nutrients, such as minerals, fats, carbohydrates, water—or even for each other!
• Vitamins themselves are not the components of our body structures.
• You cannot take vitamins, stop eating, and expect to be healthy.

4. How They Work

If you think of the body as an automobile's combustion engine and vitamins as spark plugs, you have a fairly good idea of how these amazing minute food substances work for us.

> Vitamins regulate our metabolism through
> enzyme systems. A single deficiency can
> endanger the whole body.

Vitamins are components of our enzyme systems which, acting like spark plugs, energize and regulate our metabolism, keeping us tuned up and functioning at high performance.

Compared with our intake of other nutrients like proteins, fats, and carbohydrates, our vitamin intake (even on some megadose regimens) is minuscule. But a deficiency in even one vitamin can endanger the whole human body.

5. Should You Take Supplements?

> "Everyone who has in the past eaten
> sugar, white flour, or canned food has
> some deficiency disease. . . ."

Since vitamins occur in all organic material, some containing more of one vitamin than another and in greater or lesser amounts, you could say that if you ate the "right" foods in a well-balanced diet, you would get all the vitamins you need. And you would probably be right. The problem is, very few of us are able to arrange this mythical diet. According to Dr. Daniel T. Quigley, author of *The National Malnutrition*, "Everyone who has in the past eaten processed sugar, white flour, or canned food has some deficiency disease, the extent of the disease depending on the percentage of such deficient food in the diet."

Because most restaurants tend to reheat food or keep it warm under heat lamps, if you frequently eat out you run the risk of vitamin A, B1, and C deficiencies. (And if you're a woman between the ages of 13 and 40, this sort of work-saving dining is likely to cost you invaluable calcium and iron.)

Most of the foods we eat have been processed and depleted in nutrients. Take breads and cereals, for example. Practically all of them you find in today's supermarkets are high in nothing but carbohydrates. "But they are enriched!" you say. It's written right on the label: *Enriched*.

Enriched? Enrichment means replacing nutrients in foods

that once contained them but because of heat, storage, and so forth no longer do. Foods, therefore, are "enriched" to the levels found in the natural product before processing. Unfortunately, standards of enrichment leave much to be desired nutritionally. For example, the standard of enrichment for white flour is to replace the twenty-two natural nutrients that are removed with three B vitamins, vitamin D, calcium, and iron salts. Now really, for the staff of life, that seems a pretty flimsy stick.

I think you can see why my feeling about taking supplements is clear.

6. What Are Nutrients?

They're more than vitamins, though people often think they are the same thing.

Six important nutrients

Carbohydrates, proteins (which are made up of amino acids*), fats, minerals, vitamins, and water are all nutrients—absorbable components of foods—and necessary for good health. Nutrients are necessary for energy, organ function, food utilization, and cell growth.

7. The Difference Between Micronutrients and Macronutrients

Micronutrients, like vitamins and minerals, do not themselves provide energy. The macronutrients—carbohydrates, fat, and protein—do that, but only when there are sufficient micronutrients to release them.

*See section 72

> With nutrients, *less* is often the
> same as *more*.

The amount of micronutrients and macronutrients you need for proper health is vastly different—but each is important. (See section 72 for The Protein–Amino Acid Connection.)

8. How Nutrients Get to Work

> The body simplifies nutrients in
> order to utilize them.

Nutrients basically work through digestion. Digestion is a process of continuous chemical simplification of materials that enter the body through the mouth. Materials are split by enzymatic action into smaller and simpler chemical fragments, which can then be absorbed through walls of the digestive tract—an open-ended muscular tube, more than thirty feet long, which passes through the body—and finally enter the bloodstream.

9. Understanding Your Digestive System

Knowing how your digestive system works will clear up, right at the start, some of the more common confusions about how, when, and where nutrients operate.

Mouth and Esophagus
Digestion begins in the mouth with the grinding of food and a mixture of saliva. An enzyme called ptyalin in the saliva already begins to split starches into simple sugars. The food is then forced to the back of the mouth and into the esophagus, or gullet. Here is where peristalsis begins. This is a kneading "milking" constriction and relaxation of muscles that propels material through the digestive system. To pre-

vent backflow of materials, and to time the release of proper enzymes—since one enzyme cannot do another enzyme's work—the digestive tract is equipped with valves at important junctions.

The tiny valve at the end of your esophagus opens long enough for chewed-up particles to enter the stomach. Occasionally, especially after eating, this valve relaxes—which is what enables you to belch. But a relaxed valve can also allow the acid from your stomach to be pushed back up into the esophagus, causing what's known as gastroesophageal reflux disease (GERD)—better known to those who experience it as heartburn. (See section 228.)

Stomach
This is the biggest bulge in the digestive tract, as most of us are well aware. But it is located higher than you might think, lying mainly behind the lower ribs, not under the navel, and it does not occupy the belly. It is a flexible bag enclosed by restless muscles, constantly changing form.

• Virtually nothing is absorbed through the stomach walls except alcohol.

> An ordinary meal leaves the stomach
> in three to five hours.

Watery substances, such as soup, leave the stomach quite rapidly. Fats remain considerably longer. An ordinary meal of carbohydrates, proteins, and fats is emptied from the average stomach in *three* to *five* hours. Stomach glands and specialized cells produce mucus, enzymes, hydrochloric acid, and a factor that enables vitamin B12 to be dissolved through intestinal walls into the circulation. A normal stomach is definitely on the acid side, and gastric juice, the stomach's special blend, consists of many substances:

Pepsin   The predominant stomach enzyme, a potent digester of meats and other proteins. It is active only in an acid medium.

Rennin   Curdles milk.

HCl (Hydrochloric Acid)   Produced by stomach cells and creates an acidic state.

The stomach is not absolutely indispensable to digestion. Most of the process of digestion occurs beyond it.

Small Intestine

> Virtually all absorption of nutrients
> occurs in the small intestine.

Twenty-two feet long, here is where digestion is completed and virtually all absorption of nutrients occurs. It has an alkaline environment, brought about by highly alkaline bile, pancreatic juice, and secretions of the intestinal walls. The alkaline environment is necessary for the most important work of digestion and absorption. The *duodenum,* which begins at the stomach outlet, is the first part of the small intestine. This joins with the *jejunum* (about ten feet long), which joins with the *ileum* (ten to twelve feet long). When semiliquid contents of the small intestine are moved along by peristaltic action, we often say we hear our stomach "talking." Actually our stomach lies above these rumblings (called borborygmi), but even with the truth known it's doubtful the phrase will change.

Large Intestine (Colon)

> It takes twelve to fourteen hours for
> contents to make the circuit of the large intestine.

Any material leaving the ileum and entering the cecum (where the small and large intestine join) is quite watery. Backflow is prevented at this junction by a muscular valve.

Very little is absorbed from the large intestine except water.

The colon is primarily a storage and dehydrating organ. Substances entering in a liquid state become semisolid as water is absorbed. It takes twelve to fourteen hours for contents to make the circuit of the intestine.

The colon, in contrast to a germ-free stomach, is lavishly populated with bacteria, normal intestinal flora. A large part of the feces is composed of bacteria, along with indigestible material, chiefly cellulose, and substances eliminated from the blood and shed from the intestinal walls.

Liver

The main storage organ for
fat-soluble vitamins.

The liver is the largest solid organ of the body and weighs about four pounds. It is an incomparable chemical plant. It can modify almost any chemical structure. It is a powerful detoxifying organ, breaking down a variety of toxic molecules and rendering them harmless. It is also a blood reservoir and a storage organ for vitamins such as A and D and for digested carbohydrate (glycogen), which is released to sustain blood sugar levels. It manufactures enzymes, cholesterol, proteins, vitamin A (from carotene), and blood coagulation factors.

One of the prime functions of the liver is to produce bile. Bile contains salts that promote efficient digestion of fats by detergent action, emulsifying fatty materials.

Gallbladder

> Even the sight of food may empty
> the gallbladder.

This is a saclike storage organ about three inches long. It holds bile, modifies it chemically, and concentrates it tenfold. The taste or sometimes even the sight of food may be sufficient to empty it out. Constituents of gallbladder fluids sometimes crystallize and form gallstones.

Pancreas

> The pancreas provides the body's most
> important enzymes.

This gland is about six inches long and is nestled into the curve of the duodenum. Its cell clusters secrete insulin, which accelerates the burning of sugar in the body. Insulin is secreted into the blood, not the digestive tract. The larger part of the pancreas manufactures and secretes pancreatic juice, which contains some of the body's most important digestive enzymes—*lipases,* which split fats; *proteases,* which split protein; and *amylases,* which split starches.

10. Name That Vitamin

Because at one time no one knew the chemical structure of vitamins and therefore could not give them a proper scientific name, most are designated by a letter of the alphabet. The following vitamins are known today; many more may yet be discovered.

> Known vitamins from A to U

Vitamin A (retinol, carotene); vitamin B-complex group: B (thiamine), B2 (riboflavin), B3 (niacin, niacinamide), B4 (adenine), B5 (pantothenic acid), B6 (pyridoxine), B10, B11 (growth factors), B12 (cobalamin, cyanocobalamin), B13 (orotic acid), B15 (pangamic acid), B17 (amygdalin), Bc (folic acid), Bt (carnitine), Bx or PABA (para-aminobenzoic acid); choline; inositol; C (ascorbic acid); D (calciferol, viosterol, ergosterol); E (tocopherol); F (fatty acids); G (riboflavin); H (biotin); K (menadione); L (necessary for lactation); M (folic acid); P (bioflavonoids); Pp (niacinamide); P4 (troxerutin); T (growth-promoting substances); U (extracted from cabbage juice).

11. Name That Mineral

> The top seven minerals are calcium, iodine, iron, magnesium, phosphorus, selenium, and zinc.

Although about eighteen known minerals are required for body maintenance and regulatory functions, Recommended Dietary Allowances (RDA) have only been established for seven—calcium, iodine, iron, magnesium, phosphorus, selenium, and zinc.

The active minerals in your body are calcium, chlorine, chromium, cobalt, copper, fluorine, iodine, iron, magnesium, manganese, molybdenum, phosphorus, potassium, selenium, sodium, sulfur, vanadium, and zinc. Trace minerals such as boron, silicon, nickel, and arsenic are also necessary for optimal growth and membrane function.

12. Your Body Needs Togetherness

> Vitamins alone are not enough.

As important as vitamins are, they can do nothing for you without minerals. I like to call minerals the Cinderellas of the nutrition world, because, though very few people are aware of it, vitamins cannot function and cannot be assimilated without the aid of minerals. And though the body can synthesize some vitamins, it cannot manufacture a *single* mineral.

13. Name That Antioxidant

Antioxidants (good guys) are those enzymes, amino acids, supplements, vitamins, and minerals that protect our bodies from *free radicals* (bad guys), uncontrolled oxidations that damage cells and weaken the immune system. The body generates free radicals daily simply by burning fuel for energy. In other words, they're a necessary but unwanted byproduct. Various environmental and physical stresses—from air pollution, smoking, drinking alcohol, and disease to charcoal-broiled food, old age, and vigorous exercise—generate extra free radicals. To keep free radicals in check, our bodies produce different types of natural antioxidants. The most notable among them are catalase, coenzyme-Q10, glutathione, melatonin, vitamin A, alpha- and beta-carotene, vitamin C, vitamin E, lipoic acid, selenium, superoxide dismutase (SOD), and zinc. Unfortunately, as we age, more free radicals accumulate and less natural antioxidants are produced, significantly increasing the risk of cancer and heart disease. Because of this, antioxidant-rich foods and supplements such as ginkgo biloba, grapeseed extract, green tea extract, isoflavones, lutein, lycopene, are needed in our diets, and the sooner they are included the greater the long-term benefits. (See Chapter VIII.)

14. Name That Alternative Therapy

Just as no one supplement fits all, no one alternative therapy is suited to everyone. Today, dozens of alternatives to conventional medicine are available, gaining in acceptance and evidencing remarkable results. (To locate a nutritionally oriented doctor or alternative practitioner, see section 342.) Among the better-known alternative therapies are:

Ayurveda One of the oldest recorded medical systems in the world, India's Ayurvedic medicine is still practiced in that country today. It has been dubbed the "mother of all healing" because of its profound influence on nearly all other medical systems. Ayurveda does not just treat the symptoms of a disease: the treatment must encompass the entire body—as well as mind, spirit, and lifestyle. The belief is that it's as important to keep healthy people healthy as it is to cure the sick, and that early intervention—before symptoms appear—is essential to well-being. More than two thousand different preparations are used in Ayurvedic medicine. Herbs are generally used only in combination with other herbs. In fact, Ayurvedic healers use the whole plant, as opposed to the Western concept of extracting the one or two active ingredients, because they believe that every chemical in a plant is designed to work in harmony with the body. Ayurvedic medicine is designed to bolster and support all body systems.

Acupuncture An ancient Chinese healing medicine based on the belief that a life force, *qi* (pronounced *chee*) flows through fourteen channels in the body and can be stimulated by the insertion of needles into some of the body's 360 acupuncture points to restore its energy balance. Acupuncture has been shown to have the ability in many instances to reverse temporary discomforts as well as organic disease. Acupuncturists also use herbs in healing therapies. In most states in the U.S., completion of a recognized program of study and a license to practice is required to become a doctor of acupuncture or a doctor of oriental medicine. Naturopathic doctors (N.D.s) are also licensed to practice acupuncture.

Chiropractic Chiropractic medicine focuses on spinal manipulations to achieve health. Many chiropractors (D.C.s) also practice nutritional medicine. They have had four to five years of study in an accredited chiropractic school after a minimum of two years of undergraduate school and are licensed to work in all fifty states, Australia, New Zealand, Canada, most of Europe, Africa, and the Middle East. They cannot prescribe drugs or do surgery.

Herbal Medicine   The most widely used form of medicine for thousands of years and recognized as today's leading trend in self-care. Herbal medicine is rooted in the same theory as establishment pharmacology. In fact, nearly 50 percent of all drugs commonly used and prescribed are either derived from a plant source or contain chemical imitations of a plant compound. Today, the efficacy of many herbal remedies is undisputed and well documented. (See Chapter X.)

Homeopathy   Based on the findings of Samuel Hahnemann, homeopathy uses medicines to stimulate the body's natural defense mechanisms and is based on the premise that "like cures like." For instance, a substance that can trigger symptoms in a healthy individual when taken in large doses can cure similar symptoms in a sick person when taken in extremely small doses. The homeopathic approach to treating illness—viewing the individual (mentally, physically, emotionally) as a whole—is founded on the understanding that symptoms are an expression of the body's attempt to correct an imbalance and restore health. Rather than suppressing these symptoms, homeopathic medicines (which come from naturally occurring plant, mineral, or animal substances and are nontoxic) act quickly to stimulate and regulate the body's defenses—*with no side effects when used as directed.* (See section 158.) There is no licensing at this writing for the practice of homeopathic medicine. A physician (M.D., D.O., N.D., or D.C.) can become a doctor of homeopathy (D.Ht.) after six weeks of study.

Naturopathic   Naturopathic medicine encompasses herbal medicine, massage, acupuncture, and a broad spectrum of other alternative treatments. Naturopathic doctors (N.D.s) are required to pass a national licensing exam after completing four years in a naturopathic medical college.

Orthomolecular Medicine   An alternative therapy that aims to provide optimal levels of substances normally found in the body through nutrients. Aside from using various supplements to allow the body to produce the biochemicals necessary for health, orthomolecular medicine also involves the removal of harmful substances such as drugs, pollutants, and allergens from the body. The majority, though not all, of orthomolecular practitioners are M.D.s.

Osteopathy   Osteopathic physicians (D.O.s) have the same medical education as an M.D. and are licensed to do everything an M.D. can do, including surgery. The *big* difference is that unlike traditional (allopathic) M.D.s who tend to specialize in certain diseases or organs, osteopaths are holistic in their approach to healing and, as a rule, are far better versed in preventive nutrition.

15. Eye-Opening Nutrition Facts

• One cigarette destroys 25–100 mg. of vitamin C!
• Milk with synthetic vitamin D (which means almost all store-bought milk) can rob the body of magnesium!
• People who live in smoggy cities are not getting the vitamin D that their country cousins get because the smog absorbs the sun's ultraviolet rays!
• Most elderly people are not getting enough vitamin D in their diets or just aren't making enough by not being in the sunlight.
• Daily "happy hours" of more than one cocktail can cause a depletion of vitamins B1, B6, and folic acid!
• Eighty percent of American women are deficient in calcium!
• Ten million American women take oral contraceptives and most of them are unaware that the pills can interfere with the availability of vitamins B6, B12, folic acid, and vitamin C!
• American men rank thirteenth in world health, American women sixth.
• Children need one and a half to two times more protein per pound of body weight than adults—and babies need three times more!

• Cancer researchers have found that vitamins C and E and certain chemicals called indoles, found in cabbage, brussels sprouts, and related vegetables in the crucifer family, are potent and safe inhibitors of certain carcinogens!

• Vitamin B1 can help fight air- and seasickness.

• If you're on a high-protein diet your need for B6 *increases!*

• Onions, garlic, radishes, and leeks all contain a natural antibiotic called *allicin,* which can destroy disease germs without sweeping away the friendly bacteria in the process!

• Aspirin can triple the rate of excretion of your vitamin C!

• Eighteen pecan halves can furnish an entire day's supply of vitamin F.

• Frequent consumption of foods containing artificial flavors, colors, MSG, and other additives can diminish the effectiveness of the immune system.

• Raw peanuts contain enzyme inhibitors that make it difficult for your body to digest protein.

• Bran is not a balanced food.

• Pasta packed in clear cellophane, or with large cellophane windows, is subject to nutrient loss.

• Water softeners can unhealthily increase your daily salt intake.

• A main ingredient of margarine—hydrogenated vegetable oil/trans fatty acids—is even worse for your health than the saturated fat in butter.

• Blueberries, blackberries, and red cabbage are actually better for you if cooked!

• Yellow and red onions, red grapes, and broccoli are rich in quercetin, an anticancer agent that the University of California lab studies have shown can suppress malignant cells before they form tumors.

• Olive oil and canola oil, rich in monounsaturates, are the best heart disease–fighting natural foods available.

• The easiest way to rid your body of excess sodium is to flush it out by drinking six to eight glasses of salt-free water daily.

• There may be a connection between toothpaste (with its crystalline abrasives, foaming agents, and other additives) and bowel diseases such as ulcerative colitis, Crohn's disease, and irritable bowel syndrome. It's advisable to always rinse your mouth well after brushing and to try to avoid swallowing any toothpaste.

• There is more to smoking than the average seven-year drop in life expectancy reported by the American Cancer Society. ELEVEN YEARS MORE! New studies show that life expectancy between smokers and nonsmokers differs by eighteen years!

• The mineral boron (found in apples, grapes, grape juice, and raisins) may retard bone loss in women after menopause. Also, boron helps women on ERT (estrogen replacement therapy) keep the estrogen in their blood longer.

• Avoiding black coffee may help you avoid cancer of the esophagus. Tannin, found in coffee and tea, is a suspected carcinogen. The protein in milk, though, neutralizes tannin, rendering it nonabsorbable by the body.

• Bugs Bunny was right! Carrots can help keep plaque from forming on artery walls and help prevent heart attacks in people with atherosclerosis. Eating one large carrot daily will give you approximately 11,000 IU of vitamin A from beta-carotene!

• People who drink diet sodas and eat foods with sugar substitutes have been found to make up for the loss of sugar calories by eating an average of 11 percent more fat!

• You can lower your risk of stomach cancer 50 percent by eating half an onion a day, according to a four-year study in the Netherlands. The onion's *allylic sulfides* (anticancer compounds) apparently activate enzymes that neutralize cancer-causing substances.

• Eating two to four servings a week of tomato sauce can lower a man's risk of prostate cancer because of the large amount of the antioxidant *lycopene* in tomato products.

• Most people lose the enzymes to digest milk after age twelve. That's why many adults experience gas or indigestion after drinking it.

• Use of vitamin E supplements lowers your risk of heart disease.

• Vegetarians who consume nuts five or more times a week have a lower risk of heart disease than those consuming nuts less than once a week.

• Daily vitamin C supplements have been shown to reduce the risk of developing cataracts, according to a long-term study by the USDA Human Nutrition Research Center on Aging at Tufts University.

• The flavonoids in red grapes are more than a thousand times more powerful than vitamin E in inhibiting oxidation of human LDL cholesterol.

• The amino acid arginine can help make erections stronger.

• 100 mg. of the phospholipid supplement phosphatidylserine (PS) daily can help people with normal age-related memory problems regain twelve years of brainpower.

• Recent research shows that adequate levels of selenium may slow the progression of HIV significantly.

• Carpal tunnel syndrome and hormonal imbalance may be symptoms of a vitamin B6 deficiency.

• The antioxidant *N-acetylcysteine* (NAC) may work better than vitamin C to ease flu symptoms.

• Magnesium is a muscle relaxant and nature's equivalent to calcium channel blocker drugs.

• New studies show that men who drink more than four glasses of water daily can lower their risk of colon cancer by 32 percent.

16. Any Questions About Chapter I?

I've seen quite a few amino acid supplements in health food stores. Are these considered nutrients? Are they as important as vitamins?

Emphatically yes, and yes again! Amino acids (see section 72) are the building blocks of one of our most important nutrients—protein.

Every cell in your body contains (and needs) protein. It's

used to build new tissue and repair damaged cells, as well as to make hormones and enzymes, keep the acid-alkaline blood content balanced, and eliminate the unwanted garbage, among other things. As protein is digested, it's broken down into smaller compounds called amino acids. When these amino acids reach the cells in your body, they're formed into protein again. It's a wonderful cycle.

The importance of vitamins and amino acids in nutrition is equal, because you'll get no value from one without the proper amount of the other. As for amino acid supplements and their value to you as an individual, I'd suggest looking over sections 72 and 77, which discuss some of the remarkable benefits supplementation has been shown to provide.

I know that vitamins can't work properly without minerals, but do some minerals make them work more effectively than others?

Definitely. Vitamin A, for instance, works best with the minerals calcium, magnesium, phosphorus, selenium, and zinc. The B vitamins are also potentiated by these minerals, along with cobalt, copper, iron, manganese, potassium, and sodium. For vitamin C, the five minerals found to promote the most effectiveness are calcium, cobalt, copper, iron, and sodium; for vitamin D, they are calcium, copper, magnesium, selenium, and sodium; and for vitamin E, they are calcium, iron, manganese, phosphorus, potassium, selenium, sodium, and zinc. To find out what minerals—and other vitamins—can increase the effectiveness of individual vitamins, see sections 28–51.

What is boron?

Underappreciated! It's a trace mineral needed by the body in only minuscule amounts, which is why there's no official recommended daily allowance. But this does not diminish its importance in working with calcium, magnesium, and vitamin D to help prevent osteoporosis. And it may even help your brain to work better. It's found in most fruits and vegetables; however, dried fruits such as prunes and apricots are the best source. As a supplement, I recommend 3 mg. daily. (Do not exceed 10 mg. daily.)

What are phytochemicals?

Phytochemicals are chemicals found in plants; health-promoting nutrients that give fruits, vegetables, grains, and legumes their color, flavor, and natural protection against disease. They are, essentially, the plants' immune system. They are potent antioxidants and can provide protection against free radical damage, helping the body ward off a variety of ailments, including heart disease and cancer.

I've been hearing a lot about nutraceuticals. Are they supplements?

They certainly are—and probably the most exciting breakthrough in preventive medicine! Nutraceuticals are derived from natural products (food substances or parts of a food) that have proven therapeutic benefits similar to pharmaceuticals—such as isoflavones from soy which have anticancerous properties and hypericum and polyphenols in Saint John's wort which has antidepressant properties. These naturally occurring compounds extracted from plants, algae, and other biological sources are concentrated into pills, powders, and capsules and are now being used to prevent numerous diseases as well as to treat common ailments—an area formerly ruled by prescription drugs.

Nutraceuticals can also concentrate the best of food chemicals for daily consumption. Since only 9 percent of Americans eat five servings of fruits and vegetables a day, these supplements are playing an increasingly important role in our nation's health. There are phytochemical-enriched foods, for example snack bars fortified with soy phytochemicals (phytoestrogens) to alleviate symptoms such as hot flashes in menopausal women and to prevent prostate problems in men, nutraceutical-enriched margarine to lower blood serum cholesterol, as well as phytochemical-enriched candy for children who don't care for vegetables. There are a lot more ways, these days, to get what's good for you into you.

I have a mitral valve prolapse and take antibiotics often. I've heard about probiotics, but don't know what they are. Should I be taking them?

You sure should! *Probiotic,* which means "for life," is a general term for microorganisms known as friendly bacteria, which support the body's own defenses against infection and disease. There are billions of friendly bacteria in our bodies, and they do some wonderful things, such as aid in digestion, improve immune function, help keep hormone levels normal, protect against overgrowth infection from fungi and yeasts (which may be absorbed into the bloodstream and contribute to other serious diseases), manufacture some B vitamins, and more.

Unfortunately, antibiotics can't distinguish between good and bad bacteria. Overuse can lead to an increase in drug-resistant strains and, therefore, make you more susceptible to illness. You can increase your good bacteria levels by adding more fiber to your diet (intestinal bacteria consume dietary fiber and metabolize it into acids that inhibit the growth of bad bacteria) and eating yogurt—preferably nonfat or low-fat—made with live, active cultures. (Dairy-free probiotics are also available.) But the easiest way would be to take a daily probiotic supplement during the time you're taking the antibiotics—and for about a month afterward to replenish your good bacteria. I'd suggest one capsule (or 1 tablespoon liquid) three times a day, half an hour before meals. NOTE: You may experience gas or bloating when you first start taking probiotics. This is an indication that the good bacteria are fermenting and the problem should disappear in a week or so when your body adjusts to the change.

What are carotenoids?

The most important thing to know about carotenoids is that they're good for you. (See section 103.) They're a class of compounds related to vitamin A, the best-known being beta-carotene (others include alpha-carotene, gamma-carotene, lutein, and lycopene), which has long been shown to be helpful in preventing many types of cancer. The beta-carotene in foods is converted into vitamin A, but, unlike vitamin A, large amounts are not toxic. (Too much beta-carotene could, though, make you look as if you've been overdoing it on bronzers by turning your skin an orangey yellow.)

Lycopene, the substance that gives tomatoes, watermelon, pink grapefruit, and other fruits and vegetables their distinctive red color, is the new popular carotenoid on the nutritional block. Findings from Harvard University, the U.S. Department of Agriculture, and the Dana Farber Cancer Institute indicate that tomato consumption reduces the risk of cancer in general and prostate cancer in particular. In fact, the study showed that men who consumed large amounts of tomatoes had only about half the risk of prostate cancer as did men who consumed small amounts of tomato products. Because fat helps move lycopene into the bloodstream, pizza might finally have a redeeming nutritional feature. Just don't cancel it out with pepperoni and extra cheese!

I know that antioxidants fight oxidation in the body, but what exactly is oxidation and what causes it?

Oxidation is what happens to metal when it rusts or an apple when it turns brown. Unstable oxygen molecules called free radicals steal electrons from other molecules in an attempt to become stable. In the process, the free radicals damage cells, shortening their life span and speeding up the aging process. Once oxidation begins it can be hard to stop. The consequences range from infections to various degenerative conditions including heart disease, arthritis, and cancer.

What causes oxidation? Dozens of things, but the most

common culprits are pollutants, chemicals, and toxins, such as cigarette smoke. (See section 100.)

What are "smart nutrients" and do they really make you smart?

Well, you're smart if you're getting them. They're the nutrients that have been shown to protect and enhance brain function. Our levels of naturally produced antioxidants, which protect the brain from destructive free radicals, decline with age. Because of this, antioxidant supplements—which include vitamins, minerals, amino acids, and herbs—have been deemed smart nutrients. (See Chapter VI.)

Some smart nutrients you'd be wise to look into and look for, especially in combination supplements, are: Vitamin E, grapeseed extract, lipoic acid, NADH (coenzyme I), vitamin B1 (thiamin), vitamin B3 (niacin), vitamin B6 (pyridoxine), vitamin B12, folic acid, choline, L-carnitine, phenylalanine, DHA (docosahexaenoic acid), DMAE (dimethylamino-ethanol), ginkgo biloba, gotu kola, hupA (huperzine A), magnesium, pregnenolone, phosphatidylserine, phosphatidylcholine, and inositol. None of these brain-boosters will make you an Einstein, but they can help you remember where you put your car keys.

II

A Vitamin Pill Is a Vitamin Pill Is a . . .

17. Where Vitamins Come From

> Most vitamins are extracted from
> basic natural sources.

Because vitamins are natural substances found in foods, the supplements you take—be they capsules, tablets, powders, or liquids—also come from foods. Though many of the vitamins can be synthesized, most are extracted from basic natural sources.

For example: Vitamin A usually comes from fish liver oil. Vitamin B complex comes from yeast or liver. Vitamin C is best when derived from rose hips, the berries found on the fruit of the rose after the petals have fallen off. And vitamin E is generally extracted from soybeans, wheat germ, or corn.

18. Why Vitamins Come in Different Forms

Everyone's needs are different, and for this reason manufacturers have provided many vitamins in a variety of forms.

> Vitamins come in different forms
> because people do.

Tablets are the most common and convenient form. They're easier to store, carry, and have a longer shelf life than powders or liquids—and they cannot be adulterated.

Caplets are capsule-shaped tablets. These can be enteric coated so that they dissolve in the intestine, not in the stomach (which is acid).

Capsules, like tablets, are convenient and easy to store, and are the usual supplement for oil-soluble vitamins such as A, D, and E. They contain fewer excipients than do tablets.

Gelatin capsules are made with gelatin, an animal product. They should be stored away from light in a cool, dry area to prevent against oxidation.

Vegetable capsules are free of any animal products, starches, sugars, and other allergens. They're made from cellulose and plant fiber from trees, which is resistant to fungal and bacterial problems. They can withstand storage in a high-temperature environment without melting or sticking together. They're not affected by cold, dry climates that may cause gelatin caps to become brittle. Unfortunately, they can react with the ingredients in them and are therefore not used as much as gelatin capsules. They are also more expensive.

Softgels (or *gel-caps*) are soft gelatin capsules that many people find easier to swallow than regular capsules. Like tablets and capsules, softgels must be processed through the digestive system, so they're slower acting than their liquid and powder counterparts.

Powders have the advantages of extra potency (1 tsp. of many vitamin C powders can give you as much as 4,000 mg.) and the added benefit of no fillers, binders, or additives for anyone with allergies.

Liquids are available for easy mixing with beverages and for people unable to swallow capsules or tablets.

Intra-oral sprays deliver *low-dose* concentrations of nutrients directly into the mouth, under the tongue. They are absorbed into the bloodstream through the mucous membranes and bypass the gastrointestinal tract, generally within fifteen minutes.

Sublinguals are tablets that dissolve under the tongue. (For vitamin B12, this is my recommended form of supplement because it is better absorbed by the body.)

Patches and implants supply continuous, measured amounts of nutrients, though at this writing they are available only for a limited number of nutritional supplements and are considered drug-delivery systems in the United States.

19. Oil vs. Dry or Water Soluble

The oil-soluble vitamins, such as A, D, E, and K, are available and advisable in "dry" or water-soluble form for people who tend to get upset stomachs from oil, for acne sufferers or anyone with a skin condition where oil ingestion is not advised, and for dieters who have cut most of the fat from their meals. (Fat-soluble vitamins need fat for proper assimilation. If you're on a low-fat diet and taking A, D, E, or supplements, I suggest you use the dry form.)

20. Synthetic vs. Natural and Inorganic vs. Organic

> Synthetic vitamins might be less likely to upset your budget—but not your stomach.

When I'm asked if there's a difference between synthetic and natural vitamins, I usually say only one—and that's to you. Though synthetic vitamins and minerals have produced

satisfactory results, the benefits from natural vitamins, on a
variety of levels, surpass them. Chemical analysis of both
might appear the same, but there's more to natural vitamins
because there's more to those substances in nature.

Synthetic vitamin C is just that, ascorbic acid and nothing
more. Natural C from rose hips contains bioflavonoids, the
entire C complex, which make the C much more effective.

Natural vitamin E, which can include all the tocopherols,
not just alpha, is more potent and better absorbed than its
synthetic double.

According to Dr. Theron G. Randolph, noted allergist:

*A synthetically derived substance may cause a reaction in
a chemically susceptible person when the same material of
natural origin is tolerated, despite the two substances having identical chemical structures.*

On the other hand, people who are allergic to pollen could
experience an undesirable reaction to a natural vitamin C
that had possible pollen impurities.

Nonetheless, as many who have tried both can attest, there
are fewer gastrointestinal upsets with natural supplements,
and far fewer toxic reactions when taken in higher than recommended dosage.

The difference between inorganic and organic is not the
same as the one between synthetic and natural, though that
is the common misconception. All vitamins are organic.
They are substances containing carbon.

21. Chelation, and What It Means

Only 2–10 percent of inorganic iron taken
into the body is actually absorbed.

First, pronounce it correctly. *Key' lation.* This is the process
by which mineral substances are changed into their di-

gestible form. Most mineral supplements are often not chelated and must first be acted upon in the digestive process to form chelates before they are of use to the body. The natural chelating process is not performed efficiently in many people, and because of this a good deal of the mineral supplements they take are of little use.

When you realize that the body does not use whatever it takes in, that most of us do not digest our foods efficiently, that only 2–10 percent of inorganic iron taken into the body is actually absorbed, and, even with this small percentage, 50 percent is then eliminated, you can recognize the importance of taking minerals that have been chelated. *Amino acid–bound chelated mineral supplements provide three to ten times greater assimilation than the nonchelated ones!*

22. Time Release

A major step forward in vitamin manufacturing has been the introduction of time-release supplements. Time (or sustained) release is a process by which vitamins are enrobed in micropellets (tiny time pills) and then combined into a special base for their release in a pattern that assures three- to six-hour absorption. Most vitamins are water soluble and cannot be stored in the body. Without time release, they are quickly absorbed into the bloodstream, and, no matter how large the dose, are excreted in the urine within two to three hours.

Time-release supplements can offer optimum effectiveness, minimal excretory loss, and stable blood levels during the day and through the night. (Check label for release pattern to be sure.)

23. Fillers, Binders, or What Else Am I Getting?

There's more to a vitamin supplement than meets the eye— and sometimes more than meets the label. Fillers, binders, lubricants, and the like do not have to be listed and often aren't. But if you'd like to know what you're swallowing, the following list should help.

Diluents or fillers These are inert materials added to the tablets to increase their bulk, in order to make them a practical size for compression. Dicalcium phosphate, which is an excellent source of calcium and phosphorus, is used in better brands. It is derived from purified mineral rocks. It is a white powder. Sorbitol and cellulose (plant fiber) are used occasionally.

Binders These substances give cohesive qualities to the powdered materials; otherwise, the binders or granulators are the materials that hold the ingredients of the tablet together. Cellulose and ethyl cellulose are used most often. Cellulose is the main constituent of plant fiber. Occasionally, lecithin and sorbitol are used. Another binder that can be used, but that you should be aware of—and look out for—is

Acacia (gum arabic)—a vegetable gum that has been declared GRAS (Generally Recognized As Safe) by the FDA (Food and Drug Administration) but which can cause mild to severe asthma attacks and rashes in asthmatics, pregnant women, and anyone prone to allergies.

Lubricants Slick substances, added to a tablet to keep it from sticking to the machines that punch it out. Calcium stearate and silica are commonly used. Calcium stearate is derived from natural vegetable oils. Silica is a natural white powder. Magnesium stearate can also be used.

Disintegrators Substances such as gum arabic, algin, and alginate are added to the tablet to facilitate its breakup or disintegration after ingestion.

Colors They make the tablet more aesthetic or elegant in appearance. Colors derived from natural sources, like chlorophyll, are best.

Flavors and sweeteners   Used only in chewable tablets, the sweeteners are usually fructose (fruit sugar), malt dextrins, sorbitol, or maltose. Sucrose (sugar) is rarely used in better brands.

Coating material   These substances are used to protect the tablet from moisture. They also mask unpleasant flavor or odor and make the tablet easier to swallow. Zein is one of the substances. It is natural, derived from corn protein, and a clear film-coating agent. Brazil wax, which is a natural product derived from palm trees, is also frequently used.

Drying agents   These substances prevent water-absorbing (hydroscopic) materials from picking up moisture during processing. Silica gel is the most common drying agent.

24. Storage and Staying Power

Vitamin and mineral supplements should be stored in a cool dark place away from direct sunlight in a well-closed—preferably opaque—container. They do not have to be stored in the refrigerator unless you live in a desert climate. To guard against excessive moisture, place a few kernels of rice at the bottom of your vitamin bottle. The rice works as a natural absorbent.

> Vitamins can last two to three years
> in a well-sealed container.

If vitamins are kept cool and away from light, and remain well sealed, they should last for two to three years. To insure freshness, though, your best bet is to buy brands that have an expiration date on the label. Once a bottle is opened you can expect a six-month shelf life.

Our bodies tend to excrete in urine substances we take in on a four-hour basis, and this is particularly true of water-soluble vitamins such as B and C. On an empty stomach, B and C vitamins can leave the body as quickly as two hours after ingestion.

The oil-soluble vitamins, A, D, E, and K, remain in the body for approximately twenty-four hours, though excess amounts can be stored in the liver for much longer. Dry A and E do not stay in the body as long.

25. When and How to Take Supplements

The human body operates on a twenty-four-hour cycle. Your cells do not go to sleep when you do, nor can they exist without continuous oxygen and nutrients. Therefore, for best results, space your supplements as evenly as possible during the day.

> If you take your supplements all
> at once, do so with dinner,
> not breakfast.

The prime time for taking supplements is with or after meals. Vitamins are organic substances and should be taken with other foods and minerals for best absorption. Because the water-soluble vitamins, especially B complex and C, are excreted fairly rapidly in the urine, a regimen of with breakfast, with lunch, and with dinner will provide you with the highest body level. If after each meal is not convenient, then half the amount should be taken after breakfast and the other half after dinner.

If you must take your vitamins all at once, then do so with the largest meal of the day.

And remember, minerals are essential for proper vitamin absorption, so be sure to take your minerals and vitamins together.

26. What's Right for You

Supplement needs vary depending on your sex, age, health, lifestyle, daily stresses, and dietary restrictions. Job changes, illness, physical and emotional traumas, all take a nutritional toll. With more supplements available today than ever before, and in more delivery systems than ever before, there's no reason why you can't reap maximum health benefits by selecting the nutrients you need in a form that works for you.

If you're unsure as to whether you'd be better off with a powder, a liquid, a gel-cap, or a tablet, regular vitamin E or dry, or taking supplements three times a day, my advice to you is to experiment. If the supplement you're taking doesn't agree with you, try it in another form. Vitamin C powder mixed in a beverage might be much easier to take than several large pills when you're coming down with a cold. If your face breaks out with vitamin E, try the dry form. Review section 18 to see the variety of supplement delivery systems available. Also:

• Make sure you know all you should about your supplement. (Check sections 28 through 71 and the cautions in section 334.)
• If you're taking any medications, familiarize yourself with drugs that deplete nutrients as well as nutrients that may interfere with medications. (See section 293.)
• Match your vitamin needs with those listed in Chapter XIII.

27. Any Questions About Chapter II?

When vitamins smell awful, does that mean they're spoiled, and could they be harmful?

Strong odors don't necessarily signify spoilage, but it is possible. If you've been keeping your vitamins in sunlight and warmth (great for you but not for them) it's more than possible, it's probable. But even if your vitamins have spoiled, they won't harm you. The worst that can happen is that they lose their effectiveness.

Every so often I detect a sort of alcohol smell in a bottle of vitamins. Does this indicate some sort of deterioration, and are these vitamins still safe to take?

No, the vitamins are not deteriorating, and yes they are safe to take. Alcohol is often used as a drying agent to prevent any moisture contamination. Occasionally, if the product is packed too quickly, some of the alcohol smell remains. My advice is put a few kernels of rice in the bottle. These will absorb the moisture and the smell.

Sometimes I find that a few of my B vitamin pills are cracked. Are these safe to take?

Yes they are, as are your Cs and any others. Poor tablet coating causes the cracks, but the vitamins themselves are still effective and safe.

If binders like acacia gum and alginic acid have been declared GRAS (Generally Recognized As Safe) by the FDA, why aren't they?

Just because an additive has been declared GRAS doesn't mean that it can't harm you. Here's why: when the food additive law requiring scientific testing of all chemicals for safe usage in foods went into effect in 1958, the FDA established the GRAS list to eliminate expensive testing of what were unquestionably assumed to be safe chemicals (sugar, starch, salt, baking soda, etc.). As a result of the FDA's action, all additives in use before that year were deemed GRAS; regrettably, many were later found to be otherwise.

III

Everything You Always Wanted to Know About Vitamins but Had No One to Ask

28. Vitamin A

FACTS:

Vitamin A is fat soluble. It requires fats as well as minerals to be properly absorbed by your digestive tract.

It can be stored in your body and need not be replenished every day.

It occurs in two forms—preformed vitamin A, called retinol (found only in foods of animal origin), and provitamin A, known as carotene (provided by foods of both plant and animal origin).

Vitamin A is measured in USP Units (United States Pharmacopeia), IU (International Units), and RE (Retinol Equivalents). (See section 168.)

1,000 RE (or 5,000 IU) is the recommended daily dosage for adult males to prevent deficiency. For females it's 800 RE (4,000 IU). During pregnancy the new RDIs/RDAs do not recommend an increase, but for nursing mothers an additional 500 RE is suggested for the first six months and an additional 400 RE for the second six months.

There is no formal RDI/RDA for beta-carotene, because it is not (yet) officially recognized as an essential nutrient. But anywhere from 10,000–15,000 IUs of beta-carotene are needed to meet the RDI/RDA for vitamin A.

NOTE: Throughout this book, beta-carotene will be the preferred form of vitamin A. I find it preferable because it does
not have the same toxicity potential of vitamin A. Moreover,
it has been shown to be a preventive for certain types of
cancer, helpful in lowering levels of harmful cholesterol, effective in boosting the immune system by increasing the
number of infection-fighting T lymphocytes (T cells), and a
significant factor in reducing the risk of heart disease.

WHAT IT CAN DO FOR YOU:

Counteract night blindness, weak eyesight, and aid in the
treatment of many eye disorders. (It permits formation of visual purple in the eye.)

Build resistance to respiratory infections.

Aid in the proper function of the immune system.

Shorten the duration of diseases.

Keep the outer layers of your tissues and organs healthy.

Help in the removal of age spots.

Promote growth, strong bones, healthy skin, hair, teeth,
and gums.

Help treat acne, superficial wrinkles, impetigo, boils, carbuncles, and open ulcers when applied externally.

Aid in the treatment of emphysema and hyperthyroidism.

DEFICIENCY DISEASE:

Xerophthalmia, night blindness. (For deficiency symptoms, see section 163.) Deficiency often occurs as a result of
chronic fat malabsorption. It's most commonly found in
children under five years, usually because of insufficient
dietary intake.

BEST NATURAL SOURCE:

Fish liver oil, liver, carrots, dark green and yellow vegetables, eggs, milk and dairy products, margarine, and yellow fruits. (Note: The color intensity of a fruit or vegetable

is not necessarily a reliable indicator of its beta-carotene content.)

SUPPLEMENTS:

Usually available in two forms, one derived from natural fish liver oil and the other water dispersible. Water-dispersible supplements are either acetate or palmitate and recommended for anyone intolerant to oil, particularly acne sufferers. 5,000 to 10,000 IU are the most common daily doses.

Vitamin A acid (retin A), which has often been used in the treatment of acne, and is now being marketed as a treatment for eradicating superficial wrinkles, is available only by prescription in the United States.

TOXICITY AND WARNING SIGNS OF EXCESS:

More than 50,000 IU daily, if taken for many months, can produce toxic effects in adults.

More than 18,500 IU daily can produce toxic effects in infants.

More than 34,000 IU beta-carotene daily can cause yellowing of the skin.

Symptoms of vitamin A excess include hair loss, nausea, vomiting, diarrhea, scaly skin, blurred vision, rashes, bone pain, irregular menses, fatigue, headaches, and liver enlargement. (See section 334, "Cautions.")

ENEMIES:

Polyunsaturated fatty acids with carotene work against vitamin A unless there are antioxidants present. (See sections 100–117 for antioxidants, and section 293 for drugs that deplete vitamins.)

PERSONAL ADVICE:

You need at least 10,000 IU vitamin A if you take more than 400 IU vitamin E daily.

If you are on the pill, your need for A is *decreased*.

If your weekly diet includes ample amounts of liver, carrots, spinach, sweet potatoes, or cantaloupe, it's unlikely you need an A supplement.

Vitamin A should *not* be taken with mineral oil.

Vitamin A works best with B-complex, vitamin D, vitamin E, calcium, phosphorus, and zinc. (Zinc is what's needed by the liver to get vitamin A out of its storage deposits.)

Vitamin A also helps vitamin C from oxidizing.

Don't supplement your dog's or cat's diet with vitamin A unless a vet specifically advises it.

If you are on a cholesterol-reducing drug such as Questran™ (*cholestyramine*), you'll have decreased vitamin-A absorption and may need a supplement.

Oral forms of vitamin A prescribed for skin problems are potent drugs that can cause birth defects and should not be used by pregnant women.

29. Vitamin B1 (Thiamine)

FACTS:

Water soluble. Like all the B-complex vitamins, any excess is excreted and not stored in the body. It must be replaced daily.

Measured in milligrams (mg.).

Being synergistic, B vitamins are more potent together than when used separately. B1, B2, and B6 should be equally balanced (i.e., 50 mg. of B1, 50 mg. of B2, and 50 mg. of B6) to work effectively.

The RDI/RDA for adults is 1.0 to 1.5 mg. (During pregnancy and lactation 1.5 to 1.6 mg. is suggested.)

Need increases during illness, stress, and surgery.

Known as the "morale vitamin" because of its beneficial effects on the nervous system and mental attitude.

Has a mild diuretic effect.

WHAT IT CAN DO FOR YOU:

Promote growth.

Aid digestion, especially of carbohydrates.

Improve your mental attitude.

Keep nervous system, muscles, and heart functioning normally.

Help fight air- or seasickness.

Relieve dental postoperative pain.

Aid in treatment of herpes zoster.

DEFICIENCY DISEASE:

Beriberi. (For deficiency symptoms, see section 163.)

BEST NATURAL SOURCES:

Brewer's yeast, rice husks, unrefined cereal grains, whole wheat, soybeans, egg yolks, fish, oatmeal, peanuts, organic meats, lean pork, most vegetables, bran, milk.

SUPPLEMENTS:

Available in low- and high-potency dosages—usually 50 mg., 100 mg., and 500 mg. It is most effective in B-complex formulas, balanced with B2 and B6. It is even more effective when the formula contains antistress pantothenic acid, folic acid, and B12. 100 to 300 mg. are the most common daily doses.

TOXICITY AND WARNING SIGNS OF EXCESS:

No known toxicity for this water-soluble vitamin. Any excess is excreted in the urine and not stored to any degree in tissues or organs.

Rare excess symptoms (when doses exceed 5–10 g. daily) include tremors, herpes, edema, nervousness, rapid heartbeat, and allergies. (See section 334, "Cautions.")

ENEMIES:

Cooking heat easily destroys this B vitamin. Other enemies of B1 are caffeine, alcohol, food-processing methods, air, water, estrogen, antacids, and sulfa drugs. (See section 293 for drugs that deplete vitamins.)

PERSONAL ADVICE:

If you are a smoker, drinker, or heavy sugar consumer, you need more vitamin B1.

If you are pregnant, nursing, or on the pill you have a greater need for this vitamin.

If you're in the habit of taking an after-dinner antacid, you're losing the thiamine you might have gotten from the meal.

As with all stress conditions—disease, anxiety, trauma, postsurgery—your B-complex intake, which includes thiamine, should be increased.

30. Vitamin B2 (Riboflavin)

FACTS:

Water soluble. Easily absorbed. The amount excreted depends on bodily needs and may be accompanied by protein loss. Like the other B vitamins it is not stored and must be replaced regularly through whole foods or supplements.

Also known as vitamin G.

Measured in milligrams (mg.).

Unlike thiamine, riboflavin is *not* destroyed by heat, oxidation, or acid. But it is easily destroyed by light.

For normal adults, 1.2–1.7 mg. is the RDI/RDA. During pregnancy, 1.6 mg. is suggested. For nursing mothers, 1.8 mg. is recommended for the first six months and 1.7 mg. for the second six months.

Increased need in stress situations.

America's most common vitamin deficiency is riboflavin.

WHAT IT CAN DO FOR YOU:

Aid in growth and reproduction.
Promote healthy skin, nails, hair.
Help eliminate sore mouth, lips, and tongue.
Benefit vision, alleviate eye fatigue.
Function with other substances to metabolize carbohydrates, fats, and proteins.

DEFICIENCY DISEASE:

Ariboflavinosis—mouth, lips, skin, genitalia lesions. (For deficiency symptoms, see section 163.)

BEST NATURAL SOURCES:

Milk, liver, kidney, cheese, leafy green vegetables, fish, eggs, yogurt, beans.

SUPPLEMENTS:

Available in both low and high potencies—most commonly in 100 mg. doses. Like most of the B-complex vitamins, it is most effective when in a well-balanced formula with the others.
100–300 mg. are the most common daily doses.

TOXICITY AND WARNING SIGNS OF EXCESS:

No known toxic effects.
Possible symptoms of minor excess include itching, numbness, sensations of burning or prickling. (See section 334, "Cautions.")

ENEMIES:

Light—especially ultraviolet light—and alkalies are destructive to riboflavin. (Opaque milk cartons now protect riboflavin that used to be destroyed in clear-glass milk bottles.) Other natural enemies are water (B2 dissolves in cooking liquids), sulfa drugs, estrogen, alcohol.

PERSONAL ADVICE:

If you are taking the pill, pregnant, or lactating, you need more vitamin B2.

If you eat little red meat or dairy products you should increase your intake.

There is a strong likelihood of your being deficient in this vitamin if you are on a prolonged restricted diet for ulcers or diabetes. (In all cases where you are under medical treatment for a specific illness, check with your doctor before altering your present food regimen or embarking on a new one.)

All stress conditions require additional B complex.

This vitamin works best with vitamin B6, vitamin C, and niacin.

If you're taking an antineoplastic (anticancer) drug such as *methotrexate*, too much vitamin B2 can cut down the drug's effectiveness.

If you're taking antibiotics, you're probably not getting the B2 you need.

Drinkers need more of this vitamin because alcohol interferes with proper absorption.

31. Vitamin B3 (Niacin, Niacinamide, Nicotinic Acid, Nicotinamide)

FACTS:

Water soluble and a member of the B-complex family.

Usually measured in milligrams (mg.).

Using the amino acid tryptophan, the body can manufacture its own niacin.

A person whose body is deficient in B1, B2, and B6 will not be able to produce niacin from tryptophan.

Lack of niacin can bring about negative personality changes.

The RDI/RDA for niacin is 13–19 mg. for adults. For nursing mothers the recommendation is 20 mg.

Essential for synthesis of sex hormones (estrogen, progesterone, testosterone), as well as cortisone, thyroxine, and insulin.

Necessary for healthy nervous system and brain functions.

One of the few vitamins that is relatively stable in foods and can withstand cooking and storage with little loss of potency.

WHAT IT CAN DO FOR YOU:

Help reduce cholesterol and tryglycerides.

Aid in metabolizing fats and promoting a healthy digestive system, alleviate gastrointestinal disturbances.

Give you healthier-looking skin.

Help prevent and ease severity of migraine headaches.

Increase circulation and reduce high blood pressure.

Ease some attacks of diarrhea.

Reduce the unpleasant symptoms of vertigo in Meniere's disease.

Increase energy through proper utilization of food.

Help eliminate canker sores and, often, bad breath.

DEFICIENCY DISEASE:

Pellagra, severe dermatitis. (For deficiency symptoms, see section 163.)

BEST NATURAL SOURCES:

Fish, lean meat, whole wheat products, brewer's yeast, liver, wheat germ, fish, eggs, roasted peanuts, the white meat of poultry, avocados, dates, figs, prunes.

SUPPLEMENTS:

Available as niacin, inositol hexanicotinate (IHN), also called "no-flush" niacin, and niacinamide. (Niacin—nicotinic acid—might cause flushing; niacinamide and inositol hexanicotinate—which contain niacin and inositol—will not. If you prefer niacin, you can minimize the flushing by taking your pill on a full stomach or with an equivalent amount of inositol.)

Usually found in 50–1,000 mg. doses in tablet, capsule, and powder form.

50–100 mg. are ordinarily included in the better B-complex formulas and multivitamin preparations. (Check labels.)

TOXICITY AND WARNING SIGNS OF EXCESS:

Large amounts of niacin can interfere with the control of uric acid, bringing on attacks of gout in people who are prone to this disease.

High levels of niacin can also interfere with the body's ability to dispose of sugar, causing possible deterioration of glucose control in borderline diabetes, precipitating the full-blown disease, and may promote liver abnormalities.

Except for possible side effects, such as flushing and itching resulting from doses above 100 mg., niacin is essentially nontoxic.

Do not give to animals, especially dogs. It can cause flushing and sweating and great discomfort for the animal.

(See section 334, "Cautions.")

ENEMIES:

Water, sulfa drugs, alcohol, sleeping pills, estrogen. (See section 293.)

PERSONAL ADVICE:

If you're taking antibiotics and suddenly find your niacin flushes becoming severe, don't be alarmed. It's quite common. (The flush usually disappears in about twenty minutes. Drinking a glass of water helps.) You'll probably be more comfortable, though, if you switch to a "no-flush" supplement with inositol hexanicotinate.

To avoid gastrointestinal upsets, do not take niacin on an empty stomach or with hot beverages.

If you have a cholesterol problem, increasing your niacin

intake can help. (I recommend using it under the supervision of your physician, especially if you are taking other medication.)

Skin that is particularly sensitive to sunlight is often an early indicator of niacin deficiency.

32. Vitamin B6 (Pyridoxine)

FACTS:

Water soluble. Excreted within eight hours after ingestion and, like the other B vitamins, needs to be replaced by whole foods or supplements.

B6 is actually a group of substances—pyridoxine, pyridoxal, and pyridoxamine—that are closely related and function together.

Measured in milligrams (mg.).

Requirement increased when high-protein diets are consumed.

Must be present for the production of antibodies and red blood cells.

There is some evidence of synthesis by intestinal bacteria, and that a vegetable diet supplemented with cellulose is responsible.

The recommended adult intake is 1.6–2.0 mg. daily, with 2.2 mg. doses suggested during pregnancy and 2.1 mg. for lactation.

Required for the proper absorption of vitamin B12.

Necessary for the production of hydrochloric acid and magnesium.

Dairy products are relatively poor sources of B6.

WHAT IT CAN DO FOR YOU:

In combination with folic acid, it can help break down the amino acid homocysteine, lowering the risk of heart disease *significantly*.

Strengthen the immune system.

Help prevent kidney stone formation.

Properly assimilate protein and fat.

Aid in the conversion of tryptophan, an essential amino acid, to niacin.

Help prevent various nervous and skin disorders.

Alleviate nausea (many morning-sickness preparations that doctors prescribe include vitamin B6).

Promote proper synthesis of antiaging nucleic acids.

Help reduce dry mouth and urination problems caused by tricyclic antidepressants.

Reduce night muscle spasms, leg cramps, hand numbness, certain forms of neuritis in the extremities.

Work as a natural diuretic.

DEFICIENCY DISEASE:

Anemia, seborrheic dermatitis, glossitis. (For deficiency symptoms, see section 163.)

BEST NATURAL SOURCES:

Brewer's yeast, wheat bran, wheat germ, liver, fish, soy beans, cantaloupe, cabbage, blackstrap molasses, unmilled rice, eggs, oats, peanuts, walnuts.

SUPPLEMENTS:

Readily available in a wide range of dosages—from 50 to 500 mg.—in individual supplements as well as in B-complex and multivitamin formulas.

To prevent deficiencies in other B vitamins, pyridoxine should be taken in equal amounts with B1 and B2.

Can be purchased in time-disintegrating formulas that provide for gradual release up to ten hours.

TOXICITY AND WARNING SIGNS OF EXCESS:

Daily doses of 2–10 grams can cause neurological disorders.

Possible symptoms of an oversupply of B6 are night restlessness, too vivid dream recall, numb feet, and twitching.

Doses over 500 mg. are not recommended. (See section 334, "Cautions.")

ENEMIES:

Long storage, canning, roasting or stewing of meat, freezing fruits and vegetables, water, food-processing techniques, alcohol, estrogen. (See section 293.)

PERSONAL ADVICE:

If you are on the pill, you are more than likely to need increased amounts of B6.

Heavy protein consumers need extra amounts of this vitamin.

To reduce your risk of heart attack, increase your B6 and folic acid.

Vitamin B6 might decrease a diabetic's requirement for insulin, and if the dosage is not adjusted, a low-blood-sugar reaction could result.

Arthritis sufferers being treated with Cuprimine (*penicillamine*) should be taking supplements of this vitamin.

This vitamin works best with vitamin B1, vitamin B2, pantothenic acid, vitamin C, and magnesium.

Supplements for this vitamin should *not* be taken by anyone under *levodopa* treatment for Parkinson's disease! (Ask your doctor about Sinemet™, a drug which can bypass this particular adverse vitamin interaction.)

33. Vitamin B12 (Cobalamin)

FACTS:

Water soluble and effective in very small doses.

Commonly known as the "red vitamin," also cyanocobalamin.

Cyanocobalamin is the commercially available form of vitamin B12 used in vitamin pills.

Measured in micrograms (mcg.)

The only vitamin that contains essential mineral elements.

Not well assimilated through the stomach. Needs to be combined with calcium during absorption to properly benefit the body.

Recommended adult dose is 2 mcg., with 2.2 mcg. suggested for pregnant women and 2.6 mcg. for nursing mothers.

A diet low in B1 and high in folic acid (such as a vegetarian diet) often hides a vitamin-B12 deficiency.

A properly functioning thyroid gland helps B12 absorption. Symptoms of B12 deficiency may take more than five years to appear after body stores have been depleted.

In the human diet, vitamin B12 is supplied primarily by animal products, since plant foods (with minor exceptions) don't contain it.

Unique among water-soluble vitamins, it can be stored in the body; it can take up to three years to deplete your supply.

WHAT IT CAN DO FOR YOU:

Form and regenerate red blood cells, thereby preventing anemia.

Help break down the amino acid homocysteine, lowering the risk of heart disease.

Promote growth and increase appetite in children.

Increase energy.

Maintain a healthy nervous system.

Properly utilize fats, carbohydrates, and protein.

Relieve irritability.

Improve concentration, memory, and balance.

Help protect against smoking-induced cancer.

DEFICIENCY DISEASE:

Pernicious anemia, neurological disorders. (For deficiency symptoms, see section 163.)

BEST NATURAL SOURCES:

Liver, beef, pork, eggs, milk, cheese, fish.

SUPPLEMENTS:

Because B12 is not absorbed well through the stomach, I recommend the sublingual form of the vitamin, or the time-release form—accompanied by sorbitol—so that it can be assimilated in the small intestine.

Supplements are available in a variety of strengths from 50 mcg. to 2,000 mcg.

Doctors routinely give vitamin-B12 injections. If there is a severe indication of deficiency or extreme fatigue, this method might be the supplementation that's called for.

Daily dosages most often used are 5–100 mcg.

TOXICITY AND WARNING SIGNS OF EXCESS:

There have been no cases reported of vitamin-B12 toxicity, even on megadose regimens. (See section 334, "Cautions.")

ENEMIES:

Acids and alkalies, water, sunlight, alcohol, estrogen, sleeping pills. (See section 293.)

PERSONAL ADVICE:

If you are a vegetarian and have excluded eggs and dairy products from your diet, then you need B12 supplementation.

If you keep regular "Happy Hours" and drink a lot, B12 is an important supplement for you.

Combined with folic acid, B12 can be a most effective re-vitalizer.

Surprisingly, heavy protein consumers may also need extra amounts of this vitamin, which works synergistically with almost all other B vitamins as well as vitamins A, E, and C.

Elderly people frequently have difficulty absorbing vitamin B12 and require supplementation by injection.

Women may find B12 helpful—as part of a B complex—during and just prior to menstruation.

34. Vitamin B13 (Orotic Acid)

FACTS:

Not available in the United States.
Metabolizes folic acid and vitamin B12.
No RDI/RDA has been established.

WHAT IT CAN DO FOR YOU:

Possibly prevent certain liver problems and premature aging.
Aid in the treatment of multiple sclerosis.

DEFICIENCY DISEASE:

Deficiency symptoms and diseases related to this vitamin are still uncertain.

BEST NATURAL SOURCES:

Root vegetables, whey, the liquid portion of soured or curdled milk.

SUPPLEMENTS:

Available as calcium orotate in supplemental form outside of the United States.

TOXICITY AND WARNING SIGNS OF EXCESS:

Too little is known about the vitamin at this time to establish guidelines. (See section 334, "Cautions.")

ENEMIES:

Water and sunlight.

PERSONAL ADVICE:

Not enough research has been done on this vitamin for recommendations to be made.

35. B15 (Pangamic Acid, DMG, Dimethylglycine)

FACTS:

Water soluble.

Because its essential requirement for diet has not been proved, it is not a vitamin in the strict sense.

Measured in milligrams (mg.).

Works much like vitamin E in that it is an antioxidant.

Introduced by the Russians, who are thrilled with its results, while the U.S. Food and Drug Administration has, at the time of this writing, taken it off the market.

Action is often improved by being taken with vitamins A and E.

WHAT IT CAN DO FOR YOU:*

Extend cell life span.

Neutralize the craving for liquor.

Speed recovery from fatigue.

Lower blood cholesterol levels.

---

*U.S. research in the case of B15 has been limited. The list of benefits given here is based on my study of tests performed by the former Soviet Union.

Protect against pollutants.
Relieve symptoms of angina and asthma.
Protect the liver against cirrhosis.
Ward off hangovers.
Stimulate immunity responses.
Aid in protein synthesis.

DEFICIENCY DISEASE:

Again, research has been limited, but indications point to glandular and nerve disorders, heart disease, and diminished oxygenation of living tissue.

BEST NATURAL SOURCES:

Brewer's yeast, whole brown rice, whole grains, pumpkin seeds, sesame seeds.

SUPPLEMENTS:

Usually available in 50 mg. strengths.
Daily doses most often used are 50–150 mgs.

TOXICITY AND WARNING SIGNS OF EXCESS:

There have been no reported cases of toxicity. Some people say they have experienced nausea on beginning a B15 regimen, but this usually disappears after a few days and can be alleviated by taking the B15 supplements after the day's largest meal. (See section 334, "Cautions.")

ENEMIES:

Water and sunlight.

PERSONAL ADVICE:

Despite the controversy, I have found B15 effective and believe most diets would benefit from supplementation.
If you are an athlete or just want to feel like one, I suggest

one 50 mg. tablet in the morning with breakfast and one in the evening with dinner.

36. Vitamin B17 (Laetrile, Amygdalin, Nitrilosides)

For many years, this controversial compound of two sugar molecules (one benzaldehyde and one cyanide) was erroneously called "vitamin" B17, a thoroughly misleading term. Made from apricot pits and purported to have specific cancer-controlling and preventive properties, it is—at the time of this writing—still illegal in most of the United States. I've cited it in this edition simply to clear up any residually held belief in its status as a vitamin.

37. Biotin (Coenzyme R or Vitamin H)

FACTS:

Water soluble, sulfur containing, and another member of the B-complex family.

Usually measured in micrograms (mcg.).

Synthesis of ascorbic acid requires biotin.

Essential for normal metabolism of fat and protein.

The RDI/RDA for adults is 100–300 mcg.

Can be synthesized by intestinal bacteria.

Raw eggs prevent absorption by the body.

Synergistic with B2, B6, niacin, A, and in maintaining healthy skin.

WHAT IT CAN DO FOR YOU:

Aid in keeping hair from turning gray.

Help in preventive treatment for baldness.

Ease muscle pains.

Alleviate eczema and dermatitis.

DEFICIENCY DISEASE:

Eczema of face and body, extreme exhaustion, impairment of fat metabolism, anorexia, alopecia, depression. (For deficiency symptoms, see section 163.)

BEST NATURAL SOURCES:

Beef liver, egg yolk, soy flour, brewer's yeast, milk, peanut butter, and unpolished rice.

SUPPLEMENTS:

Biotin is usually included in most B-complex supplements and multiple-vitamin tablets.

Daily doses most often used are 25–300 mcg.

TOXICITY AND WARNING SIGNS OF EXCESS:

There are no known cases of biotin toxicity. (See section 334, "Cautions.")

ENEMIES:

Raw egg white (which contains avidin, a protein that prevents biotin absorption), water, sulfa drugs, estrogen, food-processing techniques, and alcohol. (See section 293.)

PERSONAL ADVICE:

If you drink high protein shakes made with raw eggs you probably need biotin supplementation.

Be sure you're getting at least 25 mcg. daily if you are on antibiotics or sulfa drugs.

Balding men might find that a biotin supplement may keep their hair there longer.

Keep in mind that biotin works synergistically—and more effectively—with B2, B6, niacin, and A.

Biotin levels fall progressively throughout pregnancy. Although there's been no association with low birth weight, you might want to check with your doctor about a supplement which could help keep your spirits up.

38. Choline

FACTS:

A member of the B complex and a lipotropic (fat emulsifier).

Works with inositol (another B-complex member) to utilize fats and cholesterol.

One of the few substances able to penetrate the so-called blood-brain barrier, which ordinarily protects the brain against variations in the daily diet, and go directly into the brain cells to produce a chemical that aids memory.

No RDI/RDA has yet been established, though it's estimated that the average adult diet contains between 500 and 900 mg. a day.

Seems to emulsify cholesterol so that it doesn't settle on artery walls or in the gallbladder.

The utilization of choline in the body depends on vitamin B12, folic acid, and the amino acid L-carnitine.

WHAT IT CAN DO FOR YOU:

Help control cholesterol buildup.

Aid in the sending of nerve impulses, specifically those in the brain used in the formation of memory.

Assist in conquering the problem of memory loss in later years. (Doses of 1–5 g. a day.)

Help eliminate poisons and drugs from your system by aiding the liver.

Produce a soothing effect.

Aid in the treatment of Alzheimer's disease.

DEFICIENCY DISEASE:

May result in cirrhosis and fatty degeneration of liver, hardening of the arteries, and possibly Alzheimer's disease. (For deficiency symptoms, see section 163.)

BEST NATURAL SOURCES:

Egg yolks, brain, heart, green leafy vegetables, yeast, liver, wheat germ, and, in small amounts, in lecithin.

SUPPLEMENTS:

Choline may be sold under the name of phosphatidyl-choline or phosphatidylinositol.

Six lecithin capsules, made from soybeans, contain 244 mg. each of inositol and choline.

The average B-complex supplement contains approximately 50 mg. of choline and inositol.

Daily doses most often used are 500–1,000 mg.

TOXICITY AND WARNING SIGNS OF EXCESS:

None known. (See section 334, "Cautions.")

ENEMIES:

Water, sulfa drugs, estrogen, food processing, and alcohol. (See section 293.)

PERSONAL ADVICE:

Always take choline with your other B vitamins.

If you are often nervous or "twitchy," it might help to increase your choline.

If you are taking lecithin, you probably need a chelated calcium supplement to keep your phosphorus and calcium in balance, since choline seems to increase the body's phosphorus.

Try getting more choline into your diet as a way to a better memory.

If you're a heavy drinker, make sure you're giving your liver the choline it needs to do the extra work.

39. Folic Acid (Folacin, Folate)

FACTS:

Water soluble, another member of the B complex, also known as Bc or vitamin M.

Measured in micrograms (mcg.).

Essential to the formation of red blood cells.

Aid in protein metabolism.

The RDI/RDA for adults is 180 to 200 mcg., twice that amount for pregnant women, and for nursing mothers, 280 mcg. the first six months and 260 mcg. the second six months. (Babies are significantly protected from neural-tube defects, such as spina bifida, if women get the recommended double RDI/RDA at the time of conception and during early pregnancy.)

Important for the production of nucleic acids (RNA and DNA).

Essential for division of body cells.

Needed for utilization of sugar and amino acids.

Can be destroyed by being stored, unprotected, at room temperature for extended time periods.

WHAT IT CAN DO FOR YOU:

Lower homocysteine levels and reduce risk of heart disease.

Protect against birth defects.

Improve lactation.

Protect against intestinal parasites and food poisoning.

Promote healthier-looking skin.

Act as an analgesic for pain.

May delay hair graying when used in conjunction with pantothenic acid and PABA.

Increase appetite, if you are debilitated (run-down).

Act as a preventive for canker sores.
Help ward off anemia.

DEFICIENCY DISEASE:

Nutritional macrocytic anemia. (For deficiency symptoms, see section 163.)

BEST NATURAL SOURCES:

Deep green leafy vegetables, carrots, tortula yeast, liver, egg yolk, cantaloupe, apricots, pumpkins, avocados, beans, whole and dark rye flour.

SUPPLEMENTS:

Usually supplied in 400 mcg. and 800 mcg. strengths. Strengths of 1 mg. (1,000 mcg.) are available by prescription only in the United States.

400 mcg. are sometimes supplied in B-complex formulas, but often only 100 mcg. (Check labels.)

Daily doses most often used are 400 mcg. to 5 mg.

Look for supplements that contain both folate and B12.

TOXICITY AND WARNING SIGNS OF EXCESS:

No known toxic effects, though a few people experience allergic skin reactions.

Excess folic acid can mask anemia created by a B12 deficiency. (See section 334, "Cautions.")

ENEMIES:

Water, sulfa drugs, sunlight, estrogen, food processing (especially boiling), heat. (See section 293.)

PERSONAL ADVICE:

If you're a woman, be sure you're getting folic acid and vitamin B6. Just 400 mcg. folic acid with 2–10 mg. vitamin B6 can reduce your risk of heart attack by 42 percent!

If you are a heavy drinker, it is advisable to increase your folic-acid intake.

High vitamin-C intake increases excretion of folic acid, and anyone taking more than 2 g. of C should probably up his folic acid.

If you are on Dilantin™ or take estrogens, sulfonamides, phenobarbital, or aspirin, I suggest increasing folic acid.

I've found that many people taking 1–5 mg. daily, for a short period of time, have reversed several types of skin discoloration. If this is a problem for you, it's worth checking out a nutritionally oriented doctor about the possibility.

Large doses of folic acid may interfere with certain cancer drugs.

If you are getting sick, or fighting an illness, make sure your stress supplement has ample folic acid. When folic acid is deficient, so are your antibodies.

Large doses of folic acid may bring on convulsions in epileptics taking the medication phenytoin.

40. Inositol

FACTS:

Water soluble, another member of the B complex, and a lipotropic.

Measured in milligrams (mg.).

Combines with choline to form lecithin.

Metabolizes fats and cholesterol.

Daily dietary allowances have not yet been established, but the average healthy adult gets approximately 1 g. a day.

Like choline, it has been found important in nourishing brain cells.

WHAT IT CAN DO FOR YOU:

Help lower cholesterol levels.

Promote healthy hair—aid in preventing fallout.

Help in preventing eczema.

Aid in redistribution of body fat.

Produce a calming effect.

DEFICIENCY DISEASE:

Eczema. (For deficiency symptoms, see section 163.)

BEST NATURAL SOURCES:

Liver, brewer's yeast, dried lima beans, beef brains and heart, cantaloupe, grapefruit, raisins, wheat germ, unrefined molasses, peanuts, cabbage.

SUPPLEMENTS:

As with choline, six soy-based lecithin capsules contain approximately 244 mg. each of inositol and choline.

Available in lecithin powders that mix well with liquid. Most B-complex supplements contain approximately 100 mg. of choline and inositol.

Daily doses most often used are 250–500 mg.

TOXICITY AND WARNING SIGNS OF EXCESS:

No known toxic effects. (See section 334, "Cautions.")

ENEMIES:

Water, sulfa drugs, estrogen, food processing, alcohol, and coffee. (See section 293.)

PERSONAL ADVICE:

Take inositol with choline and your other B vitamins.

If you are a heavy coffee drinker, you probably need supplemental inositol.

If you take lecithin, I advise a supplement of chelated calcium to keep your phosphorus and calcium in balance, as both inositol and choline seem to raise phosphorus levels.

A good way to maximize the effectiveness of your vitamin E is to take enough inositol and choline.

41. PABA (Para-Aminobenzoic Acid)

FACTS:

Water soluble, one of the newer members of the B-complex family.

Usually measured in milligrams (mg.).

Can be synthesized in the body.

No RDI/RDA has yet been established.

Helps form folic acid and is important in the utilization of protein.

Helps in the assimilation—and therefore the effectiveness—of pantothenic acid.

WHAT IT CAN DO FOR YOU:

Reduce the pain of burns.

Keep skin healthy and smooth.

Help in delaying wrinkles.

Help to restore natural color to your hair.

DEFICIENCY DISEASE:

Eczema. (For deficiency symptoms, see section 163.)

BEST NATURAL SOURCES:

Liver, brewer's yeast, kidney, whole grains, rice, bran, wheat germ, and molasses.

SUPPLEMENTS:

30–100 mgs. are often included in good B-complex capsules as well as high-quality multivitamins.

Available in 30–1,000 mg. strengths in regular and time-release form.

Doses most often used are 30–100 mg. three times a day.

TOXICITY AND WARNING SIGNS OF EXCESS:

No known toxic effects, but long-term programs of high dosages are not recommended.

Symptoms that might indicate an oversupply of PABA are usually nausea and vomiting. (See section 334, "Cautions.")

ENEMIES:

Water, sulfa drugs, food-processing techniques, alcohol, estrogen. (See section 293.)

PERSONAL ADVICE:

Some people claim that the combination of folic acid and PABA has returned their graying hair to its natural color. It has worked on animals, so it is certainly worth a try for anyone looking for an alternative to hair dye. For this purpose, 1,000 mg. daily for six days a week is a viable regimen.

If you are taking penicillin, your PABA intake should be increased through natural foods or supplements.

42. Pantothenic Acid (Panthenol, Calcium Pantothenate, Vitamin B5)

FACTS:

Water soluble, another member of the B-complex family.

Helps in cell building, maintaining normal growth, and development of the central nervous system.

Vital for the proper functioning of the adrenal glands.

Essential for conversion of fat and sugar to energy.

Necessary for synthesis of antibodies, for utilization of PABA and choline.

The RDI/RDA (as set by the FDA) is 10 mg. for adults.

Can be synthesized in the body by intestinal bacteria.

WHAT IT CAN DO FOR YOU:

Aid in wound healing.

Fight infection by building antibodies.

Treat postoperative shock.
Prevent fatigue.
Reduce adverse and toxic effects of many antibiotics.
Lower cholesterol and triglycerides.

DEFICIENCY DISEASE:

Hypoglycemia, duodenal ulcers, blood and skin disorders. (For deficiency symptoms, see section 163.)

BEST NATURAL SOURCES:

Meat, whole grains, wheat germ, bran, kidney, liver, heart, green vegetables, brewer's yeast, nuts, chicken, unrefined molasses.

SUPPLEMENTS:

Most commonly found in B-complex formulas in a variety of strengths from 10–100 mg.
10–300 mg. are the daily doses usually taken.

TOXICITY AND WARNING SIGNS OF EXCESS:

No known toxic effects. (See section 334, "Cautions.")

ENEMIES:

Heat, food-processing techniques, canning, caffeine, sulfa drugs, sleeping pills, estrogen, alcohol. (See section 293.)

PERSONAL ADVICE:

If you frequently have tingling hands and feet, you might try increasing your pantothenic acid intake—in combination with other B vitamins.

People who need to cut their cholesterol may be given doses up to 1,000 mg. daily by their physicians.

Pantothenic acid can help provide a defense against a stress situation that you foresee or are involved in.

1,000 mg. daily has been found effective in reducing the pain of arthritis, in some cases.

If you suffer from allergies, relief could be just a vitamin B5 and C away. Try taking 1,000 mg. of each—with food—morning and evening.

43. Vitamin C (Ascorbic Acid, Cevitamin Acid)

FACTS:

Water soluble and a potent antioxidant.

Most animals synthesize their own vitamin C, but humans, apes, and guinea pigs must rely upon dietary sources.

Plays a primary role in the formation of collagen, which is important for the growth and repair of body-tissue cells, gums, blood vessels, bones, and teeth.

Helps in the body's absorption of iron.

Measured in milligrams (mg.).

Used up more rapidly under stress conditions.

The RDI/RDA for adults is 60 mg. (higher doses recommended during pregnancy and lactation—70–95 mg.).

Smokers and older persons have greater need for vitamin C. (Each cigarette destroys 25–100 mg.)

Prevents the oxidation of bad (LDL) cholesterol.

WHAT IT CAN DO FOR YOU:

Heal wounds, burns, and bleeding gums.

Increase effectiveness of drugs used to treat urinary tract infections.

Accelerate healing after surgery.

Help in decreasing blood cholesterol.

Aid in preventing many types of viral and bacterial infections and generally potentiate the immune system.

Offer protection against many forms of cancer.

Help counteract the formation of nitrosamines (cancer-causing substances).

Act as a natural laxative.
Lower incidence of blood clots in veins.
Aid in treatment and prevention of the common cold.
Extend life by enabling protein cells to hold together.
Increase the absorption of inorganic iron.
Reduce effects of many allergy-producing substances.
Help lower high blood pressure.
Prevent scurvy.

DEFICIENCY DISEASE:

Scurvy. (For deficiency symptoms, see section 163.)

BEST NATURAL SOURCES:

Citrus fruits, berries, green and leafy vegetables, tomatoes, cantaloupe, cauliflower, potatoes, and peppers.

SUPPLEMENTS:

Vitamin C is one of the most widely taken supplements. It is available in tablets, capsules, lozenges, time-release tablets, syrups, powders, chewable wafers, in just about every form a vitamin can take.

The form that is *pure* vitamin C is derived from corn dextrose (although no corn or dextrose remains).

The difference between "natural" or "organic" vitamin C and ordinary ascorbic acid is primarily in the individual's ability to digest it.

The best vitamin-C supplement is one that contains the complete C complex of bioflavonoids, hesperidin, and rutin. (Sometimes these are labeled citrus salts.)

Tablets and capsules are usually supplied in strengths up to 1,000 mg., and in powder form sometimes 5,000 mg. per tsp.

Daily doses most often used are 500 mg. to 4 g.

Rose hips vitamin C contains bioflavonoids and other enzymes that help C assimilate. They are the richest natural source of vitamin C. (The C is actually manufactured under the bud of the rose—called a hip.)

Acerola C is made with acerola berries.

TOXICITY AND WARNING SIGNS OF EXCESS:

Excessive intake may cause oxalic acid and uric acid stone formation (though taking magnesium, vitamin B6, and a sufficient amount of water daily can rectify this.) Occasionally, very high doses (over 10 g. daily) can cause unpleasant side effects, such as diarrhea, excess urination, and skin rashes. If any of these occur, cut back on your dosage.

Vitamin C should not be used by cancer patients undergoing radiation or chemotherapy. It can change test results. (See section 334, "Cautions.")

ENEMIES:

Water, cooking, heat, light, oxygen, smoking. (See section 293.)

PERSONAL ADVICE:

Because vitamin C is excreted in two to three hours, depending on the quantity of food in the stomach, and it is important to maintain a constant high level of C in the bloodstream at all times, I recommend taking it with breakfast and dinner.

Large doses of vitamin C can alter the results of laboratory tests, including Pap smears. If you're going to have any blood or urine testing, be sure to inform your doctor that you're taking vitamin C so that no errors will be made in diagnosis. (Vitamin C can mask the presence of blood in stool, compromising screening for colon cancer.)

Diabetics should be aware that testing the urine for sugar could be inaccurate if you're taking a lot of vitamin C. (But there are testing kits available that aren't affected by vitamin C. Ask your pharmacist or physician.)

Diabetes medications such as chlorpropamide (Diabinese™) and sulfa drugs may not be as effective when taken with vitamin C.

High doses are not recommended for people with genetic conditions that cause iron overload, like thalassemia and hemochromatosis.

If you're taking over 750 mg. daily, I suggest a magnesium supplement. This is an effective deterrent against kidney stones.

Carbon monoxide destroys vitamin C, so city dwellers should definitely up their intake.

You need extra C if you are on the pill.

To maximize the effectiveness of vitamin C, remember that it works best in conjunction with bioflavonoids, calcium, and magnesium.

I recommend increasing C doses if you take aspirin, which triples the excretion rate of vitamin C.

If you take ginseng, it's better to take it two hours before or after taking vitamin C or foods that are high in the vitamin.

To reduce the severity of colds, take 1,000 mg. of vitamin C twice daily. It's been shown to decrease the histamine in the blood by 40 percent. (Histamine is the substance that causes those annoying watery eyes and runny noses.)

44. Vitamin D (Calciferol, Viosterol, Ergosterol, "Sunshine Vitamin")

FACTS:

Fat soluble. Acquired through sunlight or diet. Ultraviolet sun rays act on the oils of the skin to produce the vitamin, which is then absorbed into the body.)

When taken orally, vitamin D is absorbed with fats through the intestinal walls.

Measured in International Units (IU), or micrograms of cholecalciferol mcg.).

The RDI/RDA for adults is 200–400 IU, or 5–10 mcg.

Smog reduces the vitamin-D–producing sunshine rays.

After a suntan is established, vitamin-D production through the skin stops.

WHAT IT CAN DO FOR YOU:

Properly utilize calcium and phosphorus necessary for strong bones and teeth.

Taken with vitamins A and C it can aid in preventing colds.

Help in treatment of conjunctivitis.

Aid in assimilating vitamin A.

DEFICIENCY DISEASE:

Rickets, severe tooth decay, osteomalacia, senile osteoporosis. (For deficiency symptoms, see section 163.)

BEST NATURAL SOURCES:

Fish liver oils, sardines, herring, salmon, tuna, milk and dairy products.

SUPPLEMENTS:

Usually supplied in 400 IU capsules, the vitamin itself derived from fish liver oil.

Daily doses most often taken are 400–1,000 IU.

TOXICITY AND WARNING SIGNS OF EXCESS:

20,000 IU daily over an extended period of time can produce toxic effects in adults.

Dosages of over 1,800 IU daily may cause hypervitaminosis D in children.

Signs of excess are unusual thirst, sore eyes, itching skin, vomiting, diarrhea, urinary urgency, abnormal calcium deposits in blood-vessel walls, liver, lungs, kidney, and stomach. (See section 334, "Cautions.")

ENEMIES:

Mineral oil, smog. (See section 293.)

PERSONAL ADVICE:

City dwellers, especially those in areas of high smog density, should increase their vitamin-D intake.

Night workers, and others whose lifestyle keeps them from sunlight should increase the D in their diet.

If you're taking an anticonvulsant drug, you most probably need to increase your vitamin-D intake.

Children who don't drink D-fortified milk should increase their intake of other vitamin-D–rich foods.

Dark-skinned people living in northern climates usually need an increase in vitamin D.

Do not supplement your dog's or cat's diet with vitamin D unless your vet specifically advises it.

Vitamin D works best with vitamin A, vitamin C, choline, calcium, and phosphorus.

45. Vitamin E (Tocopherol)

FACTS:

Fat soluble and stored in the liver, fatty tissues, heart, muscles, testes, uterus, blood, adrenal and pituitary glands.

Formerly measured by weight, but now generally designated according to its biological activity in International Units (IU). With this vitamin 1 IU is the same as 1 mg.

Composed of compounds called tocopherols. Of the eight tocopherols—alpha, beta, gamma, delta, epsilon, zeta, eta, and theta—alpha-tocopherol is the most effective.

An active antioxidant, prevents oxidation of fat compounds as well as that of vitamin A, selenium, two sulfur amino acids, and some vitamin C.

Enhances activity of vitamin A.

The RDI/RDA for adults is 8–10 IU. (This requirement is based on the National Research Council's latest revised allowances.)

60–70 percent of daily doses are excreted in feces. Unlike

other fat-soluble vitamins, E is stored in the body for a relatively short time, much like B and C.

Important as a vasodilator and an anticoagulant.

Products with 25 mcg. of selenium for each 200 units of E increase E's potency.

WHAT IT CAN DO FOR YOU:

Keep you looking younger by retarding cellular aging due to oxidation.

Prevent oxidation of "Bad" cholesterol.

Supply oxygen to the body to give you more endurance.

Protect your lungs against air pollution by working with vitamin A.

Help to prevent various forms of cancer.

Prevent and dissolve blood clots.

Alleviate fatigue.

Prevent thick scar formation externally (when applied topically—it can be absorbed through the skin) and internally.

Accelerate healing of burns.

Working as a diuretic, it can lower blood pressure.

Aid in prevention of miscarriages.

Help alleviate leg cramps and charley horse.

Lower risk of ischemic heart disease and stroke.

Decrease risk of Alzheimer's disease.

DEFICIENCY DISEASE:

Destruction of red blood cells, muscle degeneration, some anemias and reproductive disorders. (For deficiency symptoms, see section 163.)

BEST NATURAL SOURCES:

Wheat germ, soybeans, vegetable oils, nuts, brussels sprouts, leafy greens, spinach, enriched flour, whole wheat, whole-grain cereals, and eggs.

SUPPLEMENTS:

Available in oil-base capsules as well as water-dispersible dry tablets.

Usually supplied in strengths from 100–1,500 IU. The dry form is recommended for anyone who cannot tolerate oil or whose skin condition is aggravated by oil. It's also best for people over 40.

Daily doses most often used are 200–1,200 IU.

TOXICITY AND WARNING SIGNS OF EXCESS:

Essentially nontoxic. (See section 334, "Cautions.")

ENEMIES:

Heat, oxygen, freezing temperatures, food processing, iron, chlorine, mineral oil. (See section 293.)

PERSONAL ADVICE:

If you're on a diet high in polyunsaturated oils, you might need additional vitamin E.

High doses of vitamin E increase the action of anticoagulant drugs and can interfere with the absorption of vitamin K, which promotes blood clotting. If you are having surgery, I suggest that you discontinue vitamin-E supplements for two weeks before and after your operation, unless advised otherwise by your doctor.

The body absorbs vitamin E from natural supplements twice as well as from the synthetic ones. Natural supplements are labeled d-alpha-tocopherol; synthetics are dl.

Inorganic iron (ferrous sulfate) destroys vitamin E, so the two should not be taken together. If you're using a supplement containing any ferrous sulfate, E should be taken at least eight hours before or after.

Ferrous gluconate, peptonate, citrate, or fumerate (organic iron complexes) do not destroy E.

If you have chlorinated drinking water, you need more vitamin E.

Pregnant or lactating women, as well as those on the pill or taking hormones, need increased vitamin E.

I advise women going through menopause to increase their E intake. (If you are under forty years of age, 400 IU is fine; over forty, I suggest 800 IU daily. Dry form preferred.)

46. Vitamin F (Unsaturated Fatty Acids— Linoleic, Linolenic, and Arachidonic)

FACTS:

Fat soluble, made up of unsaturated fatty acids obtained from foods.

Measured in milligrams (mg.).

No RDI/RDA has been established, but the National Research Council has suggested that at least 1 percent of total calories should include essential unsaturated fatty acids.

Unsaturated fat helps burn saturated fat, with intake balanced two to one.

Twelve teaspoons sunflower seeds or eighteen pecan halves can furnish a day's complete supply.

If there is sufficient linoleic acid, the other two fatty acids can be synthesized.

Heavy carbohydrate consumption increases need.

WHAT IT CAN DO FOR YOU:

Aid in preventing cholesterol deposits in the arteries.

Promote healthy skin and hair.

Give some degree of protection against the harmful effects of X rays.

Aid in growth and well-being by influencing glandular activity and making calcium available to cells.

Combat heart disease.

Aid in weight reduction by burning saturated fats.

DEFICIENCY DISEASE:

Eczema, acne. (For deficiency symptoms, see section 163.)

BEST NATURAL SOURCES:

Vegetable oils—wheat germ, flaxseed, sunflower, safflower, soybean, and peanut—peanuts, sunflower seeds, walnuts, pecans, almonds, avocados.

SUPPLEMENTS:

Comes in capsules of 100–150 mg. strengths.

TOXICITY AND WARNING SIGNS OF EXCESS:

No known toxic effects, but an excess can lead to unwanted pounds. (See section 334, "Cautions.")

ENEMIES:

Saturated fats, heat, oxygen. (See section 293.)

PERSONAL ADVICE:

For best absorption of vitamin F, take vitamin E with it at mealtimes.

If you are a heavy carbohydrate consumer, you need more vitamin F.

Anyone worried about cholesterol buildup should be getting the proper intake of F.

Though most nuts are fine sources of unsaturated fatty acids, Brazil nuts and cashews are *not!*

Watch out for fad diets high in saturated fats.

47. Vitamin K (Menadione)

FACTS:

Fat soluble.

Usually measured in micrograms (mcg.).

There is a trio of K vitamins. K1 and K2 can be formed by natural bacteria in the intestines. K3 is a synthetic.

The RDI/RDA for adults is 65–80 mcg.

Essential in the formation of prothrombin, a blood-clotting chemical.

WHAT IT CAN DO FOR YOU:

Help in preventing internal bleeding and hemorrhages.
Aid in reducing excessive menstrual flow.
Promote proper blood clotting.

DEFICIENCY DISEASE:

Celiac disease, sprue, colitis. (For deficiency symptoms, see section 163.)

BEST NATURAL SOURCES:

Leafy green vegetables, yogurt, alfalfa, egg yolk, safflower oil, soybean oil, fish liver oils, kelp.

SUPPLEMENTS:

Available in 100 mcg. tablets (though the abundance of natural vitamin K generally makes supplementation unnecessary).

It is not included ordinarily in multiple vitamins.

TOXICITY AND WARNING SIGNS OF EXCESS:

More than 500 mcg. of synthetic vitamin K is not recommended. (See section 334, "Cautions.")

ENEMIES:

X rays and radiation, frozen foods, aspirin, air pollution, mineral oil. (See section 293.)

PERSONAL ADVICE:

High doses of vitamin E can interfere with vitamin K absorption.

Excessive diarrhea can be a symptom of vitamin K deficiency, but before self-supplementing, see a doctor.

Green leafy vegetables are your best defense against a vitamin-K deficiency.

If you have nosebleeds often, try increasing your K through natural food sources. Alfalfa tablets might help.

If you are taking an anticoagulant (blood thinner), be aware that this vitamin (even in natural foods) can reverse the drug's effect.

If you are on a chronic broad-spectrum antibiotic regimen, you're high risk for a vitamin-K deficiency. Increase the K-rich foods in your diet—and I suggest you check with a nutritionally oriented doctor about a supplement. (See section 342.)

48. Vitamin P (C Complex, Citrus Bioflavonoids, Rutin, Hesperidin)

FACTS:

Water soluble and composed of citrin, rutin, and hesperidin, as well as flavones and flavonals.

Usually measured in milligrams (mg.).

Necessary for the proper function and absorption of vitamin C.

Flavonoids are the substances that provide that yellow and orange color in citrus foods. (See section 104.)

Also called the capillary permeability factor. (P stands for permeability.) The prime function of bioflavonoids is to increase capillary strength and regulate absorption.

Aids vitamin C in keeping connective tissues healthy.

No daily allowances has been established, but most nutritionists agree that for every 500 mg. of vitamin C you should have at least 100 mg. of bioflavonoids.

Works synergistically with vitamin C.

WHAT IT CAN DO FOR YOU:

Prevent vitamin C from being destroyed by oxidation.

Strengthen the walls of capillaries, thereby preventing bruising.

Help build resistance to infection.

Aid in preventing and healing bleeding gums.

Increase the effectiveness of vitamin C.

Help in the treatment of edema and dizziness due to disease of the inner ear.

DEFICIENCY DISEASE:

Capillary fragility. (For deficiency symptoms, see section 163.)

BEST NATURAL SOURCES:

The white skin and segment part of citrus fruit—lemons, oranges, grapefruit. Also in apricots, buckwheat, blackberries, cherries, and rose hips.

SUPPLEMENTS:

Available usually in a C complex or by itself. Most often there are 500 mg. of bioflavonoids to 50 mg. of rutin and hesperidin. (If the ratio of rutin and hesperidin is not equal, it should be twice as much rutin.)

All C supplements work better with bioflavonoids.

Most common doses of rutin and hesperidin are 100 mg. three times a day.

TOXICITY AND WARNING SIGNS OF EXCESS:

No known toxicity. (See section 334, "Cautions.")

ENEMIES:

Water, cooking, heat, light, oxygen, smoking. (See section 293.)

PERSONAL ADVICE:

Menopausal women can usually find some effective relief from hot flashes with an increase in bioflavonoids taken in conjunction with vitamin D.

If your gums bleed frequently when you brush your teeth make sure you're getting enough rutin and hesperidin.

Anyone with a tendency to bruise easily will benefit from a C supplement with bioflavonoids, rutin, and hesperidin.

49. Vitamin T

There is very little known about this vitamin, except that it helps in blood coagulation and the forming of platelets. Because of these attributes it is important in warding off certain forms of anemia and hemophilia. No RDI/RDA has been established, and there are no supplements for the public on the market. It is found in sesame seeds and egg yolks, and there is no known toxicity.

50. Vitamin U

Even less is known about vitamin U than vitamin T. It is reputed to play an important role in healing ulcers, but medical opinions vary on this. It is found in raw cabbage and no known toxicity exists.

51. Any Questions About Chapter III?

My mother is seventy years old and healthy in most ways except she seems to catch every cold or "bug" that comes around. Is she missing a particular vitamin?

It's quite likely. Immune function declines as we age and recent studies have shown that older people with low blood-serum levels of vitamin E are often more vulnerable to developing infections. In fact, a study in *The American Journal of Clinical Nutrition* found that short-term supplementation with high doses of vitamin E significantly enhanced immune responsiveness in healthy individuals over sixty. I'd suggest that your mom do her immune system a favor and supplement her diet with a high-potency multivitamin with amino acid–chelated minerals—and at least 400–800 IU vitamin E daily.

I've read that diets high in broccoli, brussels sprouts, and carrots can help reduce the risk of cancer, but I just hate these vegetables. What vitamins can I take instead?

You can get concentrated forms of cruciferous (cabbage, broccoli, brussels sprouts, cauliflower) and carotene-rich (spinach and carrots) vegetables in tablet form. I'd advise taking these supplements daily. Since they are made from vegetables that are picked ripe, carefully washed, and quickly dehydrated without cooking—as well as being fortified with vitamins A, C, and E, beta-carotene and selenium—they'll provide you with optimal nutritional value.

Can you tell me how choline is helpful in the treatment of Alzheimer's disease?

Alzheimer's disease, which is a slow loss of mental faculties, seems to be caused by a depletion in central nervous system reserves of the neurotransmitter acetylcholine.

It has been found that patients with Alzheimer's syndrome are not only deficient in acetylcholine, but also the enzyme that catalyzes its production—choline acetyltransferase. Ingestion of more choline can apparently prevent existing acetylcholine from being broken down. Phosphatidylcholine, a new and more potent form of this is now recommended.

There is still no specific treatment for the disease, but it's been found that certain medications might worsen a patient's condition. For example, hypnotics such as *flurazepam* (Dalmane™), drugs for heart disease, and those given for intestinal cramping.

What sort of vitamin is beta-carotene? And why is there no RDA for it?

I'll answer the second part first. The reason there is no RDI/RDA for it is because it is not in itself a vitamin. Only after it's inside your body does it transform into vitamin A. Beta-carotene comes, primarily, from yellow and orange plant sources (carrots, pumpkins, sweet potatoes, cantaloupe) and has been found to be significantly helpful in the prevention of heart disease and many cancers. Levels decrease with old age, but beta-carotene can also be unnecessarily depleted by dieting, smoking, and heavy drinking. (See section 103.)

I've heard of rutin and hesperidin, but what is this bioflavonoid quercetin?

It's one you'll be hearing a lot more about. A member of the vitamin P, bioflavonoid family, quercetin is a potent antioxidant. Found in red and yellow onions, grapes, and Italian squash, it is believed to be one of the most powerful anticancer substances discovered to date. It helps to stop cancer at its earliest stage by preventing the damaging changes in the cells that initiate cancer, and also aids in inhibiting the spread of cancer cells. Additionally, quercetin has been shown to block the release of histamines and be an effective treatment for allergies and inflammatory disorders. It is available as a supplement, and the recommended dosage is one 400 mg. capsule before each meal.

IV

Your Mineral Essentials

52. Calcium

FACTS:

There is more calcium in the body than any other mineral.

Calcium and phosphorus work together for healthy bones and teeth.

Calcium and magnesium work together for cardiovascular health.

Almost all of the body's calcium (2–3 pounds) is found in the bones and teeth.

20 percent of an adult's bone calcium is reabsorbed and replaced every year. (New bone cells form as old ones break down.)

Calcium must exist in a two-to-one relationship with phosphorus. (Two parts calcium to one part phosphorus.)

In order for calcium to be absorbed, the body must have sufficient vitamin D.

The RDI/RDA for adults has been elevated from 800 mg. to 1,200 mg. And the National Institutes of Health now recommend 1,200–1,500 mg. for pregnant and nursing mothers, and 1,500 mg. for women over fifty and men over sixty-five years of age.

Calcium and iron are the two minerals most deficient in the American woman's diet.

WHAT IT CAN DO FOR YOU:

Maintain strong bones and healthy teeth.
Decrease risk of bone loss and fractures.
Help lower risk of colon cancer.
Keep your heart beating regularly.
Alleviate insomnia.
Help metabolize your body's iron.
Aid your nervous system, especially in impulse transmission.

DEFICIENCY DISEASE:

Rickets, osteomalacia, osteoporosis—commonly known as brittle bones. (See section 163 for symptoms.)

BEST NATURAL SOURCES:

Milk and milk products, all cheeses, soybeans, tofu, sardines, salmon, peanuts, walnuts, sunflower seeds, dried beans, kale, broccoli, collard greens.

SUPPLEMENTS:

Most often available in 250–500 mg. tablets.
The best form is chelated calcium tablets. (Calcium citrate provides the most usable calcium per tablet.)
Chewable calcium citrate supplements are available in flavors.
Calcium citrate is also available as effervescent tablets that dissolve in water and become a pleasant-tasting drink.
Bonemeal, formerly one of the most popular supplements, is no longer recommended—especially for children—because of its possible high lead content. (You can check with the manufacturer for an analysis.)
Calcium gluconate (a vegetarian source) or calcium lactate (a milk sugar derivative) are definitely lead-free and easy to absorb. (Gluconate is more potent than lactate.)
The letters USP (U.S. Pharmacopeia) on the label indicate

that the calcium in the product has met quality standards for dissolving within 30 minutes.

Most good multivitamin and mineral preparations include calcium.

When combined with magnesium, the ratio should be twice as much calcium as magnesium.

TOXICITY AND WARNING SIGNS OF EXCESS:

Excessive daily intake of over 2,500 mg. might lead to hypercalcemia. (See section 334, "Cautions.") Overly high intakes may also cause constipation and increase the risk of kidney stones and urinary tract infections.

ENEMIES:

Large quantities of fat, oxalic acid (found in chocolate, spinach, Swiss chard, parsley, beet greens, and rhubarb), and phytic acid (found in grains) are capable of preventing proper calcium absorption. (See section 293.)

PERSONAL ADVICE:

If you are taking antibiotics, such as tetracycline, be aware that calcium supplements may inhibit their effectiveness. (Check with your pharmacist.)

If you have chronic back pain, chelated calcium supplements might help.

Menstrual-cramp sufferers can often find relief by increasing their calcium intake.

If you enjoy chewing on chicken or turkey drumsticks, you're in luck. The tips of poultry leg bones are high in calcium.

If you're taking daily doses of 1,500 mg. calcium, and are prone to urinary tract infections, I'd advise taking your supplements with cranberry juice. This juice coats the bacteria and helps stop it from sticking to the urinary tract.

Teenagers who suffer from "growing pains" will usually

find that they disappear with an increase in calcium consumption.

Hypoglycemics could use more calcium. (I recommend calcium citrate for best absorption, in doses of 1,000–1,500 mg. daily.)

If you consume lots of soft drinks, be aware that, because they're high in phosphorus, you may be depleting your body of calcium and increasing your chances of osteoporosis.

Calcium works best with vitamins A, C, D; iron, magnesium, and phosphorus. (Too much phosphorus, as I've mentioned above, can deplete calcium.)

Calcium supplements are absorbed best when taken with meals. If you take your supplements on an empty stomach, or are over sixty years of age, calcium citrate is your best calcium choice.

You need extra calcium if you've been bedridden for a week or more. (The body loses bone density during extended bed rest.)

Taking calcium and magnesium at bedtime can help you get a good night's rest.

53. Chlorine

FACTS:

Regulates the blood's alkaline-acid balance.

Works with sodium and potassium in a compound form.

Aids in the cleaning of body wastes by helping the liver to function.

No dietary allowance has been established, but if your daily salt intake is average, you are getting enough.

WHAT IT CAN DO FOR YOU:

Aid in digestion.

Help keep you limber.

DEFICIENCY DISEASE:

Loss of hair and teeth.

BEST NATURAL SOURCES:

Table salt, kelp, olives.

SUPPLEMENTS:

Most good multimineral preparations include it.

TOXICITY AND WARNING SIGNS OF EXCESS:

Over 15 g. can cause unpleasant side effects. (See section 334, "Cautions.")

PERSONAL ADVICE:

If you have chlorine in your drinking water, you aren't getting all the vitamin E you think. (Chlorinated water destroys vitamin E.)

Anyone who drinks chlorinated water should be well advised to eat yogurt—a good natural way to replace the intestinal bacteria the chlorine destroys.

54. Chromium

FACTS:

Works with insulin in the metabolism of sugar.

Helps bring protein to where it's needed.

No official dietary allowance has been established, but 50–200 mcg. is the tentatively recommended adult intake.

As you get older, you retain less chromium in your body.

WHAT IT CAN DO FOR YOU:

Aid growth.

Help prevent and lower high blood pressure.

Work as a deterrent for diabetes.

Help prevent sugar cravings and sudden drops in energy.

DEFICIENCY DISEASE:

A suspected factor in arteriosclerosis and diabetes.

BEST NATURAL SOURCES:

Calves' livers, wheat germ, brewer's yeast, chicken, corn oil, clams.

SUPPLEMENTS:

May be found in better multimineral preparations. (Glucose tolerance factor, chromium picolinate, and chromium polynicotinate are the preferred forms.)

TOXICITY AND WARNING SIGNS OF EXCESS:

No known toxicity. (See section 334, "Cautions.")

PERSONAL ADVICE:

If you are low in chromium (90 percent of adults are not getting enough in their diet) you might try a zinc supplement. For some reason, chelated zinc seems to substitute well for deficient chromium.

The best assurance of an adequate chromium intake is a varied diet that provides a sufficient intake of other essential nutrients.

55. Cobalt

FACTS:

A mineral that is part of vitamin B12.
Usually measured in micrograms (mcg.).
Essential for red blood cells.
Must be obtained from food sources.
No daily allowance has been set for this mineral, and only very small amounts are necessary in the diet (usually no more than 8 mcg.).

WHAT IT CAN DO FOR YOU:

Stave off anemia.

DEFICIENCY DISEASE:

Anemia.

BEST NATURAL SOURCES:

Meat, kidney, liver, milk, oysters, clams.

SUPPLEMENTS:

Rarely found in supplement form.

TOXICITY AND WARNING SIGNS OF EXCESS:

No known toxicity. (See section 334, "Cautions.")

ENEMIES:

Whatever is antagonistic to B12.

PERSONAL ADVICE:

If you're a strict vegetarian, you are much more likely to
be deficient in this mineral than someone who includes meat
and shellfish in his or her diet.

56. Copper

FACTS:

Required to convert the body's iron into hemoglobin.
Can reach the bloodstream fifteen minutes after ingestion.
Makes the amino acid tyrosine usable, allowing it to work
as the pigmenting factor for hair and skin.
Present in cigarettes, birth control pills, and automobile
pollution.
Essential for the utilization of vitamin C.

No RDI/RDA has been established by the National Research Council, but 1.5–3 mg. for adults is what is currently recommended.

WHAT IT CAN DO FOR YOU:

Keep your energy up by aiding in effective iron absorption.

DEFICIENCY DISEASE:

Anemia, edema, skeletal defects, and possibly rheumatoid arthritis.

NATURAL FOOD SOURCES:

Dried beans, peas, whole wheat, prunes, organ meats, shrimp, and most seafood.

SUPPLEMENTS:

Usually available in multivitamin and mineral supplements in 2 mg. doses.

TOXICITY AND WARNING SIGNS OF EXCESS:

Rare. (See section 334, "Cautions.")

ENEMIES:

Not easily destroyed.

PERSONAL ADVICE:

As essential as copper is—and most Americans are not getting enough in their diet—I rarely suggest special supplementation. An excess seems to lower zinc level and produces insomnia, hair loss, irregular menses, and depression.

If you eat enough whole-grain products and fresh green leafy vegetables, or organ meats, you don't have to worry about your copper intake.

Cooking or storing acidic foods in copper pots can add to your daily intake.

57. Fluorine

FACTS:

Part of the synthetic compound sodium fluoride (the type added to drinking water) and calcium fluoride (a natural substance).

Decreases chances of dental caries, though too much can discolor teeth.

No RDI/RDA has been established, but most people get about 1 mg. daily from fluoridated drinking water. (1.5–4 mg. is suggested by the National Academy of Sciences-National Research Council.)

WHAT IT CAN DO FOR YOU:

Reduce tooth decay.
Strengthen bones.

DEFICIENCY DISEASE:

Tooth decay.

BEST NATURAL SOURCES:

Fluoridated drinking water, seafood, and tea.

SUPPLEMENTS:

Not ordinarily found in multimineral supplements.
Available in prescription multivitamins for children in areas without fluoridated water.

TOXICITY AND WARNING SIGNS OF EXCESS:

20–80 mg. per day. (See section 334, "Cautions.")

ENEMIES:

Aluminum cookware.

PERSONAL ADVICE:

Don't take additional fluoride unless it is prescribed by a physician or dentist.

The fluoride content of food is increased significantly if it's cooked in fluoridated water or a Teflon™-treated utensil.

58. Iodine (Iodide)

FACTS:

Two-thirds of the body's iodine is in the thyroid gland.

Since the thyroid gland controls metabolism, and iodine influences the thyroid, an undersupply of this mineral can result in slow mental reaction, weight gain, and lack of energy.

The RDI/RDA, as established by the National Research Council, is 150 mcg. for adults (1 mcg. per kilogram of body weight) and 175–200 mcg. for pregnant and lactating women respectively.

WHAT IT CAN DO FOR YOU:

Help you with dieting by burning excess fat.

Promote proper growth.

Give you more energy.

Improve mental alacrity.

Promote healthy hair, nails, skin, and teeth.

DEFICIENCY DISEASE:

Goiter, hypothyroidism.

BEST NATURAL SOURCES:

Kelp, vegetables grown in iodine-rich soil, onions, and all seafood.

SUPPLEMENTS:

Available in multimineral and high-potency vitamin supplements in doses of 0.15 mg.

Natural kelp is a good source of supplemental iodine.

TOXICITY AND WARNING SIGNS OF EXCESS:

No known toxicity from natural iodine, though intakes above 2 mg. are not recommended and iodine as a drug can be harmful if prescribed incorrectly. (See section 334, "Cautions.")

ENEMIES:

Food processing, nutrient-poor soil.

PERSONAL ADVICE:

Aside from kelp, and the iodine included in multimineral and vitamin preparations, I don't recommend additional supplements unless you're advised by a doctor to take them.

If you use salt and live in the Midwest, where iodine-poor soil is common, make sure the salt is iodized.

If you are inclined to eat excessive amounts of raw cabbage, you might *not* be getting the iodine you need, because there are elements in the cabbage that prevent proper utilization of the iodine. This being the case, you might consider a kelp supplement.

59. Iron

FACTS:

Essential and required for life, necessary for the production of hemoglobin (red blood corpuscles), myoglobin (red pigment in muscles), and certain enzymes.

Only about 8 percent of your total iron intake is absorbed and actually enters your bloodstream.

An average 150-pound adult has about 4 g. of iron in his or her body. Hemoglobin, which accounts for most of the iron, is recycled and reutilized as blood cells are replaced every 120 days. Iron bound to protein (ferritin) is stored in the body, as is tissue iron (present in myoglobin) in very small amounts.

The RDI/RDA, according to the National Research Council, is 10–15 mg. for adults, and 30 mg. for pregnant women. Nursing mothers' RDI/RDA is the same as for nonpregnant women (15 mg.).

Copper, cobalt, manganese, and vitamin C are necessary to assimilate iron.

Iron is necessary for proper metabolization of B vitamins.

Excessive amounts of zinc and vitamin E interfere with iron absorption.

Too much iron in the blood can promote formation of free radicals and increase the risk of heart disease—especially for men.

WHAT IT CAN DO FOR YOU:

Aid growth.
Promote resistance to disease.
Prevent fatigue.
Cure and prevent iron-deficiency anemia.
Bring back good skin tone.

DEFICIENCY DISEASE:

Iron-deficiency anemia. (For deficiency symptoms, see section 163.)

BEST NATURAL SOURCES:

Pork, beef, liver, red meat, clams, dried peaches, farina, egg yolks, oysters, nuts, beans, asparagus, molasses, oatmeal.

SUPPLEMENTS:

The most assimilable form of iron is amino acid chelate, which means organic iron that has been processed for fastest assimilation. This form is nonconstipating and easy on sensitive systems.

Ferrous sulfate, inorganic iron, appears in many vitamin and mineral supplements and can destroy vitamin E (they should be taken at least eight hours apart). Check labels; many drugstore formulas contain ferrous sulfate.

Supplements with organic iron—ferrous gluconate, ferrous fumerate, ferrous citrate, or ferrous peptonate—do not neutralize vitamin E. They are available in a wide variety of doses, usually up to 320 mg.

TOXICITY AND WARNING SIGNS OF EXCESS:

Rare in healthy, normal individuals. Adult doses, though, can be a hazard for children. A dose of 3 g. can be lethal for a two-year-old child. (See section 334, "Cautions.") Individuals with idiopathic hemochromatosis are genetically at risk from iron overload. Keep children's chewable vitamins with iron safely out of their reach. Teach them that these are not candies.

ENEMIES:

Phosphoproteins in eggs and phytates in unleavened whole wheat reduce iron availability to body.

PERSONAL ADVICE:

If you are a woman who experiences very heavy menstrual bleeding, a strict vegetarian, or are an extreme low-calorie dieter, you might need an iron supplement. Check the label on your multivitamin or mineral preparation and see what you are already getting so you can guide yourself accordingly. (You might want to have your blood iron status tested by your doctor to be sure you're not getting too much.)

If you're on the anti-inflammatory drug Indocin™, or take aspirin on a daily basis, you might need more iron. (Check with your physician.)

Keep your iron supplements safely out of reach of children.

Coffee drinkers, as well as tea drinkers, be aware that if you consume large quantities of either beverage you are most likely inhibiting your iron absorption.

If you are pregnant, check with your doctor before taking iron or iron-fortified vitamin supplements. (Iron poisoning has been found in children whose mothers have taken too many pills during pregnancy.)

Do not take iron supplements if you have an infection. Bacteria require iron for growth and extra iron would encourage their increase.

If you're a postmenopausal woman, you probably do not need supplemental iron.

60. Magnesium

FACTS:

Necessary for calcium and vitamin-C metabolism, as well as that of phosphorus, sodium, and potassium.

Measured in milligrams (mg.).

Essential for effective nerve and muscle functioning.

Important for converting blood sugar into energy.

Known as the antistress mineral.

Alcoholics are usually deficient.

Adults need 250–500 mg. daily. For pregnant and lactating women, the recommendation according to the National Research Council is 300–355 mg.

The human body contains approximately 21 g. of magnesium.

WHAT IT CAN DO FOR YOU:

Help burn fat and produce energy.

Aid in fighting depression.

Promote a healthier cardiovascular system and help prevent heart attacks.

Help prevent premature labor.

Keep teeth healthier.

Help prevent calcium deposits, kidney and gallstones.

Bring relief from indigestion.

Combined with calcium can work as a natural tranquilizer.

Alleviate premenstrual syndrome (PMS).

DEFICIENCY DISEASE:

(For deficiency symptoms, see section 163.)

BEST NATURAL SOURCES:

Unmilled grains, figs, almonds, nuts, seeds, dark green vegetables, bananas.

SUPPLEMENTS:

Amino acid–chelated magnesium and calcium in perfect balance (half as much magnesium as calcium) is the preferred form.

Available in multivitamin and mineral preparations.

Can be purchased as magnesium oxide. 250 mg. strength equals 150 mg. per tablet.

Commonly available in 133.3 mg. strengths and taken four times a day.

Supplements of magnesium should not be taken after meals, since the mineral does neutralize stomach acidity.

TOXICITY AND WARNING SIGNS OF EXCESS:

Large amounts, over an extended period of time, can be toxic if your calcium and phosphorus intakes are high or if you have impaired kidney function. (See section 334, "Cautions.")

ENEMIES:

Diuretics, alcohol. (See section 293.)

PERSONAL ADVICE:

If you are a drinker, I suggest you increase your intake of magnesium.

If your daily workouts are exhausting, you probably need more magnesium.

Women who are on the pill or taking estrogen in any form would be well advised to eat more magnesium-rich foods. (Keep in mind that meat, fish, and dairy products are relatively poor sources.)

If you are a heavy consumer of nuts, seeds, and green vegetables, you probably get ample magnesium—as does anyone who lives in an area with hard water.

If you are an insulin-resistant diabetic, eating a magnesium-rich diet can help lower your blood pressure. (Talk to your physician before taking a supplement.)

Magnesium works best with vitamin A, calcium, and phosphorus.

Keep in mind that because magnesium turns on the enzymes that use vitamins B1, B2, and B6, a deficiency of the mineral can cause symptoms associated with an insufficiency of B vitamins—usually convulsions.

61. Manganese

FACTS:

Helps activate enzymes necessary for the body's proper use of biotin, B1, and vitamin C.

Needed for normal bone structure.

Measured in milligrams (mg.).

Important in the formation of thyroxin, the principal hormone of the thyroid gland.

Necessary for the proper digestion and utilization of food.

No official daily allowance has been established, but 2–5 mg. is the National Research Council's recommended average adult requirement.

Important for reproduction and normal central nervous system function.

WHAT IT CAN DO FOR YOU:

Help eliminate fatigue.
Aid in muscle reflexes.
Help prevent osteoporosis.
Improve memory.
Reduce nervous irritability.

DEFICIENCY DISEASE:

Ataxia.

BEST NATURAL SOURCES:

Whole-grain cereals, nuts, green leafy vegetables, peas, beets.

SUPPLEMENTS:

Most often found in multivitamin and mineral combinations in dosages of 1–9 mg.

TOXICITY AND WARNING SIGNS OF EXCESS:

Rare, except from industrial sources. (See section 334, "Cautions.")

ENEMIES:

Large intakes of calcium and phosphorus will inhibit absorption, as can the fiber and phytic acid contained in bran and beans. (See section 293.)

PERSONAL ADVICE:

If you suffer from recurrent dizziness, you might try adding more manganese to your diet.

I advise absentminded people, or anyone with memory problems, to make sure they are getting enough of this mineral.

Heavy dairy milk drinkers and meat eaters need increased manganese.

62. Molybdenum

FACTS:

Aids in carbohydrate and fat metabolism.

A vital part of the enzyme responsible for iron utilization.

No dietary allowance has been set, but the estimated daily intake of 75–250 mcg. has generally been accepted as the adequate human requirement.

WHAT IT CAN DO FOR YOU:

Help in preventing anemia. Promote general well-being.

DEFICIENCY DISEASE:

None known.

BEST NATURAL SOURCES:

Dark green leafy vegetables, whole grains, legumes.

SUPPLEMENTS:

Not ordinarily available.

TOXICITY AND WARNING SIGNS OF EXCESS:

Rare, but 5–10 mg. a day can be considered toxic. (See section 334, "Cautions.")

PERSONAL ADVICE:

As important as molybdenum is, there seems no need for supplementation unless all the food you consume comes from nutrient-deficient soil.

63. Phosphorus

FACTS:

Present in every cell in the body.

Vitamin D and calcium are essential to proper phosphorus functioning.

Calcium and phosphorus should be balanced two to one to work correctly (twice as much calcium as phosphorus).

Involved in virtually all physiological chemical reactions.

Necessary for normal bone and tooth structure.

Niacin cannot be assimilated without phosphorus.

Important for heart regularity.

Essential for normal kidney functioning.

Needed for the transference of nerve impulses.

The RDI/RDA is 800–1,200 mg. for adults, the higher levels for pregnant and lactating women.

WHAT IT CAN DO FOR YOU:

Aid in growth and body repair.

Provide energy and vigor by helping in the metabolization of fats and starches.

Lessen the pain of arthritis.
Promote healthy gums and teeth.

DEFICIENCY DISEASE:

Rickets, pyorrhea.

BEST NATURAL SOURCES:

Fish, poultry, meat, whole grains, eggs, nuts, seeds.

SUPPLEMENTS:

Bonemeal is a fine natural source of phosphorus. (Make sure vitamin D has been added to help assimilation, *and that the bonemeal is lead-free!*)

TOXICITY AND WARNING SIGNS OF EXCESS:

No known toxicity. (See section 334, "Cautions.")

ENEMIES:

Too much iron, aluminum, and magnesium can render phosphorus ineffective. (See section 293.)

PERSONAL ADVICE:

When you get too much phosphorus, you throw your mineral balance off and decrease your calcium. Our diets are usually high in phosphorus—since it does occur in almost every natural food—and therefore calcium deficiencies are frequent. Be aware of this and adjust your diet accordingly.

If you're over forty, you should cut down on your weekly meat consumption and eat more leafy vegetables and drink milk. The reason for this is that after forty our kidneys don't help excrete excess phosphorus, and calcium is again depleted. Be on the lookout for foods preserved with phosphates and consider them as part of your phosphorus intake.

64. Potassium

FACTS:

Works with sodium to regulate the body's water balance and normalize heart rhythms. (Potassium works inside the cells, sodium works just outside them.)

Nerve and muscle functions suffer when the sodium-potassium balance is off.

Hypoglycemia (low blood sugar) causes potassium loss, as does a long fast or severe diarrhea.

No dietary allowance has been set, but 1,600–2,000 mg. is considered a sufficient daily intake for healthy adults.

Both mental and physical stress can lead to a potassium deficiency.

WHAT IT CAN DO FOR YOU:

Aid in clear thinking by sending oxygen to brain.
Help dispose of body wastes.
Assist in reducing blood pressure.
Aid in allergy treatment.

DEFICIENCY DISEASE:

Edema, hypoglycemia. (For deficiency symptoms, see section 163.)

BEST NATURAL SOURCES:

Citrus fruits, cantaloupe, tomatoes, watercress, all green leafy vegetables, mint leaves, sunflower seeds, bananas, potatoes.

SUPPLEMENTS:

Available in most high-potency multivitamin and multi-mineral preparations.

Inorganic potassium salts are the sulfate (alum), the chloride, the oxide, and carbonate. Organic potassium refers to the gluconate, the citrate, the fumerate.

Can be bought separately as potassium gluconate, citrate, or chloride in dosages up to nearly 600 mg. (99 mg. elemental potassium.)

TOXICITY AND WARNING SIGNS OF EXCESS:

An intake of 18 g. can cause toxicity. (See section 334, "Cautions.")

ENEMIES:

Alcohol, coffee, sugar, diuretics. (See section 293.)

PERSONAL ADVICE:

If you drink large amounts of coffee, you might find that the fatigue you're fighting is due to the potassium loss you're suffering from.

Heavy drinkers and anyone with a hungry sweet tooth should be aware that their potassium levels are probably low.

If you have low blood sugar, you are likely to be losing potassium while retaining water. And if you take a diuretic, you'll lose even more potassium! Watch your diet, increase your green vegetables, and take enough magnesium to regain your mineral balance.

Losing weight on a low-carbohydrate diet might not be the only thing you're losing. Chances are your potassium level is down. Watch out for weakness and poor reflexes.

Excess potassium is normally excreted by the kidneys. However, people with impaired kidney function should not eat foods high in potassium or take potassium supplements.

65. Selenium

FACTS:

Vitamin E and selenium are synergistic. This means that the two together increase the potency of each other.

Both vitamin E and selenium are antioxidants, preventing or at least slowing down aging and hardening of tissues through oxidation.

Selenium is critical for the production of glutathione peroxidase, the body's primary antioxidant that is found in every cell.

Males appear to have a greater need for selenium. Almost half their body's supply concentrates in the testicles and portions of the seminal ducts adjacent to the prostate gland. Also, selenium is lost in the semen.

The RDI/RDA for this mineral is 50 mcg. for women, 70 mcg. for men, 65 mcg. for pregnant women, and 75 mcg. for nursing mothers.

WHAT IT CAN DO FOR YOU:

Help protect against various types of cancer.
Aid in reducing risk of heart disease and stroke.
Help keep youthful elasticity in tissues.
Alleviate hot flashes and menopausal distress.
Help in treatment and prevention of dandruff.
Raise sperm count and increase fertility in men.

DEFICIENCY DISEASE:

Premature stamina loss; Keshan disease.

BEST NATURAL SOURCES:

Seafood, kidney, liver, wheat germ, bran, tuna fish, onions, tomatoes, broccoli, garlic, brown rice.

SUPPLEMENTS:

Available in small microgram doses: 25, 50, 100, and 200 mcg.

Also available combined with vitamin E and other antioxidants.

TOXICITY AND WARNING SIGNS OF EXCESS:

High doses can produce toxic effects, including gastrointestinal disorders, garlicky breath odor, brittle nails, a metallic taste in the mouth, and yellowish skin. Until more is learned, I suggest you do not exceed 300 mcg. daily. (Studies so far have shown toxicity at levels of 2,400 mcg. daily, but I suggest you err on the side of caution until safe levels have been firmly established.) (See section 334, "Cautions.")

ENEMIES:

Food-processing techniques. (See section 293.)

PERSONAL ADVICE:

If selenium-rich foods are grown in selenium-depleted soil, you're not getting enough of this mineral from food.

In addition to eating selenium-rich foods, I suggest taking selenium supplements—between 100 and 200 mcg. daily as a preventive against disease.

66. Sodium

FACTS:

Sodium and potassium were discovered together and both found to be essential for normal growth.

High intakes of sodium (salt) will result in a depletion of potassium.

Diets high in sodium usually account for many instances of high blood pressure.

There is no official allowance, but the National Research

Council's estimated sodium chloride requirement for healthy adults is 500 mg. daily. Sodium aids in keeping calcium and other minerals in the blood soluble.

WHAT IT CAN DO FOR YOU:

Aid in preventing heat prostration or sunstroke.
Help your nerves and muscles function properly.

DEFICIENCY DISEASE:

Impaired carbohydrate digestion, possibly neuralgia.

BEST NATURAL SOURCES:

Salt, shellfish, carrots, beets, artichokes, dried beef, brains, kidney, bacon.

SUPPLEMENTS:

Rarely needed, but if so, kelp is a safe and nutritive supplement.

TOXICITY AND WARNING SIGNS OF EXCESS:

Over 14 g. of sodium chloride daily can produce toxic effects. (See section 334, "Cautions.")

PERSONAL ADVICE:

If you think you don't eat much salt, see sections 311 and 312 and think again.

If you have high blood pressure, cut down on your sodium intake by reading the labels on the foods you buy. Look for SALT, SODIUM, or the chemical symbol *Na*.

Adding sodium to your diet is as easy as a shake of salt, but subtracting it can be difficult. Avoid luncheon meats, frankfurters, salted-cured meats such as ham, bacon, corned beef, as well as condiments—ketchup, chili sauce, soy sauce, mustard. Don't use baking powder or baking soda in cooking.

67. Sulfur

FACTS:

Essential for healthy hair, skin, and nails.

Helps maintain oxygen balance necessary for proper brain function.

Works with B-complex vitamins for basic body metabolism, and is part of tissue-building amino acids.

Aids the liver in bile secretion.

No RDI/RDA has been set, but a diet sufficient in protein will generally be sufficient in sulfur.

WHAT IT CAN DO FOR YOU:

Tone up skin and make hair more lustrous.

Help fight bacterial infections.

DEFICIENCY DISEASE:

None known.

BEST NATURAL SOURCES:

Lean beef, dried beans, fish, eggs, cabbage, kale, garlic, brussels sprouts.

SUPPLEMENTS:

MSM (Methylsulfonylmethane), an organic sulfur, in 1,000 mg. tablets with a vitamin-C complex is available as a supplement.

MSM is used in lotion form for skin problems.

TOXICITY AND WARNING SIGNS OF EXCESS:

No known toxicity from organic sulfur, but ill effects may occur from large amounts of inorganic sulfur. (See section 334, "Cautions.")

PERSONAL ADVICE:

Organic sulfur, MSM, is nonallergenic. Do not confuse it with the synthetic *sulfa* drugs, which can trigger allergic reactions in many people.

Taken with glucosamine, another sulfur compound, MSM can significantly reduce the pain and stiffness of arthritis.

For allergies, parasitic infections, and faster recovery after working out, MSM with a vitamin C–bioflavonoid complex is terrific.

Sulfur creams and ointments have been remarkably successful in treating a variety of skin problems. Check the ingredients in the preparation you are now using. There are many fine natural preparations available at health-food centers.

68. Vanadium

FACTS:

Inhibits the formation of cholesterol in blood vessels.
Necessary for the formation of teeth and bones.
No dietary allowance set.
Mimics the action of the hormone insulin.

WHAT IT CAN DO FOR YOU:

Aid in preventing heart attacks.
Help control insulin-resistant and Type II diabetes.
Improve nutrient transport into cells and increase energy.

DEFICIENCY DISEASE:

None known.

BEST NATURAL SOURCES:

Fish, olives, whole grains.

SUPPLEMENTS:

Available in the form of vanadyl sulfate, the biologically active form of vanadium.

Usual dose is 10 mg. half an hour before working out.

Diabetics should check with their doctor for specific dosage.

TOXICITY AND WARNING SIGNS OF EXCESS:

Can easily be toxic if taken in synthetic form. (See section 334, "Cautions.")

PERSONAL ADVICE:

This is not one of the minerals that needs to be supplemented. A good fish dinner will supply you with the vanadium you need.

There is a biologically active form of vanadium, vanadyl sulfate. It's a trace mineral that mimics the action of the hormone insulin and has been used by alternative physicians in the treatment of diabetes. (CAUTION: If you have diabetes, do not self-medicate. Vanadyl can lower blood sugar levels too quickly, causing problems. See section 342 for a listing of alternative practitioners.)

Vanadyl sulfate is available as a supplement and bodybuilders claim that it helps build muscle, increasing strength and definition. The recommended dosage for bodybuilding is 10 mg. one half hour before working out.

69. Zinc

FACTS:

Zinc acts as a traffic director, overseeing the efficient flow of body processes, the maintenance of enzyme systems and cells.

Essential for protein synthesis and collagen formation.

Governs the contractibility of muscles.

Helps in the formation of insulin.

A constituent of many vital enzymes, including the antioxidant superoxide dismutase (SOD).

Important for blood stability (keeps the proper concentration of vitamin E in the blood) and in maintaining the body's acid-alkaline balance.

Exerts a normalizing effect on the prostate and is important in the development of all reproductive organs.

Some studies indicate its importance in brain function and the treatment of schizophrenia.

Strong evidence of its requirement for the synthesis of DNA.

The RDI/RDA, as set by the National Research Council, is 12–15 mg. for adults (slightly higher allowances for nursing mothers).

Excessive sweating can cause a loss of as much as 3 mg. of zinc per day.

Most zinc in foods is lost in processing, or never exists in substantial amounts because of nutrient-poor soil.

WHAT IT CAN DO FOR YOU:

Accelerate healing time for internal and external wounds.

Get rid of white spots on the fingernails.

Help restore loss of taste.

Aid in the treatment of infertility.

Help avoid prostate problems.

Promote growth and mental alertness.

Help decrease cholesterol deposits.

Aid in the treatment of mental disorders.

Help reduce length and severity of colds.

DEFICIENCY DISEASE:

Possibly prostatic hypertrophy (noncancerous enlargement of the prostate gland), arteriosclerosis, hypogonadism.

BEST NATURAL SOURCES:

Meat, liver, seafood (especially oysters), wheat germ, brewer's yeast, pumpkin seeds, eggs, nonfat dry milk, ground mustard.

SUPPLEMENTS:

Available in all good multivitamin and multimineral preparations.

Can be bought as zinc sulfate, zinc gluconate, or zinc picolinate in doses ranging from 15 to 50 mg. of elemental zinc. Both zinc sulfate and zinc gluconate seem to be equally effective, but zinc gluconate appears to be more easily tolerated.

Amino acid–chelated zinc and zinc picolinate are the best forms of supplemental zinc.

Zinc is also available in combination with vitamin C, magnesium, and the B-complex vitamins.

Zinc lozenges, for colds, must dissolve in your mouth— otherwise they are ineffective.

TOXICITY AND WARNING SIGNS OF EXCESS:

Excessive intake can cause gastrointestinal irritation, impaired immune function, and copper deficiency. Doses of 1,000 mg. or more can produce toxic effects. (See section 334, "Cautions.")

ENEMIES:

Phytates, compounds found in grains and legumes, bind with zinc so that it cannot be absorbed. (See section 293.)

PERSONAL ADVICE:

You need higher intakes of zinc if you are taking large amounts of vitamin B6. This is also true if you are an alcoholic or a diabetic.

Men with prostate problems—and without them—would be well advised to keep their zinc levels up.

I have seen success in cases of impotence with a supplement program of B6 and zinc.

Elderly people, concerned about senility, might find a zinc and manganese supplement beneficial.

If you are bothered by irregular menses, you might try a zinc supplement before resorting to hormone treatment to establish regularity.

Your zinc levels may be lowered by diarrhea and consumption of large amounts of fiber.

Remember, if you are adding zinc to your diet, you will increase your need for vitamin A. (Zinc works best with vitamin A, calcium, and phosphorus.)

If you're taking both iron and zinc supplements, take them at different times as they can interfere with each other's activity.

CAUTION: Although zinc is an immune system booster, doses over 150 mg. daily may inhibit immune response.

70. Water

FACTS:

The simple truth is that this is our most important nutrient. One-half to four-fifths of the body's weight is water.

A human being can live for weeks without food, but only a few days without water.

Water is the basic solvent for all the products of digestion.

Essential for removing wastes.

There is no specific dietary allowance since water loss varies with climate, situations, and individuals, but under ordinary circumstances 6–8 glasses daily is considered healthy. Nursing mothers have increased water requirements because of the amount that's secreted in their milk.

Regulates body temperature.

WHAT IT CAN DO FOR YOU:

Keep all your bodily functions functioning.
Aid in dieting by depressing appetite before meals.
Help prevent constipation.
Aid in preventing kidney stones.

DEFICIENCY DISEASE:

Dehydration.

BEST NATURAL SOURCES:

Drinking water, juices, fruits, and vegetables.

SUPPLEMENTS:

All drinkable liquids can substitute for our daily water requirements.

TOXICITY AND WARNING SIGNS OF EXCESS:

No known toxicity, but an intake of one and a half gallons (that's 16–24 glasses) in about an hour could be dangerous to an adult. It could kill an infant.

PERSONAL ADVICE:

I advise 6–8 glasses of filtered water daily, to be drunk a half hour before meals, for anyone who's dieting.

If you're running a fever, be sure to drink lots of water to prevent dehydration and to flush the system of wastes.

The more water you drink with a drug that can cause stomach distress—aspirin, ibuprofen, antibiotics—the less your chance of stomach upset.

Don't drink water from your hot water tap. Hot water dissolves more lead than cold water. And in the morning, always let the water run a few minutes to get the lead out of overnight accumulations.

If you live in an area where there is hard water, you're

probably getting more calcium and magnesium than you think.

SPECIAL WATER CAUTIONS:

If you live in an old home containing lead pipes, have your water analyzed by the local county health department. Water with the wrong pH can dissolve lead from pipes, subjecting children to possible lead poisoning. (Even homes with copper plumbing can have lead-soldered joints that might affect tap water.)

If there are chlorinated solvents or pesticides in your water, they can be absorbed through the skin and are volatile. *Taking a fifteen-minute shower can be as toxic as drinking eight glasses of contaminated water!*

Most home water-filtering systems have drawbacks, and many can be hazardous to your health. For instance:

• Activated carbon filters can become fouled with harmful contaminants if they are not changed on a regular basis.
• Reverse-osmosis systems, which remove chemicals, but not necessarily inorganic contaminants, must be tested periodically because the filter can be loaded with bacteria without evidencing a reduced flow rate.
• Distillers, which are generally more effective in removing inorganic than organic contaminants, must be descaled regularly. If not, the product water can be *worse* instead of better! If you use a home filtering system, remember that it must be properly maintained and checked periodically. Stick to well-known or national brands.

71. Any Questions About Chapter IV?

I'm a forty-year-old woman and drink three glasses of milk every day. Do I still need more calcium?

If that's your sole source of calcium, you do! Three 8-ounce glasses of whole milk give you only 776 mg. of calcium—not enough and certainly not worth the 360 mg. of sodium, 33 mg. of cholesterol, 15 g. of saturated fat, and 577 calories that you also get. Skim, low-fat milk, or buttermilk will lower the amount of calories and fat, but still won't provide you with sufficient calcium. (See section 52 for other natural sources.)

I've read that chlorinated drinking water can cause cancer. Is this true? If so, why do they chlorinate water?

Unfortunately, chlorination has indeed been linked to a group of cancer-causing chemicals (trihalomethanes) in our water. But according to the Environmental Protection Agency, the risk to the public is far outweighed by the benefits—primarily the prevention of widespread outbreaks of typhoid and other waterborne diseases. Home water-filtering systems can remove chlorine from tap water after bacteria have been killed, but see section 70 for water cautions to be aware of.

I'm worried about all the pollution in our rivers and streams. How do I know that my tap water is safe to drink?

The best thing to do if you want to find out if there are contaminants in your water is to contact your local water superintendent and ask for the results of water-sampling tests and sanitary surveys. Ask to see the Public Health Service standards, too, so that you'll be able to compare the former with the latter. You can also have your water tested for contaminants at most local hospital laboratories.

Meanwhile, until you are sure that your water is safe, I recommend taking the following emergency measures:

• Let your water run for 3–4 minutes before using it. This helps flush out any lead, cadmium, and cobalt that may lodge in your pipes.
• Boil your water (uncovered) for at least 20 minutes before using it. Boiling can kill bacteria and remove some organic chemicals.

• If you're worried abut trihalomethanes (which are carcinogens found in chlorinated water), whip your water in a blender for 15 minutes with the top off. Aeration removes chlorine and chlorinated organics.
• Buy a water filter.

I get very confused in the supermarket. Is mineral water better for me than springwater?

Better? Not really. Some bottled mineral waters may actually have fewer dissolved minerals than many city water supplies. In fact, the term mineral water is frequently used to describe all bottled water, with the exception of bulk water, club soda, and seltzer. Springwater must, under truth-in-labeling laws, come from a spring. But that spring has minerals in it, too. What you want to watch out for are mineral waters without the word *natural* on the label. This means that minerals may have been removed or added—and if you're going to buy a nutrient cocktail, you're better off making it yourself!

I know I need calcium, but I'm allergic to dairy products. Can you recommend alternative dietary sources?

Lots! Orange juice (6 oz.) fortified with calcium will give you approximately 200 mg. A 3-ounce can of sardines or salmon (with bones) will give you another 200–300 mg. Tofu, made with calcium sulfate, will also supply calcium (150 mg. per 4-oz. serving) as will almonds, Brazil nuts, and hazelnuts (approximately 200–300 mg. per cup). You might also want to try nori and other seaweeds. They're an acquired taste, but they are high in calcium.

V

Protein—and Those Amazing Amino Acids

72. The Protein–Amino Acid Connection

Protein is a life necessity in the diet of man and all animals. Actually, though, it is not protein itself that is required, but the amino acids which are the building blocks of protein.

> If any essential amino acid is low or missing, the effectiveness of all the others will be proportionately reduced.

Amino acids, which combined with nitrogen form thousands of different proteins, are not only the units from which proteins are formed, but are also the end products of protein digestion.

There are twenty-three commonly known amino acids. Eight of these are called *essential amino acids*. These essential amino acids *cannot,* like the others, be manufactured by the human body and *must* be obtained from food or supplements. A ninth amino acid, histidine, is considered essential only for infants and children.

In order for the body to effectively use and synthesize protein, all the essential amino acids must be present and in the proper proportions. Even the temporary absence of a single essential amino acid can adversely affect protein synthesis. In fact, whatever essential amino acid is low or missing will proportionately reduce the effectiveness of all the others.

THE AMINO ACIDS
(Essential amino acids are marked with asterisks.)

Alanine	*Leucine
Arginine	*Lysine
Asparagine	*Methionine
Aspartic acid	Ornithine
Cysteine	*Phenylalanine
Cystine	Proline
Glutamic acid	Serine
Glutamine	Taurine
Glycine	*Threonine
*Histidine (for infants and children)	*Tryptophan
	Tyrogine
*Isoleucine	*Valine

73. How Much Protein Do You Need, Really?

Everyone's protein requirements differ, depending on a variety of factors including health, age, and size. Actually, the larger and younger you are, the more you need. To estimate your own personal daily recommended allowance, see the chart below.

AGE	1–3	4–6	7–10	11–14	15–18	19 and over
POUND KEY	0.82	0.68	0.55	0.45	0.40	0.36

- Find the pound key under your age group.
- Multiply that number by your weight.
- The result will be your daily protein requirement in grams

Example: You weigh 100 pounds and are 33 years old. Your pound key is 0.36.

0.36 x 100 = 36g.—your daily protein requirement.

An average minimum protein requirement is around 45 g. a
day. That's 15 g. or about half an ounce per meal. And you
don't need to eat a lot of meat to get it. A 4-ounce serving of
chicken breast has about 30–35 grams, a cup of yogurt will
give you 12 grams, and a cup of 2 percent milk with two
shredded wheat biscuits will give you a breakfast boost of
14 grams.

74. Types of Protein—What's the Difference?

All proteins are not the same, though they're manufactured
from the same twenty-three amino acids. They have different functions and work in different areas of the body.

There are basically two types of protein—complete protein and incomplete protein.

Complete protein provides the proper balance of eight
necessary amino acids that build tissue, and is found in
foods of animal origin such as meats, poultry, seafood, eggs,
milk, and cheese.

Incomplete protein lacks certain essential amino acids and
is not used efficiently when eaten alone. However, when it
is combined with small amounts of animal-source protein, it
becomes complete. It is found in seeds, nuts, peas, grains,
and beans.

Mixing complete and incomplete proteins can give you
better nutrition than either one alone. A good rice-and-beans
dish with some cheese can be just as nourishing, less expensive, and lower in fat than a steak.

75. Protein Myths

A lot of people seem to think that protein is nonfattening.
This misconception has frustrated many a determined dieter

who forgoes bread but eats healthy portions of steak and wonders where the weight is coming from. The fact is

- 1 g. protein   = 4 calories
- 1 g. carbohydrate = 4 calories
- 1 g. fat   = 9 calories

In other words, protein and carbohydrates have the same gram-for-gram calorie count.

It is also thought that protein can burn up fat. This is another erroneous assumption that leaves dieters staring uncomprehending at their scales. It just is not true that the more protein you eat the thinner you'll get. And, believe it or not, one homemade beef taco or a slice of cheese pizza will give you more protein than two eggs or four slices of bacon or even a whole cup of milk. (Of course, if the taco or pizza is made with all sorts of additives, you're better off taking a cut in protein and sticking with the eggs.)

76. Protein Supplements

> Two tablespoons of supplement equal
> the protein in a three-ounce steak.

For anyone who isn't able to get his or her daily protein requirement from whole food, protein supplements are helpful. The best formulas are derived from soybeans, egg white, whey, and nonfat milk, which contain all the essential amino acids. They come in liquid and powdered form, are available without carbohydrates or fats, and generally supply about 26 g. of protein an ounce (two tablespoons). That would be about the same amount of protein you get from a 3-ounce T-bone.

Supplements can easily be added to beverages and foods. Texturized vegetable protein (TVP) can be added to ground beef to extend and enhance hamburgers, which will be more economical and better for you because of the cut in saturated fat.

77. Amino Acid Supplements

Free-form amino acids are now available in balanced formulas or as individual supplements, because so many have been found to offer specific health-enhancing properties—from improving the immune system to reducing dependence on drugs. (See individual listings, sections 78 through 84.)

It's wise, when taking amino acid supplements, to also take the major vitamins that are involved in their metabolisms, for instance: vitamins B6, B12, and niacin. And if you're going to take an amino acid formula, make sure it's well-balanced. *Read the label!* For protein synthesis to occur, there must be a balance between "essential" and "nonessential" amino acids, and the essentials in proper proportion to one another. (Lysine should be in a 2:1 ratio to methionine, 3:1 to tryptophan, and so on. When in doubt, ask your pharmacist or consult a reliable nutritionist. See section 342.) What you want is a formula that's modeled after naturally occurring proteins so that you can get the proper therapeutic value.

CAUTION: It's dangerous for any supplement to be used in place of food on a regular basis or taken in megadoses without the advice of a physician. Always keep them out of the reach of children.

78. Let's Talk Tryptophan—and 5-HTP

Tryptophan is an essential amino acid that's used by the brain—along with vitamin B6, niacin (or niacinamide), and magnesium—to produce serotonin, a neurotransmitter that carries messages between the brain and one of the body's biochemical mechanisms of sleep.

WHAT IT CAN DO FOR YOU:

Help induce natural sleep.
Reduce pain sensitivity.
Act as a nondrug antidepressant.
Alleviate migraines.
Aid in reducing anxiety and tension.
Help relieve some symptoms of alcohol-related body-chemistry disorders and aid in control of alcoholism.

BEST NATURAL SOURCES:

Cottage cheese, milk, meat, fish, turkey, bananas, dried dates, peanuts, all protein-rich foods.

SUPPLEMENT GUIDE:

L-tryptophan is no longer available as an over-the-counter supplement, and can be obtained only by prescription. (It was recalled by the U.S. FDA in 1988 after a tainted batch from Japan caused several deaths. The problem was not with the tryptophan itself but with seriously flawed manufacturing procedures.)

But let's talk 5-HTP (5-hydroxytryptophan), a new supplement, very similar to tryptophan, that is also being hailed as a natural alternative to Prozac™. It is a selective serotonin reuptake inhibitor (SSRI) that, like Prozac™, enhances the activity of serotonin. But unlike prescription antidepressants and sleep aids, 5-HTP does not cause unpleasant side effects, such as dry mouth and loss of libido. *And* not only has 5-HTP been found to alleviate depression and function as a sleep aid, it's been shown to help suppress appetite as well. (For dieters, that can be a mood elevator right there.)

As a supplement, I recommend one or two 50 mg. capsules daily on an empty stomach.

PERSONAL ADVICE AND COMMENTS:

For best results with 5-HTP (or L-tryptophan), be sure that you are also taking a complete balanced B-complex formula (50–100 mg. of B1, B2, and B6) with your morning and evening meals.

79. The Phenomenal Phenylalanine

Phenylalanine is an essential amino acid that is a neurotransmitter, a chemical that transmits its signals between the nerve cells and the brain. In the body it's turned into norepinephrine and dopamine, excitatory transmitters, which promote alertness and vitality. (Do not confuse with DL-phenylalanine; see section 80.) It is also half of the artificial sweetener aspartame (phenylalanine and aspartic acid) and in virtually all diet soft drinks with the exception of Dr Pepper™, as well as most dietetic foods and medicines.

WHAT IT CAN DO FOR YOU:

Reduce hunger.
Increase sexual interest.
Improve memory and mental alertness.
Alleviate depression.

BEST NATURAL SOURCES:

All protein-rich foods, bread stuffing, soy products, cottage cheese, dry skim milk, almonds, peanuts, lima beans, pumpkin and sesame seeds.

SUPPLEMENT GUIDE:

Available in 250–500 mg. tablets. For appetite control, tablets should be taken one hour before meals with juice or water (no protein).

For general alertness and vitality, tablets should be taken between meals, but again with water or juice (no protein).

CAUTION: Phenylalanine is contraindicated during pregnancy and for people with PKU (phenylketonuria) or skin cancer.

PERSONAL ADVICE AND COMMENTS:

Before resorting to prescription or recreational drugs, I'd advise giving this natural "upper" a chance. (Keep in mind, though, that it cannot be metabolized if you are deficient in vitamin C.)

Phenylalanine is nonaddictive, *but it can raise blood pressure!* If you are hypertensive or have a heart condition, I'd advise checking with your doctor before using phenylalanine. (In most cases, persons with high blood pressure are able to take phenylalanine *after* meals, but clear it with your doctor first.)

80. DL-Phenylalanine (DLPA)

This form of the essential amino acid phenylalanine is a mixture of equal parts of D (synthetic) and L (natural) phenylalanine. By producing and activating morphinelike hormones called *endorphins,* it intensifies and prolongs the body's own natural painkilling response to injury, accident, and disease.

Certain enzyme systems in the body continually destroy endorphins, but DL-phenylalanine effectively inhibits these enzymes, allowing the painkilling endorphins to do their job.

> Many people who do not respond to such
> conventional painkillers as Empirin™
> and Valium™ *do* respond to DLPA.

People who suffer from chronic pain have lower levels of endorphin activity in their blood and cerebrospinal fluid. Since DLPA can restore normal endorphin levels, it can thereby assist the body in reducing pain naturally—without the use of drugs.

Moreover, because DLPA is capable of selective painblocking, it can effectively alleviate chronic long-term discomfort while leaving the body's natural defense mechanisms for short-term acute pain (burns, cuts, etc.) unhindered.

The effect of DLPA often equals or exceeds that of morphine and other opiate derivatives, but DLPA differs from prescription and over-the-counter medicines in that—

• it is nonaddictive;
• pain relief becomes *more* effective over time (without development of tolerance);
• it has strong antidepressant action;
• it can provide continuous pain relief for up to a month without additional medication;
• it's nontoxic;
• it can be combined with any other medication or therapy to increase benefits without adverse interactions.

WHAT IT CAN DO FOR YOU:

Act as a natural painkiller for conditions such as whiplash, osteoarthritis, rheumatoid arthritis, lower back pain, migraines, leg and muscle cramps, postoperative pain, and neuralgia.

SUPPLEMENT GUIDE:

DL-phenylalanine is generally available in 375 mg. tablets. Correct dosages vary according to the individual's own experience of pain.

Six tablets per day (2 tablets taken approximately 15 minutes before each meal) is the best way to begin a DLPA regimen. Pain relief should occur within the first 4 days, though it may, in some cases, take as long as 3–4 weeks. (If no substantial relief is noticed in the first 3 weeks, double the initial dosage for an additional 2–3 weeks. If treatment is still not effective, discontinue the regimen. It's been found that 5–15 percent of users do not respond to DLPA's analgesic properties.)

CAUTION: DLPA is a contraindicated during pregnancy and for people with phenylketonuria. Because it elevates blood pressure, people with heart conditions or hypertension should check with a doctor before starting any DLPA regimen. Usually, though, it's allowed if taken *after* meals.

PERSONAL ADVICE AND COMMENTS:

On a DLPA regimen, pain usually diminishes within the first week. Dosages can then be reduced gradually until a minimum requirement is determined. Whatever yours turns out to be, doses should be regularly spaced throughout the day.

Some people require only one week of DLPA supplements a month; others need it on a continuous basis. (I found it interesting to discover that many people who do not respond to such conventional prescription painkillers as Empirin™ and Valium™ *do* respond to DLPA.)

81. Looking at Lysine

This essential amino acid is vital in the makeup of critical body proteins. It's needed for growth, tissue repair, and the production of antibodies, hormones, and enzymes.

WHAT IT CAN DO FOR YOU:

Help reduce the incidence of and/or prevent herpes simplex infection (fever blisters and cold sores).
Promote better concentration.
Properly utilize fatty acids needed for energy production.
Aid in alleviating some fertility problems.

BEST NATURAL SOURCE:

Fish, milk, lima beans, meat, cheese, yeast, eggs, soy products, all protein-rich foods.

SUPPLEMENT GUIDE:

L-lysine is generally available in 500 mg. capsules or tablets. The usual dose is 1–2 daily, half an hour before mealtimes.

PERSONAL ADVICE AND COMMENTS:

If you're often tired, unable to concentrate, prone to bloodshot eyes, nausea, dizziness, hair loss, and anemia, you could have a lysine deficiency.

Older persons, particularly men, require more lysine than younger ones.

Lysine is lacking in certain cereal proteins such as gliadin (from wheat) and zein (from corn). Supplementation of wheat-based foods with lysine improves their protein quality. (See complete and incomplete protein in section 74.)

If you have herpes, lysine supplements in doses of 3–6 grams daily—plus lysine-rich foods—are strongly recommended. For cold sores or fever blisters, 500–1,000 mg. daily, between meals, is a good preventive.

82. All About Arginine, "The Natural Viagra"

This amino acid is necessary for the normal function of the pituitary gland. Along with ornithine, phenylalanine, and other neurochemicals, arginine is required for the synthesis and release of the pituitary gland's growth hormone. (See section 84.) It is frequently recommended by natural healers as a supplement for men who have problems maintaining an erection long enough to engage in sex. It increases the blood flow to the penis, which results in harder erections. Regrettably, it does not work for everyone and the effect is short-lived, but for maximum effectiveness in improving sexual performance it should be taken about 45 minutes before having sex. Arginine can also increase sperm count (seminal fluids contain as much as 80 percent of this protein building block) and may help in treating male infertility. Additionally, arginine can improve immune function by stimulating the thymus gland, where disease-fighting T cells (T lymphocytes) are stored until they are called into action. In fact, studies show that arginine can increase the number of T cells, and may even trigger the production of natural killer cells that can aid in the body's defense against cancer.

WHAT IT CAN DO FOR YOU:

Increase sperm count and enhance sexual performance in men.

Aid in immune response and healing of wounds.

Help metabolize stored body fat and tone up muscle tissue.

Promote physical and mental alertness.

BEST NATURAL SOURCES:

Nuts, popcorn, carob, gelatin desserts, chocolate, brown rice, oatmeal, raisins, sunflower and sesame seeds, whole wheat bread, and all protein-rich foods.

SUPPLEMENT GUIDE:

L-arginine is available in tablets or powder and should be taken on an empty stomach, with juice or water (no protein). As an immune booster and to promote physical and mental alertness, take a 2 gram (2,000 mg.) dose immediately before retiring. For muscle-toning, take 2 grams (2,000 mg.) one hour prior to engaging in vigorous physical exercise. For sex-enhancing benefits, take 3–6 grams (3,000–6,000 mg.) of L-arginine 45 minutes before having sex.

CAUTIONS: Do not give to growing children (could cause giantism) or persons with schizophrenic conditions. Arginine supplements—and arginine-rich foods—are contraindicated for anyone who has herpes. Dosages exceeding 20–30 grams daily are not recommended. (Could cause enlarged joints and deformities of bones.)

PERSONAL ADVICE AND COMMENTS:

Arginine is necessary for adults because after the age of thirty there is almost a complete cessation of its secretion from the pituitary gland.

If you notice a thickening or coarsening of your skin, you're taking too much arginine. Several weeks of extremely high doses can cause this side effect, but it is reversible. Just cut back on your intake.

Any physical trauma increases your need for dietary arginine.

L-arginine taken in conjunction with L-ornithine can help stimulate weight loss.

83. Taurine

Synthesized in the body, this nonessential amino acid is the building block of all the other amino acids. Taurine is abundant in the tissues of the heart, the skeletal muscles, and the central nervous system. It is needed for the digestion of fats, the absorption of fat-soluble vitamins, and the control of serum cholesterol levels. It also has a protective effect on the brain.

WHAT IT CAN DO FOR YOU:

Strengthen heart function.
Help bolster vision and prevent macular degeneration.
Aid in treatment of anxiety and epilepsy.

BEST NATURAL SOURCE:

Eggs, fish, meat, milk.

SUPPLEMENT GUIDE:

Taurine is available in 500 mg. capsules. Take up to three 500 mg. capsules daily, with juice or water (no protein), half an hour before mealtimes.

PERSONAL ADVICE AND COMMENTS:

Taurine is not in vegetable proteins. But it can be effectively synthesized in the body as long as there are sufficient quantities of vitamin B6.

Excessive alcohol consumption causes the body to lose its ability to utilize taurine properly.

Diabetes increases requirements for taurine.

Taurine taken in conjunction with cystine may decrease the need for insulin.

84. Growth Hormone (G.H.) Releasers

Growth Hormone (G.H.) Releasers are nutrients that stimulate the production of growth hormone in the body. The human growth hormone is stored in the pituitary gland and the body releases it in response to sleep, exercise, and restricted food intake.

WHAT GROWTH HORMONE CAN DO FOR YOU:

Help burn fat and convert it into energy and muscle.

Improve resistance to disease.

Accelerate wound-healing.

Aid in tissue repair.

Strengthen connective tissue for healthier tendons and ligaments.

Enhance protein synthesis for muscle growth.

Reduce urea levels in blood and urine.

> By supplementing your diet with the
> amino acids and vitamins that stimulate
> release of growth hormone, production
> can be brought back up to
> young-adult levels.

Important G.H. releasers are the amino acids ornithine, arginine, tryptophan, glutamine, glycine, and tyrosine, which work synergistically (more effectively together than separately) with vitamin B6, niacinamide, zinc, calcium, magnesium, potassium, and vitamin C to trigger the nighttime release of growth hormone. Peak secretion of G.H. is reached about 90 minutes after we fall asleep.

Natural growth hormone levels decrease as we grow older. Somewhere around age 50, G.H. production virtually stops completely. But by supplementing your diet with the amino acids and vitamins that stimulate release of growth hormone, production can be brought back up to the levels of a young adult.

THE DYNAMIC AMINO DUO:
ORNITHINE & ARGININE

Ornithine and arginine, two of the amino acids involved in the release of human growth hormone, are among the most popular amino acid supplements today, essentially because they can help you slim down and shape up while you sleep (which is when G.H. is secreted). While some hormones encourage the body to store fat, growth hormone acts as a mobilizer of fat, helping you to not only look trimmer but have more energy as well.

Ornithine stimulates insulin secretion and helps insulin work as an anabolic (muscle-building) hormone, which has increased its use among bodybuilders. Taking extra ornithine will help increase the levels of arginine in your body. (Actually, arginine is constructed from ornithine, ornithine is released from arginine in a continuing cyclic process.)

Because ornithine and arginine are so closely related, the characteristics and cautions for one apply to the other. (See section 82, "All About Arginine.") As a supplement, ornithine works best when taken at the same time and in the same manner as arginine (on an empty stomach, with juice or water—no protein).

85. Other Amazing Amino Acids

GLUTAMINE & GLUTAMIC ACID

Glutamic acid serves primarily as a brain fuel. It has the ability to pick up excess ammonia—which can inhibit high-performance brain function—and convert it into the buffer glutamine. Since glutamine produces marked elevation of glutamic acid, a shortage of the former in the diet can result in a shortage of the latter in the brain.

Glutamine is also a component of glutathione, the body's primary antioxidant, which is present in virtually every cell. So if you are deficient in glutamine, you're likely to be deficient in glutathione. And glutamine can also help boost the level of human growth hormone.

Aside from improving intelligence (even the IQs of mentally deficient children), glutamine has been shown to help in the control of alcoholism. It has also been found to shorten healing time for ulcers and alleviate fatigue, depression, and impotence. Additionally, it has helped promote healing in burn victims and may prevent muscle wasting in the chronically ill. Most recently it's been used successfully in the treatment of schizophrenia, senility, and on cancer patients undergoing bone marrow transplants, shortening their hospital stay and reducing their risk of infection. It has also been shown to enhance muscle size in healthy people who work out.

L-glutamine (the natural form of glutamine) is available as a supplement in 500 mg. capsules. My recommended dosage is up to three 500 mg. capsules or tablets either half an hour before or two hours after eating. (I'd suggest starting with 500–1,000 mg. for the first few weeks and building up to 1,500 mg. over the course of a month.)

CAUTION: Though glutamine and glutamic acid are not the same as monosodium glutamate (MSG), persons with a sensitivity to the latter could experience an allergic reaction and are advised to consult a physician before using these supplements.

ASPARTIC ACID

Aspartic acid aids in the expulsion of harmful ammonia from the body. (When ammonia enters the circulatory system, it acts as a highly toxic substance.) By disposing of ammonia, aspartic acid helps protect the central nervous system. Recent research indicates that it may be an important factor in increased resistance to fatigue. When salts of aspartic acid were given to athletes, they showed decidedly improved stamina and endurance.

L-aspartic acid (the natural form of aspartic acid) is available as a supplement in 250 mg. and 500 mg. tablets. The usual dosage is 500 mg. 1–3 times daily with juice or water (no protein).

CYSTINE & CYSTEINE

Cystine is the *stable form* of the sulfur-containing amino acid cysteine (an important antiaging nutrient). The body readily converts one into the other as needed, and the two forms can be considered as a single amino acid in metabolism. When cystine is metabolized, it yields sulfuric acid, which reacts with other substances to help detoxify the system.

Sulfur-containing amino acids, particularly cystine and methionine, have been shown to be effective protectors against copper toxicity. (An excessive accumulation of copper in humans is a sign of Wilson's disease.) Cystine/cysteine can also help "tie up" and protect the body from other harmful metals as well as destructive free radicals that are formed by smoking and drinking. A cysteine supplement (L-cysteine) taken daily with vitamin C (3 times as much vitamin C as cysteine) is the regimen that's been suggested for smokers and alcohol drinkers. (Supplements need not be taken on an empty stomach.) Recent research also indicates that therapeutic doses of cysteine can offer an important degree of protection against X-ray and nuclear radiation.

CAUTION: Large doses of cysteine/cystine, vitamins C and B1 are not recommended for anyone with diabetes mellitus, and should only be undertaken on the advice of a physician. (The combination of these nutrients could negate insulin effectiveness.)

METHIONINE

An essential amino acid that helps in the breakdown of fats, methionine is a powerful antioxidant. Like cystine, it is another sulfur-containing amino acid, and helps protect the body from toxic substances as well as destructive free radicals. Methionine helps in some cases of schizophrenia by lowering the blood level of histamine, which can cause the brain to relay wrong messages. When combined with choline and folic acid, it has been shown to offer protection against certain tumors. It is also beneficial for women who take oral contraceptives because it promotes the excretion of estrogen.

An insufficiency of methionine can break down the body's ability to process urine and result in edema (swelling due to retention of fluids in tissues) and susceptibility to infection. A methionine deficiency has also been linked to cholesterol deposits, atherosclerosis, and hair loss in laboratory animals.

Because methionine is not synthesized in the body, it must be obtained from food or supplements. Good food source of this amino acid are beans, fish, eggs, garlic, soybeans, meat, onions, seeds, and yogurt.

GLYCINE

Sometimes referred to as the simplest of the amino acids, glycine has been shown to yield quite a few remarkable benefits. It has been found helpful in the treatment of low pituitary gland function, and, because it supplies the body with additional creatine (essential for muscle function), it has also been found effective in the treatment of progressive muscular dystrophy. Interestingly, having too much of this amino acid can cause fatigue, but the proper amount produces more energy.

Glycine is necessary for central nervous system function, and has been used in the treatment of manic depression, hyperactivity, and can help in preventing epileptic seizures.

Many nutritionally oriented doctors now use glycine in the treatment of hypoglycemia. (Glycine stimulates the release of glucagon, which mobilizes glycogen, which is then released into the blood as glucose.)

Additionally, it is effective as a treatment for gastric hyperacidity (and is included in many gastric antacid drugs). It has also been used to treat certain types of acidemia (low pH of the blood), especially one caused by a leucine imbalance which results in an offensive body and breath odor (a condition formerly treated only by a dietary restriction of leucine).

TYROSINE

Though this is a nonessential amino acid, it's a high-ranking neurotransmitter, and important because of its role in stimulating and modifying brain activity. For instance, in order for phenylalanine to be effective as a mood elevator, appetite depressant, etc. (see section 79), it must first convert into tyrosine. If this conversion does not take place, either because of some enzyme insufficiency or a great need elsewhere in the body for phenylalanine, insufficient quantities of norepinephrine will be produced by the brain and depression will result.

Tyrosine promotes healthy functioning of the adrenal, pituitary, and thyroid glands. It also stimulates the release of growth hormone and it produces norepinephrine, which suppresses appetite.

Clinical studies have shown that tyrosine supplementation has helped control medication-resistant depression and anxiety, as well as enable patients taking amphetamines (as mood elevators or diet drugs) to reduce their dosages to minimal levels in a matter of weeks.

Tyrosine has also helped cocaine addicts to kick their habit by helping to avert the depression, fatigue, and extreme irritability which accompany withdrawal. A regimen of tyrosine, dissolved in orange juice, taken along with vitamin C, tyrosine hydroxylase (the enzyme that lets the body use tyrosine), and vitamins B1, B2, and niacin seems to work.

Supplements of L-tyrosine should be taken with high-carbohydrate meals, or at bedtime, so as not to compete for absorption with other amino acids. Good natural sources are dairy products, bananas, avocados, lima beans, almonds, pumpkin and sesame seeds.

86. Any Questions About Chapter V?

I'm prone to convulsions, and my doctor put me on Dilantin™ (phenytoin) a year ago. Recently, a friend told me about taurine, which she said was a nonessential amino acid that was natural and could help me the same way. What I want to know is, if it's nonessential why would I need it? And why would it work?

Let me begin by clearing up a major point of misunderstanding: where amino acids are concerned, nonessential does *not* mean unnecessary. All the amino acids are necessary, it's just that the ones that are deemed essential can't be synthesized by the body in sufficient quantities to promote effective protein synthesis. If these essential ones are not supplied in the diet, *all* amino acids are reduced in the same proportion as the one that's low or missing. As for substituting taurine for an anticonvulsant medication, that's a decision only your doctor can make. I can say though that taurine has been shown to be quite successful as an anticonvulsant when taken in combination with glutamic and aspartic acids, but would not recommend undertaking it without consulting a doctor. (For listings of nutritionally oriented doctors in your area, see section 342.)

I've read that exercise stimulates the release of growth hormone. I do at least twenty minutes of dance exercises every day, so does this mean that I probably don't need a G.H. supplement?

On the contrary, you probably do. Only certain exercises, such as weight lifting, where there is what's known as muscular "peak output" (even briefly sustained), promote a significant release of G.H. Other exercises, even prolonged ones, produce negligible amounts (if any) of growth hormone—unless they are performed with peak muscular effort. In fact, because amino acids are lost through the skin when you sweat, exercise *increases* your need for amino acids that will stimulate growth hormone.

I take Dexatrim™ to control my weight. On the label it says that it contains phenylpropanolamine. Is this the same as L-phenylalanine, and are they equally effective?

Phenylpropanolamine (PPA), which is found in many diet pills, is definitely *not* the same as L-phenylalanine. PPA is an appetite depressant (of dubious effectiveness, according to the American Medical Association) with a high incidence of side effects, including adverse interactions with MAO inhibitors and some oral contraceptives. Unlike the amino acid phenylalanine, which stimulates the brain to produce norepinephrine (which has been shown to reduce hunger), and alleviate those down-in-the-dumps diet blues, PPA depletes the brain of norepinephrine—usually in about two weeks—and leaves dieters fatigued and often depressed.

PPA is a poor substitute for a good diet (see section 161), while L-phenylalanine, which is found naturally in such protein-rich foods as cottage cheese, soy products, almonds, dry skim milk, and many more, can aid in appetite control (while nourishing the brain) if taken one hour before meals with juice or water.

Is there such a thing as an antiaging amino acid?

As a matter of fact, L-glutathione (GSH) has been called a triple threat antiaging amino acid. It's actually a tripeptide, synthesized from three amino acids—L-cysteine, L-glutamic acid, and glycine, and it has been shown to act as an antioxidant and deactivate free radicals which speed up the aging process. It is also an antitumor agent, a respiratory accelerator in the brain, and has been used to help in the treatment of allergies, cataracts, diabetes, hypoglycemia, and arthritis, as well as in helping to prevent the harmful side effects of high-dose radiation in chemotherapy and X rays. Additionally, it helps to protect against the harmful effects of cigarette smoke and alcohol.

Glutathione is present in fruits and vegetables; however, cooking can reduce its potency. I recommend taking a 50 mg. capsule once or twice daily.

What is this amino acid L-carnitine that I have been hearing about?

It's a potential life extender. Its primary job is to provide heart and skeletal cells with energy. It can help in the treatment of heart disease, reduce angina attacks, aid in the control of hypoglycemia, and may help slow the progression of Alzheimer's disease as well as benefit patients with diabetes, liver, or kidney disease.

It plays an important role in converting stored body fat into energy and is being used by athletes, enabling longer periods of intense workouts.

Meat and dairy products are the major natural sources of L-carnitine. There is no recommended daily allowance for this amino acid, but the average American consumes between 100 and 300 mg. of it daily. As a supplement, I suggest two 500 mg. capsules a day. In rare cases, people taking over 1 gram of carnitine daily may develop a fishy odor (caused by the breakdown of carnitine by intestinal bacteria). This usually disappears when the dose is cut back.

CAUTION: There are two kinds of carnitine: L-carnitine and D-carnitine. Stick to products containing only L-carnitine, as some studies suggest that D-carnitine may be toxic. If you have an existing heart condition, do not take this or any other supplement without first consulting your physician.

With diseases such as cancer, AIDS, and what have you on the rampage these days, is there anything that can be done to improve an individual's immune system?

Fortunately, lots! (See section 340 for an extensive list.) But when it comes to amino acids, growth hormone releasers are your best defense.

What happens is that as we get older, our immune system—that ever-ready army of white blood cells (called T cells because they're under the command of the thymus gland) which are told where and when to attack and what antibodies their cofighters (called B cells because they're made in the bone marrow) should produce—begins to break down due to the decreasing power and size of the thymus gland. This not only causes an ineffectual defense system, but often dangerous confusion where the T cells mistake friends for enemies and attack you, resulting in autoimmune disorders. (It's been suggested that diseases such as multiple sclerosis, myasthenia gravis, and arthritis may be due to this.)

What's been discovered recently, though, is that this is most likely due to a reduced rate of growth hormone, which is produced by the pituitary gland and necessary to the function of the thymus gland and therefore the immune system. But supplements of antioxidants, vitamin C, alpha- and beta-carotene, lutein, lycopene, selenium, grapeseed extract, green tea extract, alpha lipoic acid, soy isoflavonoids (genistein and daidzein), zinc, and enzymes such as papain have been found to work wonders in reversing this degenerative syndrome.

I'm a professional bodybuilder and would like to know if there are any legal, natural supplement alternatives to steroids?

There certainly are. Branched chain amino acids (BCAAs)—which are compromised of leucine, valine, and isoleucine—are natural anabolic muscle-building supplements. They regulate how protein is used by the body and play a unique role in protein metabolism in muscles. While all other amino acids are broken down in the liver, BCAAs are oxidized in peripheral muscle.

BCAAs are, in effect, a principal source of calories for human muscle. Intense physical exercise produces a rapid excretion of nitrogen, which causes a decrease in muscle protein synthesis. BCAAs limit this decrease.

During strenuous exercise, such as weight training, the stress on a muscle causes it to break down (catabolism). BCAAs not only act to prevent this, but actually reverse the process. They are, therefore, *anabolic* because they build up muscle.

BCAA facts that can help your workout:

- BCAAs can reduce appetite while preserving basic protein storage in the body.
- One-half of your body weight is muscle, and 15–20 percent of muscle is branched chain amino acids.
- 50 percent of ingested BCAA is available to your muscles in one hour, 100 percent in two hours.
- BCAAs produce glycogen, which helps balance insulin secretion.
- BCAAs directly affect muscle and body weight changes, promoting lean muscle distribution.

Supplements should only be taken half an hour before workouts.

I'm a bit confused about N-acetyl cysteine (NAC) and what it does. Is it a worthwhile amino acid supplement?

You bet it is! NAC is an amino acid and a precursor to glutathione, the body's most abundant antioxidant. Studies have shown that NAC can help protect against such respiratory ailments as bronchitis, bronchial asthma, emphysema, chronic sinusitis—and may even help protect against lung damage caused by cancer-causing chemicals in cigarette smoke. NAC has also been used successfully to treat people with serious inner ear infections. And bodybuilders have found that it helps them recover faster from their workouts. As a supplement, 1–3 capsules or tablets (500 mg.) can be taken with meals.

CAUTION: Do *not* use NAC if you have peptic ulcers, or use drugs known to cause gastric lesions.

VI

Fat and Fat Manipulators

87. Lipotropics—What Are They?

Methionine, choline, inositol, and betaine are all lipotropics, which means their prime function is to prevent abnormal or excessive accumulation of fat in the liver.

Lipotropics also increase the liver's production of lecithin, which keeps cholesterol more soluble, detoxifies the liver, and increases resistance to disease by helping the thymus gland carry out its functions.

88. Who Needs Them and Why

We all need lipotropics, some of us more than others. Anyone on a high-protein diet falls into the latter category. Methionine and choline are *necessary* to detoxify the amines that are by-products of protein metabolism.

Because nearly all of us consume too much fat (the average consumption in the United States is now 36–42 percent of total calories), and a substantial part of that is saturated fat, lipotropics are indispensable. By helping the liver produce lecithin, they're helping to keep cholesterol from forming dangerous deposits in blood vessels, lessening chances of heart attacks, arteriosclerosis, and gallstone formation as well.

> Lipotropics keep cholesterol
> moving safely.

We also need lipotropics to stay healthy, since they aid the thymus in stimulating the production of antibodies, the growth and action of phagocytes (which surround and gobble up invading viruses and microbes), and in destroying foreign or abnormal tissue.

89. The Cholesterol Story

Like everything else, there's a good and bad side to fats. The general misconception that all of them are bad for you, prevalent as it may be, simply is not true. And the most maligned of all is cholesterol.

Practically everyone knows that cholesterol can be responsible for arteriosclerosis, heart attacks, a variety of illnesses, but very few are aware of the ways that it is *essential* to health.

At least two-thirds of your body cholesterol is produced by the liver or in the intestine. It is found there as well as in the brain, the adrenals, and nerve fiber sheaths. And when it's good, it's very, very good:

• Cholesterol in the skin is converted to essential vitamin D when touched by the sun's ultraviolet rays.

• Cholesterol aids in the metabolism of carbohydrates. (The more carbohydrates ingested, the more cholesterol produced.)

• Cholesterol is a prime supplier of life-essential adrenal steroid hormones, such as cortisone.

• Cholesterol is a component of every membrane and necessary for the production of male and female sex hormones.

Differences in the behavior of cholesterol depend upon the protein to which it is bound. Lipoproteins are the factors in our blood which transport cholesterol.

Low-density lipoproteins (LDL) carry about 65 percent

of blood cholesterol and are the bad guys who deposit it in the arteries where, joined by other substances, it becomes artery-blocking plaque.

Very-low-density lipoproteins (VLDL) carry only about 15 percent of blood cholesterol but are the substances the liver needs and uses to produce LDL. The more of them, the more LDL the liver sends out and the greater your chance of heart disease.

High-density lipoproteins (HDL) carry about 20 percent of blood cholesterol and, composed principally of lecithin, are the good guys whose detergent action breaks up plaque and can transport cholesterol through the blood without clogging arteries. (A recent study found that people with big hips and trim waists have higher HDL cholesterol levels than do those with potbellies, which might explain why females, on the average, live eight years longer than males.)

In short: the higher your HDL the lower your chances of developing heart disease.

> Eggs might not be as bad
> as you thought.

It is also worth mentioning that though the egg consumption in the United States is one-half of what it was in 1945, there has *not* been a comparable decline in heart disease. And though the American Heart Association deems eggs hazardous, a diet without them can be equally hazardous. Not only do eggs have the most perfect protein components of any food, but they contain lecithin, which aids in fat assimilation. And, most important, they *raise* HDL levels!

90. Leveling About Cholesterol Levels

When people talk about their cholesterol levels, they're referring to the total amount of cholesterol in their blood (serum cholesterol). The amounts are measured in milligrams per deciliter; the accepted levels—for *everyone*—should not exceed 200 mg/dl.

The ratio of HDL (good cholesterol) to LDL (bad cholesterol) is as important as the ratio of HDL to your total cholesterol level. The more HDL you have, therefore, the more protection you have against clogged arteries.

Blood cholesterol tests will usually also measure your levels of *triglycerides*. These fats differ from cholesterol, but there is a connection between them; although you can have high triglyceride levels without high cholesterol (and vice versa), lowering triglyceride levels does seem to help bring down cholesterol.

Keeping your daily fat intake to no more than 30 percent (and preferably 20 percent) of total calories consumed is vital to leveling off elevated cholesterol levels. And no more than 10 percent of that fat should be saturated.

91. Saturated Fat vs. Unsaturated Fat

Saturated fat comes from animal sources (with a few exceptions, notably coconut and palm oils, and hydrogenated or partially hydrogenated vegetable oils) and *all* animal fats contain cholesterol.

Unsaturated fat (be it mono- or polyunsaturated) comes from vegetable sources—and *no* vegetables or fruits contain cholesterol.

BUT, and this is a big "but," even if foods don't contain cholesterol, that doesn't mean they don't contain fat. Avocados, for instance, are free of cholesterol, but just one used for guacamole will give you more than 30 grams of fat!

92. Foods, Nutrients, and New Supplements That Can Lower Your Cholesterol Naturally

The following is a list of natural foods, nutrients, and cholesterol-lowering supplements. (*Name-brand supplements are in italics. Their inclusion is to provide informa-*

*tion about what they are and should not be construed as any
sort of product endorsement.*)

Before using any supplement to reduce high cholesterol,
consult your doctor. Switching from prescription drugs to
supplements or adding a supplement to a drug regimen on
your own is potentially dangerous. And remember, no food,
nutrient, or supplement is a magic bullet; a low-fat diet and
regular exercise are still necessary to lower high cholesterol.

- Barley
- Chromium picolinate (Most absorbable form of chro-
mium; works particularly well with "no-flush" niacin. Take
up to three 200 mcg. tablets daily.)
- *Cholestatin*™ (Contains phytosterols, compounds in food
such as rice and soybeans, mainly sitosterol. Suggested
dosage is 6–8 capsules daily, taken before meals.)
- Corn bran
- Cruciferous vegetables (broccoli, cauliflower)
- Eggplant
- Evening primrose oil (Contains gamma-linolenic acid
[GLA]. I'd suggest 250 mg. 1–3 times daily.)
- *Evolve*® (Contains tocotrienols extracted from rice bran.
Recommended dosage is 1–2 25 mg. capsules daily.
NOTE: Vitamin E supplements may reduce this supple-
ment's cholesterol-lowering effect.
- Fenugreek seed (CAUTION: Do not use fenugreek during
pregnancy.)
- Fiber (25–30 grams daily)
- Fish oils: EPA and DHA (omega-3 fatty acids; take up to
six 1,000 mg. capsules daily. CAUTION: Can interfere with
normal blood clotting. Do not use if you are taking blood
thinners, such as coumadin or heparin, unless advised by
your physician.)
- Garlic (As a supplement, take 1 capsule up to 3 times
daily.)
- Ginger (As a supplement, take 1 capsule up to 3 times
daily.)

• Guar gum (An extract from the seeds of the guar plant. Tablets must be chewed thoroughly or sucked gradually, and taken with lots of water. CAUTION: Should not be taken by anyone who has difficulty swallowing or who's had gastrointestinal surgery.)

• Gugulipid (An extract from the mukul myrrh tree, native to India, and used for centuries in Ayurvedic medicine. Take one 25 mg. capsule with meals three times daily. CAUTION: May cause a rash or hives in susceptible individuals.)

• Lemongrass oil

• Lentils: pinto beans, lima beans, navy beans, kidney beans

• *LipoGuard*™ (Contains a combination of fish oil and garlic. The recommended dosage is 4–10 capsules daily. CAUTION: Should not be taken by anyone with a bleeding disorder, or on blood thinners, unless advised by a physician.)

• Monounsaturated oils (olive, peanut, canola)

• Niacin (Use "no-flush" supplements with inosital hexanicotinate, IHN. Take up to three 500 mg. capsules daily. CAUTION: May bring on attacks of gout in people prone to the disease, and high doses may promote liver abnormalities.)

• Oat bran

• Onions

• Pectin (apples, grapefruit)

• *PhytoQuest*™ (Contains phytosterols, mainly sitosterol, which blocks cholesterol's absorption sites in the small intestine. Suggested dosage is 6–8 capsules daily, before meals.)

• Phytosterols: beta-sitosterol, stigmasterol, campesterol (Naturally occurring compounds in plant foods such as rice and soybeans.)

• Polyunsaturated oils (sunflower, corn, safflower)

• Psyllium husk (Three rounded teaspoons supply 10 grams of cholesterol-lowering soluble fiber.)

• Raw carrots

• Red pepper

• Rice bran

- Soybeans and soy foods (see section 129)
- Vitamin C
- Vitamin E
- Yogurt

93. Do You Know What's Raising Your Cholesterol?

Many things that you might not be aware of can be raising your cholesterol levels or undermining your efforts to lower them. Here are a few you should think about:

- Smoking
- Caffeine
- Stress
- The pill
- Refined sugar
- Food additives
- Environmental pollutants

If you're watching your cholesterol, you probably know that turkey is a good dinner choice. Just remember that although three ounces of light-meat turkey has only about 67 mg. of cholesterol, the same amount of dark meat, as 75 mg. And a cup of chopped turkey liver has abut 830 mg.!

94. Any Questions About Chapter VI?

I'd like to know if there is any difference in being hyperlipidemic and hypercholesterolemic?

There is, but unfortunately, not much when it comes to being a candidate for coronary heart disease. A person who is hyperlipidemic has elevated fats in general in the blood, and someone who is hypercholesterolemic just has elevated cholesterol levels. It's sort of a semantic moot point where health is concerned.

I'm confused. Some products say low-fat and some low-cholesterol. Is there a difference?

You bet there is! In fact, a product that's marked cholesterol-free can be loaded with fat! You have to understand that cholesterol and fat are not synonymous. Unlike fat, cholesterol is not used for energy; it's used primarily to transport fat to cells through the body.

What's the difference, as far as lowering cholesterol is concerned, between polyunsaturated and monounsaturated oils?

Polyunsaturated oils (sunflower, corn, safflower, soy) lower both the bad and the good (LDL and HDL) cholesterol. Monounsaturated oils (olive, peanut, canola), on the other hand, not only reduce the bad cholesterol, but raise the good (HDL) levels. Most medical authorities, though, according to Robert E. Kowalski, author of *The 8-Week Cholesterol Cure,* are not ready to commit on which is better and suggest using both.

I've heard that polyunsaturated oils, which I use frequently, can cause cancer. Is there any truth to this?

Perhaps. Studies have found that large amounts of "processed" polyunsaturates in the diet can increase the formation of carcinogens. This seems to happen when vegetable oils are "hydrogenated" to make them into solid shortenings—a process that, in effect, turns unsaturated fats into saturated ones. I'd suggest you supplement your diet with vitamin E (200–400 IU daily) to help prevent lipid peroxidation (fats rusting in the body); avoid products containing hydrogenated oils; increase your intake of cruciferous vegetables; and switch your polyunsaturated oils for monounsaturated ones, such as olive and canola.

Are lipotropics available as supplements, and if so, what's the recommended dosage and are there any special instructions for taking them?

Lipotropics are available as supplements in tablet form. (Usually 3 tablets equal 1,000 mg.—or 1 gram of each lipotropic agent.) The dosage most often recommended is 1–2 tablets taken 3 times daily, *with* food.

Do you consider lipotropic supplements more important for some people than others?

Definitely, especially meat eaters. Lipotropics are the substances which can liquefy or homogenize fats. I feel that supplementation is particularly important for anyone on a high-protein diet, the reason being that lipotropics detoxify amines, which are by-products of protein metabolism. Also, anyone worried about gallstone formation would be wise to consider these supplements.

My daughter-in-law is taking a hemp oil supplement, which I know nothing about. I know marijuana comes from a hemp plant. Does this supplement have similar hallucinogenic effects?

Not at all! Unfortunately, because hemp is a member of the *Cannabis sativa* family, it is illegal to grow the hemp plant in the U.S., even though the products derived from it are not hallucinogenic. Because of its important health benefits, hemp is now being imported from other countries, and hemp products are available at natural-food stores.

Hemp oil is a rich source of the two essential fatty acids, omega-3 and omega-6 (particularly omega-3), "good" fats that are required for a healthy body and mind. (See previous question for potential benefits.) Most people get adequate amounts of omega-6 through their diet, but not enough omega-3. In fact, it's very difficult to get enough omega-3 through food alone, especially since it's destroyed by heating. Hemp oil can be used in salad dressings and other food, but only after cooking. The hemp oil capsules that your daughter-in-law is taking are the easiest way to reap some pretty "essential" health benefits.

Can you explain, simply, what omega-3 fatty acids are and what they can do for me?

Simply, omega-3 fatty acids are a unique component of fish and fish oils, EPA and DHA (eicosapentaenoic and docosahexaenoic acid) and there are many things that they've been found to do. As for what they can do for you, take your pick. They can:

- help retard atherosclerosis
- lower LDL cholesterol and triglycerides
- reduce blood viscosity and help prevent heart attacks and strokes
- keep skin, hair, and nails healthy
- lower blood pressure
- enhance the immune system
- possibly prevent depression
- alleviate rheumatoid arthritis
- help protect the body from lupus erythematosus
- offer protection against migraines and kidney disease

If you're a vegetarian, omega-3 fatty acids can also be found in vegetable oils such as soybean, canola, flaxseed, and hemp—but the conversion to EPA and DHA is much slower.

What's the difference between omega-3 and omega-6 fatty acids on a cholesterol-lowering regimen?

Only the omega-3 fatty acids lower triglycerides as well as cholesterol.

I've been using margarine for years because I was told to stay away from saturated fat. Now, I hear that margarine can be worse for me than butter. Is this true?

Not exactly. Let me put it this way: margarine isn't worse for you than butter—but it isn't much better. We all know that saturated fats give an unhealthy boost to cholesterol levels and unsaturated fats don't. But recent studies have shown that when unsaturated fats are "hydrogenated" (a process which solidifies them so they resemble butter at room temperature) they not only continue to raise cholesterol levels, they do something that saturated fats don't—they *lower* the levels of the body's HDL (good cholesterol)! Look for nonhydrogenated or trans-fatty acid–free margarine. Better yet, use olive or canola oil instead.

What's the skinny on these new fake fats, like olestra and Z-Trim™?

Still pretty thin nutritionally. The synthetic fat called olestra (also known as Olean™ and sucrose polyester) is made with sucrose and fatty acids and was designed so that it couldn't be broken down by our body's enzymes and would, therefore, not be absorbed by the body. Great in theory, but this faux fat, which is currently being used primarily in snacks such as chips and cheese puffs, has some not-so-great side effects. Aside from the widely publicized "brown stain" effect (from many reports of people experiencing loose stools and fecal urgency), it depletes the body of fat-soluble vitamins A, D, E, and K—and carotenoids. Olestra is now fortified with these vitamins—but only to the U.S. government's determinations of the bare minimum amount to prevent deficiency, not to maximize health. (Early studies of olestra found that six chips a day could reduce a person's beta-carotene level by 50 percent!) Admittedly, olestra does reduce the total grams of fat consumed, but it's a risky nutritional price to pay for reducing a serving of potato chips from 150 to 70 calories.

Z-Trim™ is the newest entry into the fake fat foray. Developed by the U.S. Department of Agriculture, it's made from oat hulls, which they feel could cut down calories and bulk up fiber—and it can be used in cooking. At this writing, it doesn't appear to have any side effects, but until long-term safety is assured, I'd recommend lowering your fat intake the old-fashioned way—by cutting back on products that contain it.

As for other fake fats such as Simpless™, which is a milk and egg white fat substitute used primarily in low-calorie frozen desserts, they are unstable in heat and, at least at this time, cannot be used in cooked products. Considering most of our fats come from cooked foods, the percentage of fat saved by eating products with this type of fake fat is *not* impressive. What's worse is that these fake fats can lull you into a false sense of low-fat security and get you to indulge in products you ordinarily wouldn't eat—and they don't get you to change your basic fat-eating patterns at all!

What's the difference between foods labeled cholesterol-free and those labeled low cholesterol?

Approximately anywhere between 18 mg. and 20 mg. per typical serving. Cholesterol-free foods have 2 mg. or less of cholesterol per serving, and less than 2 grams of saturated fat per serving. (Saturated fat stimulates the production of cholesterol in the body.) Low cholesterol on a label means the food contains no more than 20 mg. of cholesterol per serving. Just remember that while you're watching your cholesterol, it's important to keep your eye on serving sizes as well!

VII

Carbohydrates and Enzymes

95. Why Carbohydrates Are Necessary

Carbohydrates, the scourge of misinformed dieters, are the main suppliers of the body's energy. During digestion, starches and sugars, the principal kinds of carbohydrates, are broken down into glucose, better known as blood sugar. This blood sugar provides the essential energy for our brain and central nervous system.

You need carbohydrates in your daily diet so that vital tissue-building protein is not wasted for energy when it might be needed for repair.

> They have the same calories
> as protein.

If you eat too many carbohydrates, more than can be converted into glucose or glycogen (which is stored in liver and muscles), the result, as we know all too well, is fat. When the body needs more fuel, the fat is converted back to glucose and you lose weight.

Don't be too down on carbohydrates. They're as important for good health as other nutrients—and gram for gram they have the same 4 calories as protein. Though no official requirement exists, a minimum of 50 g. daily is recommended to avoid ketosis, an acid condition of the blood that can happen when your own fat is used primarily for energy.

96. Look Up Your Carbs on the Glycemic Index

All carbohydrates are not equal when it comes to their ranking on a scale known as the glycemic index, a calculation based on how fast and how high blood glucose is elevated after a particular food is eaten. Foods with a high glycemic index are carbohydrate-rich (high in sugar and starch), and allow glucose to enter the bloodstream quickly. There's nothing wrong with glucose (it's the fuel used by every cell in the body), but to process it, the pancreas has to produce insulin. The more high-glycemic foods you eat, the harder your pancreas has to work. And if it has to work too hard too often, it can wear down and diabetes can result.

Additionally, high-glycemic refined carbohydrates cause a surge in blood sugar and, consequently, insulin; insulin then turns all the extra glucose into fat. This is why so many low-fat and no-fat foods are still making so many Americans fat.

The key to keeping healthy and trim is replacing high-glucose starches with slowly digested high-fiber carbohydrates. To score high nutritionally, look for foods on the low-glycemic index.

HIGH-GLYCEMIC FOODS (Decrease)

- Refined white sugar
- Snack candies, cakes, and cookies
- Potato chips, pretzels, and related snacks
- White-flour pastas
- Instant rice
- Bagels
- Potatoes
- Carbonated soft drinks

LOW-GLYCEMIC FOODS (Increase)

• Whole-grain pasta
• Hard beans—pinto, soy, tepary, mung
• Whole-wheat bread
• Oatmeal, bran
• High-fiber fruits and vegetables
• Soy products

97. The Truth About Enzymes

Enzymes are necessary for the digestion of food, releasing valuable vitamins, minerals, and amino acids which keep us alive and healthy.

Enzymes are catalysts, meaning they have the power to cause an internal action without themselves being changed or destroyed in the process.

Enzymes are destroyed under certain heat conditions.

Enzymes are best obtained from uncooked or unprocessed fruits, vegetables, eggs, meats, and fish.

Each enzyme acts upon a specific food; one cannot substitute for the other. A deficiency, shortage, or even the absence of one single enzyme can mean the difference between sickness and health.

Enzymes that end in -ase are named by the food substance they act upon. For example, with phosphorus the enzyme is called phosphatase; with sugar (sucrose) it is known as sucrase.

Pepsin is a vital digestive enzyme that breaks up the proteins of ingested food, splitting them into usable amino acids. Without pepsin, protein could not be used to build healthy skin, strong skeletal structure, rich blood supply, and strong muscles.

Rennin is a digestive enzyme which causes coagulation of milk, changing its protein, casein, into a usable form in the body. Rennin releases the valuable minerals from milk, calcium, phosphorus, potassium, and iron that are used by the body to stabilize the water balance, strengthen the nervous system, and produce strong teeth and bones.

Lipase splits fat, which is then utilized to nourish the skin cells, protect the body against bruises and blows, and ward off the entrance of infectious virus cells and allergic conditions.

Hydrochloric acid in the stomach works on tough foods such as fibrous meats, vegetables, and poultry. It digests protein, calcium, and iron. Without HCl, problems such as pernicious anemia, gastric carcinoma, congenital achlorhydria, and allergies can develop. Because stress, tension, anger, and anxiety before eating, as well as deficiencies of some vitamins (B complex primarily) and minerals, can all cause a lack of HCl, more of us are short of it than realize it. If you think that you have an overacid problem or heartburn, for which you are dosing yourself with an antacid such as Maalox™, Di-Gel™, Tums™, Rolaids™, or Alka-Seltzer™, you are probably unaware that *the symptoms of having too little acid are exactly the same as having too much,* in which case the taking of antacids could be the worst possible thing for you to do.

Dr. Alan Nittler, author of *A New Breed of Doctor,* has stated emphatically that everyone over the age of forty should be using a HCl supplement.

Betaine HCl and glutamic acid HCl are the best forms of commercially available hydrochloric acid.

CAUTION: If you have an ulcer condition, consult your doctor before using these supplements.

98. The Twelve Tissue Salts and Their Functions

Tissue salts are inorganic mineral components of your body's tissues. They are also known as Schuessler biochemical cell salts, after Dr. W. H. Schuessler, who isolated them in the late nineteenth century. Dr. Schuessler found that if the body was deficient in any of these salts, illness occurred, and that if the deficiency was corrected, the body could heal itself. In other words, tissue salts are *not a cure,* but merely a remedy.

The twelve tissue salts are:

Fluoride of lime (calc. fluor.)—Part of all the connective tissues in your body. An imbalance can be the cause of varicose veins, late dentition, muscle tendon strain, carbuncles, and cracked skin.

Phosphate of lime (calc. phos.)—Found in all your body's cells and fluids, an important element in gastric juices as well as bones and teeth. An imbalance or deficiency can be the cause of cold hands and feet, numbness, hydrocele, sore breasts, and night sweats.

Sulfate of lime (calc. sulf.)—A constituent of all connective tissue in minute particles, as well as in the cells of the liver. An imbalance or deficiency can be the cause of skin eruptions, deep abscesses, or chronic oozing ulcers.

Phosphate of iron (ferr. phos.)—Part of your blood and other body cells, with the exception of nerves. An imbalance or deficiency can be the cause of continuous diarrhea or, paradoxically, constipation. It has also been used as a remedy for nosebleeds and excessive menses.

Chloride of potash (kali. mur.)—Found under the surface body cells. An imbalance or deficiency can be the cause of granulation of the eyelids, blistering eczema, and warts.

Sulfate of potash (kali. sulf.)—The cells that form your skin and internal organ linings interact with this salt. An imbalance or deficiency can be the cause of skin eruptions, a yellow coating on the back of the tongue, feelings of heaviness, and pains in the limbs.

Potassium phosphate (kali. phos.)—Found in all your body tissues, particularly nerve, brain, and blood cells. An imbalance or deficiency can be the cause of improper fat digestion, poor memory, anxiety, insomnia, and a faint, rapid pulse.

Phosphate of magnesia (mag. phos.)—Another mineral element of bones, teeth, brain, nerves, blood, and muscle cells. An imbalance or deficiency can be the cause of cramps, neuralgia, shooting pains, and colic.

Chloride of soda (nat. mur.)—Regulates the amount of moisture in the body and carries moisture to cells. An imbalance or deficiency can be the cause of salt cravings, hay fever, watery discharges from eyes and nose.

Phosphate of soda (nat. phos.)—Emulsifies fatty acids and keeps uric acid soluble in the blood. An imbalance or deficiency can be the cause of jaundice, sour breath, an acid or coppery taste in the mouth.

Sulfate of soda (nat. sulf.)—A slight irritant to tissues and functions as a stimulant for natural secretions. An imbalance or deficiency can be the cause of low fevers, edema, depression, and gallbladder disorders.

Silicic acid (silicea)—Part of all connective tissue cells, as well as those of the hair, nails, and skin. A deficiency or imbalance can be the cause of poor memory, carbuncles, falling hair, and ribbed, ingrowing nails. Eating whole-grain products should supply the normal need for this tissue salt.

99. Any Questions About Chapter VII?

My father-in-law suffers terribly from heartburn and takes Mylanta so often that it's virtually his dessert after meals. Isn't there some natural alternative?

There sure is, and it tastes a lot better than any chalky liquid. Chewable papaya enzyme tablets, made from nature's "magic melon" fruit, can actually digest 2,230 times their weight of starch. They do this because they contain pepsin and prolase, enzymes which assist in protein digestion and combine with mylase, a potent starch digestive enzyme. (Papain, by the way, is the chief ingredient in meat tenderizers, which work on foods before they even reach your stomach.) The U.S. Department of Agriculture has attested to the fact that papaya contains valuable digestive properties, so your father-in-law would be well-advised (and probably a lot happier) to take 1 or 2 of these pleasant-tasting natural tablets after his meals.

I'm on a diet. Am I better off eating pasta or steak?

Personally, I'd recommend fish. It's high in protein, low in calories, and a 3-ounce serving of flounder or sole has a mere 80 calories with only 1 gram of fat. Carbohydrates, though they have the same caloric value as protein, are less fattening than fat (which steak has a lot of). It works this way: in order to convert 100 calories of carbohydrates, you use up 25 calories; in order to convert 100 calories of fat, you use up only 3 calories. Keep in mind, though, that a serving of pasta doesn't mean a bowlful. In fact, a one-cup serving is about the size of two scoops of ice cream.

VIII

Antioxidants on Purpose

100. Do I Need to Take Antioxidants?

The answer is an unqualified *yes!* With every breath you take you generate free radicals, the uncontrolled oxidants that damage cells. The older you get, the less natural antioxidants your body produces to keep these destructive molecules in check. As they accumulate, health deteriorates and aging accelerates—leaving you more susceptible to everything from wrinkles to serious degenerative diseases.

Though we get antioxidants from food, many people have increased antioxidant needs that diet alone cannot meet. Smokers, for instance, need two to three times as much vitamin C to achieve the same antioxidant blood levels as nonsmokers. Other factors that can increase free radicals are: air pollution, chronic disease, secondhand smoke, dietary carcinogens (foods fried at high temperatures or charcoal-broiled, nitrites, cured meats), inherited susceptibility to a disease, infection, vigorous exercise, menopause, mental stress, sun exposure, and X rays. Additionally, it's not always what foods you eat but how the food is prepared. For example, cooked carrots supply more bioavailable beta-carotene than raw ones. Your best free radical defense is to know your antioxidants and how to maximize their effectiveness in your diet and supplements.

101. What Antioxidants Can Do for You

• Retard the aging process.
• Lower cholesterol levels.
• Decrease risk of atherosclerosis.
• Help protect against heart disease and stroke.
• Reduce the risk of all types of cancer.
• Help slow down progression of Alzheimer's disease.
• Aid in suppressing the growth of tumors.
• Help the body detoxify carcinogens.
• Protect eyes from macular degeneration, a disease that causes vision loss.
• Aid in defending the body against damage from cigarette smoking.
• Help protect against chronic obstructive pulmonary disease (CPOD)—such as asthma, bronchitis, and emphysema.
• Offer protection against environmental pollution.

102. Phytochemicals

These are natural chemical substances found in plants; health-promoting nutrients (sometimes referred to as phytonutrients) that give fruits, vegetables, grains, and legumes their color, flavor, and protection against disease. They form the plant's immune system. Potent antioxidants, they have been shown to have a protective effect against many ailments including heart disease, diabetes, high blood pressure, osteoporosis, lung ailments, and cancer.

103. Carotenoids

Carotenoids are powerful phytochemicals that act as antioxidants and have strong anticancer properties. They are the fat-soluble pigments found in orange, yellow, red, and green fruits and vegetables that protect them from constant exposure to the sun's ultraviolet (UV) rays and other environmental carcinogens, preventing the formation of dangerous free radicals. There are at present 600 known carotenoids, and about 50 can be found in edible fruits and vegetables. The 5 being touted as antioxidant stars for the twenty-first century are alpha-carotene, beta-carotene, lycopene, lutein, and zeaxanthin.

ALPHA-CAROTENE: Converted into vitamin A as the body needs it, alpha-carotene has been shown to drastically reduce tumors in animals and may be *ten times* more powerful than beta-carotene in protecting skin, eye, liver, and lung tissue against free-radical damage.

Food and Supplement Advice: Your best food sources are cooked carrots and pumpkin. As a supplement, alpha-carotene is sold alone, but it is also included in mixed carotenoid and antioxidant formulas. My recommendation is 3–6 mixed carotenoids daily.

BETA-CAROTENE: Converted into vitamin A only as the body needs it, leaving the remainder to act as an antioxidant. Studies have shown beta-carotene to play a significant role as a cancer preventive by inhibiting the formation of free radicals. Additionally, it has been found to help strengthen the immune system, reduce the risk of atherosclerosis, heart attack, and stroke, and protect against the formation of cataracts.

Food and Supplement Advice: Look for brightly colored fruits and vegetables, such as apricots, sweet potatoes, broccoli (even better steamed), cantaloupe, pumpkin, carrots, mangoes, peaches, and spinach. Supplements are sold separately, but beta-carotene is included in mixed carotenoid formulas as well as most multivitamins and antioxidant formulas. Beta-carotene is available in two forms: all-*trans*- and 9-*cis*-beta-carotene. The 9-*cis* form may be better absorbed by the body.

CAUTION: If you have hypothyroidism, your body probably cannot convert alpha- or beta-carotene into vitamin A, so it's best to avoid these supplements.

LYCOPENE: A carotenoid that does not have any pro–vitamin A activity (meaning that it is not converted into vitamin A as the body needs it), and has significantly more antioxidant capability than beta-carotene. Lycopene is the substance that gives tomatoes, watermelon, pink grapefruit, and other fruits and vegetables their red color, and has been shown to inhibit the growth of many types of cancer cells. In fact, men who eat pizza have been found to have a reduced risk of prostate cancer because of the lycopene-rich tomato sauce. Lycopene has also been found to protect against the carcinogens in tobacco smoke and exposure to the sun's ultraviolet rays.

Food and Supplement Advice: Blood levels of lycopene decline with age. Also, lycopene is a fat-soluble pigment and not well absorbed by the body unless it is heated and combined with a small amount of fat, such as olive oil. For this reason cooked tomato sauce provides more of this carotenoid than plain tomatoes. So, if you are over fifty, and not eating tomato products on a daily basis, one 6–10 mg. capsule a day with meals might be advisable.

LUTEIN: Another carotenoid that does not convert to vitamin A in the body but is an impressive antioxidant. Especially helpful in protecting the eyes, lutein has been found to clear away free radicals caused by harmful ultraviolet rays and retard macular degeneration, the most common cause of blindness in people sixty-five and over.

Food and Supplement Advice: Lutein is abundant in spinach and collard greens, so if you eat plenty of those daily you probably do not need a supplement. But if you're not a fan of those particular veggies, you can find lutein in tablets and combination products (which should contain at least 6 mg. of it). If taken separately, I'd suggest one 6–20 mg. tablet a day with a meal.

ZEAXANTHIN: This carotenoid, like lutein, also protects the eye from free radical induced macular degeneration. (Damage to the macular, a tiny dimple on the retina responsible for fine vision, can cause blurry vision and eventually lead to loss of central vision. Though surgery may slow its progress, there is no cure for macular degeneration, which is why prevention is so important.) Zeaxanthin may also help protect against different forms of cancer by scavenging free radicals and decreasing the growth of tumor cells.

Food and Supplement Advice: Zeaxanthin is found in substantial concentrations in watercress, Swiss chard, chicory leaves, beet greens, spinach, and okra. If your diet does not frequently include these greens, a good mixed carotenoid or antioxidant supplement with 30–130 mg. zeaxanthin taken daily with meals should be considered.

104. Flavonoids

These antioxidant phytochemicals form the water-soluble colors of vegetables, fruits, grains, leaves, and bark. (Biologically active antioxidant flavonoids are bioflavonoids.) There are many types of flavonoids, and different plants contain varying concentrations of them. In fact, studies have shown that some flavonoids possess up to 50 times more antioxidant activity than vitamins C and E—and those in red grapes are more than 1,000 times more powerful than vitamin E in inhibiting oxidation of human LDL cholesterol! The following are just some of the flavonoids you should at least know a little about because they can do a lot for your health!

CATECHINS: These members of the polyphenol-flavonoid family have been found to inhibit the growth of antibiotic-resistant *Staphylococcus* bacteria, which can cause life-threatening infections, as well as help people who eat a high-cholesterol diet maintain normal cholesterol levels and aid in preventing dental caries and gum disease. There is also strong evidence that they may help in reducing the rate of stomach and lung cancer, prevent DNA damage, and delay the onset of arteriosclerosis.

Food and Supplement Advice: Catechins are found in large concentrations in green tea. They are also in grapes, grape juices, and the wines made from them. Excessive ingestion of catechins can be toxic. I've found, however, that a cup or two a day of green tea appears to be both safe and beneficial.

CAUTION: Women who are pregnant or nursing or anyone with a heart arrhythmia should limit their intake to no more than two cups of green tea daily. (Caffeine-free green tea extract supplements are available.)

RESERVERATROL: Another important polyphenol-flavonoid family member. Studies have shown it can reduce the risk of heart disease and stroke by inhibiting the formation of blood clots and LDL, the bad cholesterol. It has also been found capable of helping to block the formation of cancer cells, and being able to turn malignant cells back to normal.

Food and Supplement Advice: Reserveratrol is a compound found in the skin and seeds of grapes. Along with catechins and anthocyanidin, the antioxidant responsible for deep purple color in red grapes, it may account for "The French Paradox." Despite the fact that the French eat a diet of extremely high-fat, high-cholesterol food, they have one of the lowest rates of heart disease in the world. Researchers believe this is because of the red wine they drink with meals. If you're not a drinker, don't want the negative effects of alcohol overconsumption, and still want to reap the health benefits, there are alternatives. Purple grape juice also contains reserveratrol, though in much smaller quantities, and supplements are available. I'd suggest taking either one 1,000 mcg. reserveratrol capsule daily or two 30 mg. polyphenol capsules.

PROANTHOCYANIDINS AND ANTHOCYANIDINS (PCOs): [also known as oligomeric proanthocyanidins (OPCs)] These flavonoids (technically, "flavonals"), are powerful vascular protectors and remarkable in their ability to connect and strengthen the body's many strands of collagen protein—particularly in soft tissues, tendons, ligaments, and bones. Because of this, they help promote good circulation to all glands and organs (crucial to preventing and overcoming disease), act therapeutically for fragile capillary conditions such as bruising, varicose veins, and hemorrhoids, and may offer significant aid in preventing osteoporosis. Additionally, they may be beneficial to athletes and fitness buffs because they are water-soluble and, therefore, capable of neutralizing the free radicals in tissue fluids generated by heavy exercise.

Food and Supplement Advice: PCOs or OPCs (you say "tomato" I say "toMAHto") are derived primarily from grapeseed and pine bark extract. Pycnogenol™, which is one of the few antioxidants that crosses the blood-brain barrier to help protect brain and nerve tissue from oxidation, has become synonymous with pine bark benefits, though it is actually a trademarked name for the patented process of extracting flavonoids and other substances from pine bark and consists of 50–60 percent proanthocyanidins. These flavonoids are present in other fruits and vegetables, too, but because bark, stems, leaves, and skins are not high on most people's must-eat lists, they are usually discarded. Fortunately, supplements are available. My recommendation would be to take up to three 30–100 mg. PCO tablets daily *between* meals. Preferably, grapeseed and grape skin extract tablets. (Use the lower dose unless you are over sixty-five or have a compromised immune system.)

105. Isoflavones

Found in soybeans and other legumes, these phytonutrients are related to flavonoids. In the body they are converted into phytoestrogens (plant estrogens), hormonelike compounds that may help block the growth of hormone-dependent—and other—cancers. They also seem to help lower total cholesterol levels and reduce high blood triglycerides, providing protection against heart disease. (They may even prevent hot flashes in menopausal women.) The best-known isoflavones are genistein and daidzein.

GENISTEIN: Helps block the spread of cancerous tumors by preventing the growth of new blood vessels to nourish the cancer cells. May reduce the risk of breast and prostate cancer.

Food and Supplement Advice: Genistein is found exclusively in soy foods, such as soy milk, tofu, miso, and tempeh. If you're not a tofu fan, and your feeling about soy is just soy-so, it is available in pill and powdered supplement form with daidzein and other isoflavones. One soy protein shake or two soy concentrate supplement tablets (containing 10 mg. genistein and daidzein) is what I would recommend.

DAIDZEIN: Works with genistein to block enzymes that promote tumor growth. May be especially beneficial to women in controlling the effects of potent estrogens that could stimulate the growth of breast cancer cells. Helps reduce blood-alcohol levels and relieve hangovers (see section 205).

Food and Supplement Advice: Like genistein, daidzein is found in soy products. As an antioxidant, cancer-fighting supplement, one soy protein shake daily or two soy concentrate tablets (containing genistein and other isoflavones) is recommended. Daidzein is also the isoflavone in the oriental herb kudzu (*Pueraria lobata*) that has been shown to help prevent hangovers and reduce the desire for alcohol. Kudzu supplements are available in capsules. If you'd like help getting "on the wagon"—or getting over the night before—my recommendation is three 500 mg. capsules daily before or after drinking alcohol.

106. Vitamins

The major vitamins that act as antioxidants are vitamin A, vitamin C, and vitamin E.

VITAMIN A: A potent and important free radical scavenger, vitamin A—particularly its precursors alpha- and beta-carotene—destroys carcinogens and has been found to protect against many forms of cancer.

Food and Supplement Advice: (See section 28.)

VITAMIN C: This water-soluble wonder worker could well be called the antioxidant's antioxidant because it helps protect other antioxidants in the body. It inhibits the production of cancer-causing nitrosamines, cuts the risk of many types of cancer, increases the activity of vital immune cells, prevents dangerous oxidation of LDL cholesterol, and reduces your chances of heart attack.

Food and Supplement Advice: (See section 43.)

VITAMIN E: A fat-soluble free-radical fighter that protects cell membranes and other lipid-containing tissues. It has been found to help prevent cataracts, enhance the body's immune response, protect against many types of cancer, and significantly reduce the risk of fatal heart attacks.

Food and Supplement Advice: (See section 45.)

107. Minerals

All minerals are antioxidants, but, unlike some vitamins, not a single one can be manufactured by the body and all must be acquired through diet. Their presence in the body in proper amounts cannot be overemphasized, since vitamins cannot function, be assimilated, without the help of minerals. The major mineral free-radical scavengers are selenium and zinc.

SELENIUM: Synergistic with vitamin E, meaning the two together increase each other's effectiveness, it has been shown to be an important cancer preventive, particularly helpful in protecting against damage caused by radiation and chemical carcinogens. It also stimulates increased antibody response to infection, aids in the prevention of blood clots which can cause a stroke, and may help reduce the pain and stiffness of arthritis. Additionally, it is reputed to increase the male sex drive.

Food and Supplement Advice: (See section 65.)

ZINC: A potent fighter of the common cold, it has been shown to enhance the immune system, increasing the level of infection-fighting T cells, particularly in older people. It may also help retard vision loss caused by macular degeneration as well as aid in protecting the prostate from enlargement and even cancer.

Food and Supplement Advice: (See section 69.)

108. Allium Vegetables

There are over 500 plants in the genus *Allium*, but the antioxidant superstars are garlic (see section 122), onions, shallots, and leeks. These vegetables contain flavonoids, vitamin C, selenium, and sulfur compounds that have been shown to have potent cancer-fighting properties—particularly in helping cells dispose of carcinogens. They may also help prevent heart attack and stroke by lowering cholesterol and blood pressure and preventing blood clots. Additionally, they benefit the liver by helping activate detoxification enzyme systems, and may be helpful, too, in the prevention of allergies and asthma.

Food and Supplement Advice: You don't have to eat raw onions or garlic to reap benefits from this group; even when cooked, they seem to have antioxidant capabilities. And if you'd rather not chance heartburn or bad breath, odorless garlic caps are available. Parsley sprigs are natural breath fresheners, but internal breath freshening capsules made from parsley seed oil might be easier to carry around.

109. Bilberry

This herb, also known as European blueberry, is a potent antioxidant. It contains anthocyanosides, that have been found to help keep capillaries strong, protect against cataracts, night blindness, and other vision problems, and improve circulation. It may also inhibit the growth of bacteria and act as an anti-inflammatory, as well as have anticarcinogenic effects.

Food and Supplement Advice: As a supplement, bilberry is available in capsules and liquid extract. Take one 500 mg. capsule up to 3 times daily. Or, mix 15–40 drops in water or juice, and drink 3 times daily. Bilberry works best when combined with vitamin C (up to 500 mg. vitamin C daily).

CAUTION: Do not exceed recommended dosages! Although commercially prepared extracts are safe, bilberry leaves can be poisonous if consumed over a long period of time.

110. Coenzyme-Q10 (Co-Q10, Ubiquinone)

This antioxidant nutrient is found in every living cell and is essential for providing us with energy necessary to carry out bodily functions effectively. As we age, levels of coenzyme-Q10 fall, which may directly relate to numerous diseases and illnesses associated with age. (See section 320.) Poor eating habits, stress, and infection can also affect the body's ability to provide adequate amounts. Sharing many of vitamin E's antioxidant properties, it has been shown to increase energy, improve heart function, help reverse gum disease, and improve the immune system.

Food and Supplement Advice: Coenzyme-Q10 is found in meat, cereals, vegetables, eggs, and dairy products, but it is significantly reduced by the length of storage, processing, and methods of cooking. As a supplement, I'd suggest one 30 mg. capsule twice daily. The gel form of Co-Q10 is the best absorbed and easiest to swallow.

111. Cruciferous Vegetables

This group of antioxidant-rich vegetables (broccoli, brussels sprouts, cabbage, kale, etc.) contains—along with vitamin C and other flavonoids—phytochemicals called indoles and sulforaphane. Indoles inactivate estrogens that can promote the growth of tumors, particularly those in the breast. Sulforaphane has been found to stimulate cells to produce cancer-fighting enzymes. The combination of all these potent antioxidants in cruciferous vegetables has been found to help protect against many forms of cancer.

Food and Supplement Advice: Despite the nutritional benefits of cruciferous vegetables like broccoli, kale, cauliflower, brussels sprouts, bok choy, and others, they're not high on most people's favorite foods list. Fortunately, many of the beneficial substances in these vegetables can now be obtained in supplement form. Swallowing a pill won't provide you with fiber and all the other nutrients in fresh vegetables, but it's better than passing these health benefits by altogether. I find that taking a combination supplement of mixed fruits and vegetables that contains broccoli isolates or extracts is a terrific pick-me-up between meals—and a great way to cover my nutritional bases!

112. Ginkgo Biloba

This potent antioxidant herb is best known for improving circulation. By increasing the supply of oxygen to the heart, brain, and all other body parts, it aids in mental functioning and the ability to concentrate, helps relieve muscle pain, and may alleviate impotency. In fact, quite a few men have told me they think of it as nature's Viagra™. It can relieve symptoms of vertigo and tinnitus (ringing in the ears), and may improve perception and social function in victims of Alzheimer's disease. Because it helps protect cells from free radical damage, it may also aid in slowing the aging process and preventing cancer.

Food and Supplement Advice: Standardized ginkgo biloba is available in 40 mg. and 60 mg. strengths. You can take up to three 60 mg. capsules or tablets daily.

CAUTION: Taking this herb with aspirin may cause bloodshot eyes.

113. Glutathione

This triple-powered antioxidant is produced in the liver from three amino acids—cysteine, glutamic acid, and glycine. It protects cells throughout the body, as well as all organ tissues, and may help prevent cancer, especially of the liver. Glutathione functions as an immune system booster, a detoxifier of heavy metals and drugs, and may also protect against radiation poisoning and the detrimental effects of cigarette smoke and alcohol abuse. It has also been used as an anti-inflammatory treatment for arthritis and allergies.

Food and Supplement Advice: Glutathione is found in fruits and vegetables, but cooking can reduce its potency. As a supplement, I'd suggest a 50 mg. capsule one or two times daily. The amino acid methionine helps protect against glutathione depletion, so a diet that includes natural food sources of methionine—such as beans, eggs, fish, garlic, lentils, soybeans, and yogurt—is a good idea. Taking an amino acid supplement containing L-cysteine and L-methionine can also boost the body's own production of glutathione.

114. Lipoic Acid

A unique defender against free radicals, frequently called the universal antioxidant, lipoic acid is a vitamin-like substance that the body produces naturally. Unlike other internally produced antioxidants that have specific jobs, lipoic acid is neither exclusively fat soluble nor water soluble, enabling it to enhance the activity of other antioxidants in the body as well as be an all-around pinch hitter. If, for example, your stores of antioxidant vitamins C or E are low, lipoic acid can fill in for them temporarily. Because of its ability to pass through the blood-brain barrier, it can also help reverse the negative effects to the brain caused by strokes. Lipoic acid also helps normalize blood sugar levels and can prevent serious complications from diabetes.

Food and Supplement Advice: As we age, our bodies stop producing lipoic acid in sufficient quantities to provide benefits. If you've passed the big 4-0, you might *not* want to pass on a supplement. Lipoic acid is available in tablets and included in antioxidant formulas. I'd suggest one or two 50 mg. tablets daily.

115. Melatonin

This antioxidant hormone is produced by the brain's pineal gland during sleep and helps maintain the body's natural biorhythms. Because of its control of our body clock (sleep-wake cycles), I've found it helpful as a treatment for jet lag as well as insomnia.

As we age, our levels of melatonin decline. Supplements may help retard the aging process, particularly by helping to prevent the oxidative damage to brain cells that contributes to a variety of illnesses, including Alzheimer's disease. Melatonin has also been found to reduce the incidence of cluster headaches and can boost immune function by activating cancer-fighting cells that help stop malignancies from spreading.

Food and Supplement Advice: Melatonin is found in foods such as tomatoes, which is why, even though it is a hormone, it can be sold as a supplement and not a drug. My recommendation for avoiding jet lag is 1–3 mg. (sublingual form) dissolved under tongue half an hour before you want to go to sleep at your arrival destination. If taking tablets or capsules, which are not as fast-acting, I'd suggest 1–3 mg. 1½ hours before desired sleep time. For insomnia, 1–5 mg. before bedtime. (Start with 1 mg. and increase if necessary. Do not exceed 5 mg.) As a general antiaging supplement, I'd recommend 0.5–1 mg. (sublingual form) taken before bedtime.

CAUTIONS: Melatonin may make you very sleepy and should be taken at bedtime. Do not drive or operate heavy machinery after taking it. If you are taking *any* medication, have a serious illness, are pregnant or breastfeeding, are diabetic, have a hormonal imbalance from another illness, or are menopausal and on hormone replacement therapy (HRT), melatonin should **not** be taken without consulting your doctor. Because it may overstimulate immune function, anyone with an autoimmune disease or on immune-suppressing medication *should not take melatonin!*

116. Superoxide Dismutase (SOD)

An enzyme that acts as a powerful antioxidant, especially with skin tissue, revitalizing cells and reducing the rate of cell destruction. In fact, SOD injections have been shown to help in the treatment of scleroderma, a hardening of the skin. SOD helps the body utilize essential zinc, copper, and manganese but can become inactive if these minerals are not supplied. As we age, our bodies produce less and less SOD, so supplementation may prove an important factor in reducing wrinkles and retarding the aging process on all levels.

Food and Supplement Advice: Among the best natural sources of SOD are barley grass, broccoli, brussels sprouts, cabbage, and wheatgrass. SOD is destroyed in the stomach, so supplements must be enteric coated in order for them to pass through the stomach intact so that the enzyme can reach and be absorbed in the small intestine. As part of an antiaging regimen (see section 320), take 125 mcg. daily.

117. Any Questions About Chapter VIII?

My sister, who's a nurse, told me that taking beta-carotene supplements can diminish the effectiveness of my vitamin E. Is this true?

It's true but unlikely. Vitamin E's absorption may be reduced if you have high levels of vitamin A and beta-carotene in your body, but unless you are overdoing your supplements

(or your skin looks a little orange from carotenoid overload)
I wouldn't worry.

Is there any way to tell if I'm low on antioxidants?

As a matter of fact, there is. It's called an oxidative stress
test and uses urine and blood samples to determine your
body's free-radical levels and glutathione reserves. If you're
in good health with no distressing symptoms or serious concerns, I don't feel there is a need to incur the expense of a
test. But, of course, if you are worried, your best bet is to
consult a nutritionally oriented doctor. (See section 342.)

*What can I take to increase the levels of my body's antioxi-
dants naturally?*

A couple of supplements come to mind. Silymarin is one
that contains three bioflavonoids extracted from the milk
thistle plant: silybin, silydianin, and silychristin. It is a natural antioxidant that enhances liver function (milk thistle
has been used for centuries to treat liver disorders) and also
increases the levels of two of the body's own most important
antioxidants, glutathione and superoxide dismutase (SOD).
You can take up to three 500 mg. silymarin capsules a day.

There is also an ancient Chinese tonic herb called cordy-
ceps, traditionally used to fight fatigue and promote vitality,
that can raise levels of the body's own antioxidants. I'd suggest taking two 525 mg. capsules daily with meals.

IX

Other Wonder Workers

118. Acidophilus

Lactobacillus acidophilus, or acidophilus, as it is commonly known, is a source of friendly intestinal bacteria and more potent as a capsule or granule supplement than yogurt. It is available as acidophilus culture, incubated in soy, milk, or yeast bases.

> Regular use of acidophilus
> keeps the intestines clean.

Many doctors prescribe acidophilus in conjunction with oral antibiotic treatment because antibiotics destroy beneficial intestinal flora, often causing diarrhea as well as an overgrowth of the fungus Candida albicans. This fungus can grow in the intestines, vagina, lungs, mouth (thrush), on the fingers, or under the nails. It will usually disappear after a few days' use of generous amounts of acidophilus culture.

Regular use of acidophilus culture keeps the intestines clean. It can eliminate bad breath caused by intestinal putrefaction (the sort resistant to mouthwash or breath spray), constipation, foul-smelling flatulence, and aid in the treatment of acne and other skin problems. It can also boost the immune system, which weakens as we age, and help menopausal women who are more susceptible to vaginal yeast infections because of the dryness that accompanies the drop in estrogen.

Keep in mind that lactose, complex carbohydrates, pectin, and vitamin C plus roughage (see fiber, section 123) encourage additional growth of intestinal flora. This is important since friendly bacteria can die within five days unless they are continuously supplied with some form of lactic acid or lactose.

As a general diet supplement, take 2 acidophilus capsules—or 2 tablespoons liquid—three times daily one half hour before or after meals. Or, 1 packet of acidophilus granules in 6 ounces of juice once or twice a day.

119. Bromelain

Pineapple is good for more than dessert! Bromelain, an enzyme derived from the stem of the pineapple plant, is a mixture of protein-processing enzymes that aids in digestion while enhancing the absorption of nutrients from food *and* supplements. It can also help reduce pain and swelling due to arthritis or injury, similar to nonsteroidal anti-inflammatory drugs (NSAIDs) but without their gastrointestinal side effects. (NSAIDs such as aspirin, ibuprofen, and Naprosyn™ inhibit prostaglandins, compounds that cause inflammation but also have a protective effect on the stomach lining.) Bromelain may also prevent abnormally high levels of fibrinogen, which can cause blood clots to form spontaneously and lead to heart attack or stroke.

As a digestive aid, I recommend one or two 500 mg. tablets after meals. As an anti-inflammatory, one to three 500 mg. tablets daily.

120. Curcumin

If you eat Indian food often, you've been spicing up your health in more ways than you probably realized. Derived from turmeric, the spice that gives curry powder its distinctive yellow color, curcumin (not the same as cumin, which is also in curry powder) is a potent antioxidant that's been shown to be particularly helpful in reducing the free-radical damage inflicted on smokers by the carcinogenic chemicals in cigarettes. It also may reduce inflammation from rheumatoid arthritis. In fact, for some arthritis sufferers it has produced improvement that's comparable to phenylbutazone, a prescription nonsteroidal anti-inflammatory, with none of the unpleasant side effects of NSAIDs. Additionally, it appears to inhibit the activity of certain proteins that may trigger the growth of breast tumors and may also lower high blood cholesterol levels.

Turmeric, the spice itself, has long been used by Indian healers in the practice of Ayurvedic medicine to strengthen liver function, and many alternative practitioners today prescribe curcumin to people with the common liver ailment hepatitis C. Turmeric also helps prevent the formation of blood clots that can lead to heart attack. As a supplement, one to three 500 mg. curcumin capsules daily with food is the suggested dosage. Many commercial preparations combine curcumin with bromelain, another anti-inflammatory. The two appear to work best together and bromelain may increase the absorption of curcumin.

121. Ginseng

It is generally well accepted that ginseng is a stimulant of both mental and physical energy. The Chinese have been using it for nearly five thousand years and still revere it as a preventive and cure-all. It is a mild laxative and helps the body pass poisons through more rapidly. It may also help reduce LDL (bad) cholesterol, improve circulation, alleviate discomfort caused by menopause by increasing estrogen levels (it is a rich source of phytoestrogen), inhibit the growth of cancerous tumors, normalize blood pressure, and help cure colds. Purported to be an aphrodisiac for centuries, many women say that it does enhance their sexual desire. Because of its stimulating effect, men may find it improves their sexual performance as well.

The big nutritional plus for ginseng is that it helps you assimilate vitamins and minerals by acting as an endocrine-gland stimulant. For maximum effectiveness, it is best to take on an empty stomach—preferably before breakfast—or at least an hour before or after eating. Vitamin C may interfere with the absorption of ginseng. If you take a vitamin C supplement, wait two hours before or after taking your ginseng to do so. (A time-release vitamin C supplement makes any counteraction less likely.)

The primary types of ginseng available are Asian ginseng (*Panax ginseng*), also called oriental, Chinese, or Korean ginseng, American ginseng (*Panax quinquefolius*), and Siberian ginseng (*Eleutherococcus senticosus*), which is not a true (*Panax*) ginseng but is enough of a relative to provide many of the same benefits—particularly increasing stamina and helping to lower cholesterol levels.

Ginseng is available in capsule form in 500–650 mg. (10-grain) doses. I don't recommend more than six 500 mg. capsules daily. It can also be purchased as a tea, powder, or liquid concentrate. It is now considered a class A adaptogen (a nontoxic substance which increases the body's resistance to a wide variety of stress factors, whether they be physical, chemical, or biological in nature.) If you use Asian or American ginseng, look for products containing 4–7 percent ginsenosides (biologically active ingredients); for Siberian ginseng, find products that contain eleutherosides equal to 1 percent of the total weight.

CAUTION: In rare cases, ginseng may cause vaginal bleeding in menopausal women. Though not dangerous, it could be mistaken as a symptom of uterine cancer. In any event, if bleeding does occur you should notify your doctor and don't forget to tell him that you're taking ginseng. Also, some people may develop headaches or high blood pressure from *Panax* ginseng, so it's advisable to check with your doctor before starting a ginseng regimen. I'd also advise avoiding products that combine ginseng with another herbal stimulant, ma huang (ephedra), which may cause jitters and palpitations in some people.

122. Alfalfa, Garlic, Chlorophyll, and Yucca

A natural diuretic.

Alfalfa has been dubbed "the great healer" by noted biologist and author Frank Bouer, who discovered that the green leaves of this remarkable legume contain *eight* essential enzymes. Also, for every 100 g., it contains 8,000 IU of vitamin A and 20,000–40,000 units of vitamin K, which protects against hemorrhaging and helps in blood clotting. It is additionally a fine source of vitamins B6 and E, rich in calcium, magnesium, potassium, and beta-carotene, and contains enough vitamin D, lime, and phosphorus to secure strong bones and teeth in growing children.

A good laxative and a natural diuretic, alfalfa is often used to treat urinary tract infections. Also, it is reputed to provide relief from rheumatoid arthritis, improve poor appetite, and has been used for treating stomach ailments and gas pains. It is available as a supplement in capsules and tablets—3–6 daily is my recommended dosage.

CAUTION: Alfalfa has been known to aggravate lupus and should be avoided by anyone with that disease or any other autoimmune disorder.

Garlic contains potassium, phosphorus, a significant amount of B and C vitamins, as well as calcium, protein, and some amazing health-giving compounds that have finally become recognized by traditional doctors for their remarkable medicinal value. A natural antibiotic, once relied on so heavily by the Soviet army that it became known as "Russian penicillin," it has now been found to lower cholesterol—specifically LDL (bad) cholesterol—and also act as a natural blood thinner, helping to prevent the formation of blood clots, offering protection against heart attack and stroke.

Recent research has shown that a component of garlic oil, diallyl sulfide (DAS), may inactivate potent carcinogens and suppress the growth of cancerous tumors. Garlic has also been found effective in lowering blood pressure, cleansing the blood of excess glucose (blood sugar ranks with cholesterol as a causative factor in arteriosclerosis and heart attacks), and alleviating bronchial congestion, sore throat, and flu symptoms.

The best way to take garlic as a supplement is in the form of aged, raw, odorless capsules. These leave no after-odor on the breath. For extra breath-friendly assurance, you might want to also take an internal breath freshener made from parsley seed oil.

Chlorophyll, according to G. W. Rapp in the *American Journal of Pharmacy*, possesses positive antibacterial action. It also appears to act as a wound-healing agent, and, while stimulating the growth of new tissue, it reduces the hazard of bacterial contamination.

Nature's deodorant, it is used in commercial air fresheners, as a topical body deodorant, and as an oral breath refresher. It is available in tablets and in liquid preparations.

Yucca extract comes from the genus of trees and shrubs belonging to the *Liliaceae* family. (The Joshua tree is a yucca.) The Indians used the yucca for many purposes and revered it as a plant that guaranteed their health and survival. Dr. John W. Yale, a botanical biochemist, extracted the steroid saponin from the plant and used the extract in a tablet for the treatment of arthritis. The treatment proved safe and effective, the average dose being four tablets daily, and there was no gastrointestinal irritation. Yucca-extract tablets and liquid are nontoxic and available in most health-food and vitamin stores. To help reduce inflammation and joint pain caused by arthritis or rheumatism, I'd suggest 1 tablet or capsule— or 10–30 drops liquid—up to 3 times daily.

CAUTION: Long-term use may slow the absorption of fat-soluble vitamins such as A, D, E, and K. If you are using yucca over an extended period of time, check with your physician to see if you need supplements of these oil-soluble vitamins.

123. Fiber and Bran

When research appeared in the *Journal of the American Medical Association* indicating that we would all be a great deal healthier and live longer if we ate coarser diets that sent more indigestible dietary fiber through our digestive tracts, a lot of people, wisely, jumped on the fiber bandwagon, though most weren't aware (and still aren't) that all fiber is not the same and that different types perform different functions.

TYPES OF FIBER YOU SHOULD KNOW ABOUT

Cellulose This is found in whole-wheat flour, bran, cabbage, young peas, green beans, wax beans, broccoli, brussels sprouts, cucumber skins, peppers, apples, and carrots. (Provides insoluble fiber.)

Hemicelluloses These are found in bran, cereals, whole grains, brussels sprouts, mustard greens, and beets. (Provide insoluble and soluble fiber.)

Cellulose and hemicelluloses absorb water and can smooth functioning of the large bowel. Essentially, they "bulk" waste and move it through the colon more rapidly. This not only can prevent constipation, but may also protect against diverticulosis, spastic colon, hemorrhoids, cancer of the colon, and varicose veins.

CAUTION: Increased fiber is contraindicated in certain bowel disorders. A physician should be consulted before starting any high-fiber diet.

Gums These are usually found in oatmeal and other rolled oat products as well as in dried beans. (Provide soluble fiber.)

Pectin This is found in apples, citrus fruits, carrots, cauliflower, cabbage, dried peas, green beans, potatoes, squash, and strawberries. (Provides soluble fiber.)

Gums and pectin primarily influence absorption in the stomach and small bowel. By binding with bile acids, they decrease fat absorption and lower cholesterol levels. They delay stomach-emptying by coating the lining of the gut, and by so doing they slow sugar absorption after a meal, which is helpful to diabetics since it reduces the amount of insulin needed at any one time.

CAUTION: Gums and pectin can interfere with the effectiveness of certain antifungal medications containing *griseofulvin*, such as Grifulvin V™, Grisactin™, and Fulvicin™.

Lignin This type of fiber is found in breakfast cereals, bran, older vegetables (when vegetables age, their lignin content rises, and they become less digestible), eggplant, green beans, strawberries, pears, and radishes. (Provides insoluble fiber.)

Lignin reduces the digestibility of other fibers. It also binds with bile acids to lower cholesterol and helps speed food through the gut.

CAUTION: While it's true that most of us still don't have enough fiber in our diet, too much can cause gas, bloating, nausea, vomiting, diarrhea, and possibly interfere with the body's ability to absorb certain minerals, such as zinc, calcium, iron magnesium, and vitamin B12, though this is easily prevented by varying your diet along with your high-fiber foods.

HOW MUCH IS ENOUGH? The recommended intake of fiber for adults is 20–35 grams a day. The following chart should help you locate sources that offer the most fiber-bang for your food buck.

FINDING FIBER FAST

Serving	Food	Grams of Fiber
1 cup	All-Bran™ cereal	23
¾ cup	Bran Buds™ Cereal	18
1 medium	Avocado	12
1 cup	Acorn squash	9
½ cup	Black beans	8
1 cup	Raspberries	8
1 cup	Blackberries	7.2
½ cup	Lima beans	7
½ cup	Kidney beans	6.9
1 large	Apple	6
1 cup	Seedless raisins	6
¾ cup	Parsnips, cooked	5.9
1 cup cooked	Whole-wheat spaghetti	5.4
5 dried	Peach halves	5.3
1½ cups popped	Low-fat popcorn	5
3 medium	Figs	5
1 large	Pear	5
1 medium	Potato with skin	5
1 cup	Yams	5
⅔ cup	Corn kernels	4.2
½ cup	Peas	4
1 average	Whole-wheat muffin	4
1 medium	Carrot, raw	3.7

124. Kelp

This amazing seaweed contains more vitamins (especially Bs) and valuable minerals than any other food! Because of its natural iodine content, kelp has a normalizing effect on the thyroid gland. In other words, thin people with thyroid trouble can gain weight by using kelp, and obese people can lose weight with it. In fact, one of the most widespread fads for many years has been the kelp, lecithin, vinegar, and B6 diet. (See section 300.) Kelp has also been used by homeopathic physicians in the treatment of obesity, poor digestion, flatulence, obstinate constipation, and to protect against effects of radiation. It is reported to be very beneficial to brain tissue, the membrane surrounding the brain, the sensory nerves, and the spinal cord.

Kelp can be eaten raw, but it is usually dried and ground into a powder, which can be used as a flavoring or a salt substitute. It is also available in tablets and as a liquid.

125. Mushrooms

Revered for centuries in China and Japan for their flavor and unique medicinal properties, mushrooms have finally come into the health spotlight in the West. They have been shown to strengthen the immune system, inhibit tumor growth, lower cholesterol, reduce blood pressure, help prevent heart attacks, work as an effective cancer therapy in combination with chemotherapy drugs, and more.

Mushrooms are high in water and low in fat, carbohydrates, and calories (a *fresh* pound has only 125 calories.) But when they are dried, they have almost as much protein as veal, ounce for ounce. Cooking also removes moisture and concentrates protein. No mushrooms should be eaten raw in quantity.

Maitake mushroom (*Grifola frondosa*) This basketball-size mushroom, whose name literally means "dancing mushroom" because legend has it that those who find it start dancing with joy, works as an adaptogen, meaning it helps the body adapt to stress and normalize bodily functions. It has been shown to shrink tumors, enhance chemotherapy effectiveness, reduce chemo side effects such as nausea and fatigue, lower blood pressure as well as blood sugar, and prevent the destruction of T cells by HIV, the virus that causes AIDS—with little or no side effects. (Large doses of maitake on an empty stomach should be avoided.) Taking vitamin C along with mushroom supplements provides better absorption and enhances effectiveness. Dosages will vary according to individual health needs. For basic preventative purposes, I suggest one 100 mg. tablet daily.

Reishi mushroom (*Ganoderma lucidum*)   Known as an "elixir of immortality" and one of the most valued plants in the Chinese pharmacopoeia for over 2,000 years, the reishi mushroom has been prescribed by Asian healers for hundreds of years for people suffering from angina or chest pain. Considered an adaptogen, increasing the body's resistance to stress and general well-being, reishi has been used with success as an analgesic, a natural anti-inflammatory agent, a remedy for insomnia, and as a cancer treatment. (Compounds in reishi activate macrophages and T cells, the disease-fighters that help rid the body of all foreign invaders, including cancer cells.) Reishi has also been used to treat high cholesterol, liver disorders, chronic fatigue syndrome, and altitude sickness. It is available in capsule, pill, and extract form, as well as fresh or dried for use in foods. (Soak dried mushrooms in warm water or broth for half an hour before using.) Recommended dosages increase according to the severity of individual health needs. Though there is no known toxicity, for treating serious illness a nutritionally oriented practitioner always should be consulted. To ease joint pain, reduce inflammation, or as a general immune system booster, I advise 100 mg. extract of reishi daily.

Shiitake mushroom (*Lentinus edodes*)   Another fungal wonder worker, the shiitake contains a polysaccharide called lentinan that strengthens the immune system by increasing T-cell function. It has also been found to inhibit tumor growth, according to studies reported by scientists from Japan's National Cancer Center. It may also lower cholesterol, prevent heart disease, and have antiviral properties equal to the prescription drug amantadine—without the serious side effects. Like reishi mushrooms (see above), shiitakes are available fresh, dried, and as supplements in capsule, pill, and extract form.

126. Shark Cartilage

It's taken a while, but shark cartilage is finally getting establishment recognition as a potential treatment for many different types of cancer. Purified shark cartilage, derived from the tough, elastic material that makes up the skeleton of the shark, contains a compound that inhibits the development of new blood vessels that tumors need in order to grow, basically starving them. The cartilage supplement, Benefin®, has been shown to have a similar mechanism to the prescription drugs angistatin and endostatin in the treatment of Kaposi's sarcoma and various forms of cancer. It has also been found to boost the immune system, help reduce arthritic pain and joint inflammation, as well as help treat psoriasis, scleroderma, eczema, and a host of other skin diseases. It is available in capsules and powder forms, but read labels carefully; not all products contain 100 percent pure shark cartilage.

CAUTION: Shark cartilage blocks the body's ability to generate new blood vessels and should *not* be taken by children, bodybuilders, pregnant women, women attempting to conceive, anyone who has recently suffered a heart attack or had major surgery.

127. Propolis

A bee-smart wonder worker rich in bioflavonoids that appears to help protect against viruses, especially in the elderly and others with weakened immune systems. A by-product of honey, propolis has been valued for its medicinal wound-healing properties for thousands of years. It has natural antibiotic, antiviral, and anti-inflammatory compounds; and, in addition, recent studies show that it may inhibit the growth of cancerous cells in the colon.

Propolis can be used both externally and internally. It has been shown to be an excellent treatment for sore throats and gum disease. Additionally, it is effective against the herpes virus; when applied to herpes lesions, it can help relieve pain, when taken orally in capsule form, it can help stimulate immune function. As a supplement, propolis is available as a salve (to be used externally), as a lozenge (good for sore throats), and in capsule form. My supplement recommendation is one 200 mg. capsule daily. (As part of an antiaging regimen, 500 mg. capsules may be taken up to three times daily.)

128. Yeast

One of the richest sources
of organic iron.

It's known as nature's wonder food, and it does a lot to deserve its reputation. Yeast is an excellent source of protein and a superior source of the natural B-complex vitamins. It is one of the richest sources of organic iron and a gold mine of minerals, trace minerals, and amino acids. It has been known to help lower cholesterol (when combined with lecithin), help reverse gout, and ease the aches and pains of neuritis.

There are various sources of yeast:

brewer's yeast (from hops, a by-product of beer), sometimes called nutritional yeast *torula yeast,* grown on wood pulp used in the manufacture of paper or from blackstrap molasses

whey, a by-product of milk and cheese (best-tasting and most potent nonyeast product)

liquid yeast from Switzerland and Germany, fed on herbs, honey malt, and oranges or grapefruit.

Avoid live baker's yeast! Live yeast cells deplete the B vitamins in the intestines and rob your body of all vitamins. In nutritional yeast, these live cells are heat-killed, thus preventing that depletion.

Yeast has all the major B vitamins (except B12), which can be especially bred into it. It contains sixteen amino acids, fourteen or more minerals, and seventeen vitamins (except for A, E, and C). It can be considered a whole food.

Because yeast, like other protein foods, is high in phosphorus, it is advisable when taking it to add extra calcium to the diet. Phosphorus, though a coworker of calcium, can take calcium out of the body, leaving a deficiency. The remedy is simple: increase your calcium (calcium lactate assimilates well in the body). *B-complex vitamins should be taken together with yeast to be more effective. Together they work like a powerhouse.*

Yeast can be stirred into liquid, juice, or water and taken between meals. Many people who feel fatigued take a tablespoon or more in liquid and feel a return of energy within minutes, and the good effects last for several hours. Yeast can also be used as a reducing food. Stir into liquid and drink just before a meal. It takes the edge off a large appetite and saves you a lot in calories.

129. The Soy Phenomenon

The biggest wonder about this wonder food is why more of us aren't eating it! For centuries, the Chinese and Japanese have been eating a diet high in soy foods and reaping impressive longevity benefits as well as much lower rates of death from cancer and heart disease than Americans. In fact, researchers now believe that adding as little as 2 ounces of soy food to your daily balanced diet can be a powerful protective weapon against disease!

Soy is high in fiber and rich in phytoestrogens, particularly the two important isoflavones, genistein and daidzein. (See section 105.) It is also one of the few plant foods that is a complete protein containing the proper balance of the eight essential amino acids. (See section 72.) The U.S. government recognizes it as a protein alternative equivalent to meat, and, according to the *American Journal of Clinical Nutrition*, "except for premature infants, soy protein can serve as a sole protein source in the human body." As with other vegetable proteins, the nutritional value of soy is enhanced by eating it with a grain such as rice or pasta.

SOY ADVANTAGES OVER ANIMAL PROTEIN

- Lower in fat
- No cholesterol
- High in phytochemicals
- Good source of fiber
- Good source of minerals such as calcium, iron, magnesium, phosphorus, and the B vitamins thiamin, riboflavin, and niacin.

{Note: Soybeans—with the exception of tempeh, a fermented whole soybean product—are a poor source of vitamin B12. Vegetarians should take supplementary vitamin B12.}

POTENTIAL SOY BENEFITS

- Antioxidants present in soy foods may protect against many forms of cancer as well as premature aging.

- May slow down or prevent kidney damage in people with impaired kidney function.

- Can help lower cholesterol levels.

- Help retain bone density and prevent osteoporosis.

• Aid in boosting the immune system.

• May alleviate hot flashes in menopausal women.

SOY FOODS AND PRODUCTS TO CHOOSE AND CHOOSE FROM

Soy nuts These are deep-fried or dry-roasted soybeans, often salted or flavored with seasoning. An excellent source of protein, fiber, and isoflavones. Keep in mind, though, like real nuts they are high in fat and calories.

Soy sprouts Whole soybeans that have been sprouted for up to six days. Good source of protein and fiber. Easy to add to vegetable dishes.

Fresh green soybeans These are the bean and fuzzy green pod. Unlike dried soybeans, they are eaten young, steamed like fresh vegetables, and a good source of protein, fiber, and isoflavones. A popular Japanese snack known as *edamame*, soybean in the pod, is also served in many natural-foods restaurants in the United States.

Soy milk Lactose free, soy milk is made by soaking and grinding whole soybeans with water. It is also made by adding water to whole, full-fat soy flour. It is a great source of isoflavones, protein, B vitamins, and minerals. (Only fortified soy milk, however, contains as much calcium, vitamin D, or B12 as regular milk.)

Tofu A white, cheeselike cake made from soy milk. (Also called bean curd.) Available in many different forms, it can literally soak up any flavor that is added to it. In fact, it's so versatile it can be used as a cheese as well as a meat substitute. Firm tofu (cotton tofu) is higher in protein, fat, and calcium than other forms; it's best in cooked dishes when you want it to retain its shape and consistency. Soft tofu (silken tofu) is creamier and good puréed or blended. Yakidofu is firm tofu that's been lightly broiled, and koyodofu is freeze-dried tofu that must be reconstituted before being used in cooking. Powdered instant tofu mix is also available.

Miso A versatile, fermented bean paste that can be used as a condiment, made into soup, or used as a base for salad dressings and sauces. It is low in fat, but high in sodium, and can keep in the refrigerator for up to a year.

CAUTION: It's advisable to avoid miso if you have high blood pressure or are sodium sensitive.

Soy sauce One of the world's most popular condiments, this salty sauce—made from a fermented mixture of soybeans, wheat, and *aspergillus* spores—does not contain isoflavones, but some studies suggest it does have other anticarcinogenic compounds. Though low-sodium soy sauce is available, at 605 mg. per tablespoon it isn't "no-sodium sauce"; I'd suggest you pass on it if you have high blood pressure or are sodium sensitive.

Soy protein isolate (or isolated soy protein) is sold as a plain or flavored powder that contains at least 90 percent protein. Frequently found in meal-replacement bars, infant formulas, and "muscle-building" protein powders, it is a powerful cholesterol-lowering agent, and can be used as a fat-reducing meat extender in baking, sprinkled on cereal, or blended with fruit or juice for a nondairy shake. If you can't find soy protein isolate, look for a protein powder that has soy protein isolate as the first or second ingredient. (Note: Products labeled "soy protein" could merely refer to soy flour, which is lower in protein than isolated soy protein and often higher in fat. Read labels carefully.)

Soy flour A terrific source of isoflavones, soy flour contains no less than 50 percent protein. Made from the "meat" of the roasted soybean, full-fat soy flour can be very full in fat, so look for defatted or low-fat flour, which is actually a more concentrated source of protein. Though it is good for microwave baking because it helps retain moisture, keep in mind that soy flour is gluten-free, which means it cannot be used as a substitute for wheat or rye flour in yeast-raised breads. (In non-yeast-raised products, you can substitute 20 percent of the total flour with the heavier soy flour.)

Texturized soy protein Made from soy flour, texturized soy protein (TSP) is low in fat and calories and high in protein, isoflavones, calcium, iron, and zinc. It can be used to replace part or all of the meat in ground beef dishes such as meat loaf, chili, or hamburgers, but must be rehydrated before use in recipes.

Soybean oil Though it does not contain isoflavones, soy oil—unlike most other vegetable oils—is rich in omega-3 and omega-6 fatty acids similar to those found in marine fish oils. (See section 94.) It also contains linoleic acid, which is essential for life but cannot be produced by the body. Nonetheless, like all oils, it should be used sparingly.

Soy supplements Tablets rich in the isoflavones genistein and daidzein are available. The recommended daily dose is 2 10 mg. tablets for men and 4 10 mg. tablets for women.

130. Any Questions About Chapter IX?

What's the difference between red and white ginseng?

The red is considered to be of superior quality. The natural color of the ginseng root is white. When it is simply cleaned and dried, it retains its natural color. Red ginseng, on the other hand, is the result of being steamed with a solution of herbs. Adulteration and dilution of ginseng products are not uncommon, so be sure you buy from a reputable company and look for standardized, guaranteed potency products.

I'm a thirty-eight-year-old woman. I take vitamins and exercise, but I want better muscle tone. I've heard about creatine, but I'm not sure what it is or what it does. Is it right for me?

It might be; it's already a favorite of bodybuilders and athletes. Creatine monohydrate is a synthetic version of an amino acid found naturally in the body, primarily in skeletal muscles. It is essential for the production of adenosine triphosphate (ATP), the fuel for motion involving muscle contraction. When ATP is depleted, you become fatigued. By increasing your creatine levels, you produce more ATP fuel for longer intense workouts, which leads to increased fat-burning muscle mass. You might not lose weight—muscle weighs more than fat—but you'll lose fat, and reduced blood lipid levels may protect you against heart disease.

Creatine occurs naturally in meats and fish, but serious athletes use it up faster than it can be replenished through diet. If, though, you're involved in endurance sports such as long-distance running or swimming, creatine may be counterproductive since the extra muscle mass might slow you down. Creatine is available as a powder or as chewable wafers. One tablespoon of the powder (5,000 mg.) mixed with juice or water should give your muscles a boost. Look for supplements that promise 99 percent creatine. Cheaper brands may have only about 60 percent. {Note: Studies have shown that some individuals who try creatine are unable to absorb the extra amounts into their muscles and, as a result, experience no improvement in muscle mass or athletic performance. If you don't notice *any* improvement in two or three weeks, creatine is probably not the supplement for you.}

I'm trying to reduce my cholesterol by upping my intake of soy foods. How many isoflavones should I be getting on a daily basis and am I getting enough—or too much—from tofu?

Most researchers feel that staying in the 30–50 mg. isoflavone range is enough to reap health benefits. For your reference, a cup of tofu, or tempeh, contains about 70 mg., a cup of soy milk 30 mg., and ½ cup roasted soy nuts about 120 mg. Asians—and many vegetarians in this country who use soy products as diet mainstays—consume in the neighborhood of 100 mg. of isoflavones per day, according to Dr. Stephen Barnes, Ph.D., a leading soy researcher and professor of pharmacology and toxicology at the University of Alabama. Staying within this range is advisable since long-term intakes at much higher levels have not been studied.

Is shark liver oil better than shark cartilage as a supplement?

They're both pretty impressive, but researchers are now saying that the liver oil may be a more potent cancer fighter. Shark liver oil is rich in vitamins A and D and also contains the compounds squalene and alkyglycerol (AKG), which seem to have a powerful strengthening effect on the immune system. It is a strong antioxidant and may be helpful in protecting cancer patients before, during, and after radiation treatment. Daily supplements of 1 capsule or 1 teaspoon oil appear to help minimize colds and other infections. Be sure to look for minimally processed oils that list their squalene and AKG content.

What's the scoop on spirulina? Is it some sort of wonder drug?

It's not a drug at all. Spirulina is a natural, easily assimilated complete protein. (It's known as spirulina plankton or blue-green algae.) It's nature's highest source of chlorophyll pigment, rich in such chelated minerals as iron, calcium, zinc, potassium, and magnesium, a fine source of vitamin A and B-complex vitamins, and it contains phenylalanine, which acts on the brain's appetite center to decrease hunger pangs—while also keeping your blood sugar at the proper level.

And if you'd like to slim down, this is a wonderful aid for weight reduction. Take three 500 mg. tablets one-half hour before meals. Once the dosage begins to work, decrease to two or one tablet before meals.

I've been told about an alga (not spirulina) that's supposed to have amazing health and healing properties. Have you heard of it and can you tell me what it is?

I have, and it's chlorella. Chlorella (the emerald alga) has been touted as the perfect whole food. Aside from being a complete protein and containing all the B vitamins, vitamin C, vitamin E, and the major minerals (with zinc and iron in amounts large enough to be considered supplementary), it has been found to improve the immune system, improve digestion, detoxify the body, accelerate healing, protect against radiation, aid in the prevention of degenerative diseases, help in treatment of Candida albicans, relieve arthritis pain and, because of its nutritional content, aid in the success of numerous weight loss programs.

It is available in tablets, powder, and water-soluble extracts (which contain the highest concentrations of chlorella growth factor [CGF]). Be aware, though, that although chlorella products are widely available, they differ depending on the particular strain of chlorella used.

The average dosage is 5–8 tablets 3 times daily. I'd suggest starting with only 1 tablet 3 times daily and working up, just to make sure you have no allergic reactions. Possible adverse reactions include: gas, bloating, bowel irregularity, nausea, green stools, and mild skin breakouts or eczema. (These reactions, unless severe, are not unusual and should clear up in a few days. If not, discontinue supplementation and consult a nutritionally oriented doctor. See section 342.)

Dr. David Steenblock, author of *Chlorella, Natural Medicinal Algae*, has found that for detoxification purposes, chlorella is best taken on an empty stomach; however, because it is a food, it can also be taken with other foods as well as medications.

I know that bran is good for me. I just don't know which bran is best.

It depends on what you're looking for nutritionally. The following bran name guide may help:

Barley bran is high in soluble fiber and helpful in lowering cholesterol.

Corn bran is high in insoluble fiber and may be helpful in reducing the risk of colon cancer.

Oat bran is high in soluble fiber and helpful in lowering cholesterol. (In fact, studies have shown that just 2 ounces daily can help reduce cholesterol levels by 7–10 percent!)

Rice bran is high in soluble fiber and may be helpful in lowering cholesterol. (It's similar to oat bran in nutritional benefits, but less of it is needed to produce the same results. Two tablespoons of rice bran will give you as much soluble fiber as one-half cup oat bran.)

Wheat bran is high in insoluble fiber and may be helpful in reducing the risk of colon cancer. (For natural sources of these types of fiber—and cautions—see section 123.)

Could you tell me about royal jelly? How is it different from propolis?

Propolis is a by-product of honey. Royal jelly is the bees' "milk," a nutrient-dense white secretion produced by worker bees. All bee larvae eat this concentrated superfood for the first three days of life, but after that only the designated queen bee does. It is her only food—and she grows to be 50 percent larger than her sister bees, lives up to 40 times longer, and is highly fertile! Royal jelly contains all the essential amino acids, as well as vitamins A, C, D, E, 9 B-complex vitamins (including vitamin B12, cyanocobalamin), and the minerals calcium, copper, iron, phosphorus, potassium, silicone, and sulfur. A complete protein, it is also a mild, natural antibiotic and has a stimulating effect on the adrenal glands, which affect metabolism, mood, appetite, and sex drive. It can help you increase energy and naturopathic doctors often recommend it for treating symptoms of menopause and to improve sexual performance in men. Additionally, many women believe that it definitely helps reduce the appearance of fine lines and wrinkles. As a daily energizer, I recommend taking one or two 500 mg. capsules daily.

X

Herbs, Folk Remedies, Essential Oils, and Homeopathic Medicines

131. What You Should Know About Natural Remedies

Just because herbs are natural doesn't mean that they can be used indiscriminately. Before trying any herbal remedy, be sure you know what it does, how to prepare and use it—and what cautions or side effects you should be aware of.

> Never try any natural or herbal remedy without knowing what it does, how it should be prepared and taken, what cautions should be observed, and what its possible side effects could be!

As a rule, few medical problems occur from ingesting herbal remedies, but the potential for an allergic or toxic response is always there.

IMPORTANT: If you are now taking any drugs, or have any medical problems, it's wise to consult a nutritionally oriented physician who is aware of herb-drug interactions, as well as any potentially dangerous side effects.

132. Aloe Vera

The aloe vera plant contains a wound-healing substance called aloe vera gel, a mixture of antibiotic, astringent, and coagulating agents.

Taken internally, it works as a mild laxative. One tablespoon taken at regular intervals (preferably on an empty stomach) totaling a pint a day, can help in the treatment of stomach ulcers.

External uses of aloe vera gel are many.

• It acts as an immediate and effective wound-healer, aiding in the treatment of burns, insect stings, and poison ivy. Split a leaf and apply pulp directly to the injured area, or soak cloth with aloe vera gel and bind on.
• Aloe vera gel ointments, creams, and lotions can prevent blistering and peeling from sunburn.
• It can help soften corns and calluses on the feet.
• Applied to the face and throat, it can soften skin and hold aging lines in check.
• It can alleviate the pain and itching of hemorrhoids and bleeding piles.
• It can be used as an effective hair conditioner.

CAUTION: As an ointment it can cause hives, rashes, itching and other allergic reactions in sensitive individuals— and can be extremely dangerous if taken internally by pregnant women.

133. Anise (seed)

This is a natural diuretic and gastric stimulant and is often used to relieve flatulence. It's also been used in home remedies as a treatment for dry cough.

134. Astragalus

This herb has been found to alleviate fatigue and lessen the frequency of colds. It's an immune system booster that improves resistance to viruses and bacterial infections and also accelerates healing. It may also prevent the spread of malignant cancer cells to healthy tissue. It works best with zinc and vitamins A and C.

CAUTION: If you are undergoing chemotherapy, do not take astragalus—or any other medication—without first consulting your doctor.

135. Basil

Sweet basil is a plant that can be used as a poultice to draw poison from the skin. It is frequently used to alleviate bee stings and to draw underskin pimples to a head.

136. Black Cohosh

Used to induce menstruation, relieve menstrual cramps, and promote labor and ease delivery. It is also used to treat persistent coughs and to reduce the swelling and soreness of rheumatism. Combined with skullcap, wood betony, passionflower, and valerian, it works as a natural tranquilizer.

CAUTION: Do not use during pregnancy until in labor and then only under a doctor's supervision. Large doses can cause symptoms of poisoning.

137. Blessed Thistle

Often used as an appetite stimulant and in the treatment of digestive problems, it can reduce fevers and break up congestion.

CAUTION: In high doses, this can cause burns of the mouth and esophagus, as well as diarrhea.

138. Chamomile

This plant has antispasmodic and gastric-stimulant properties, and is usually taken internally for migraines, gastric cramps, and anxiety. Externally it's used as a treatment for wounds, skin ulcers, and conjuctivitis.

CAUTION: May cause severe allergic reactions—including fatal shock—in individuals with hay fever, or those sensitive to ragweed, asters, and related plants.

139. Comfrey

When used in teas, comfrey has been found to alleviate stomach ailments, coughs, diarrhea, arthritis pain, liver and gallbladder conditions.

CAUTION: A possible side effect of using this herb is that it can reduce your absorption of iron and vitamin B12.

140. Echinacea

This herb has been found to protect healthy cells from viral and bacterial attack by stimulating activity of the immune system in general and T cells—which attack pathogens and toxins—in particular. Helpful in lessening the severity of colds and flu, and in speeding recovery.

141. Ephedra

Known as ma huang in China, it is used as a remedy for asthma, colds, and other respiratory ailments. Ephedra contains ephedrine and pseudoephedrine, two alkaloids used in many over-the-counter cold and allergy medications. It speeds up metabolism and is found in some herbal weight-loss formulas.

CAUTION: If taken in excess, ma huang can have an amphetamine-like effect, causing rapid heartbeat and a dangerous rise in blood pressure. It should definitely *not* be used by anyone with heart problems.

142. Juniper (berries)

These are often used as a stomach tonic, can act as appetite and digestion enhancers, as well as a diuretic and a disinfectant of the urinary tract.

CAUTION: Excessive ingestion of the berries, or beverages and tonics containing them, can cause hallucinations.

143. Kava Kava

This plant, grown in the Polynesian and South Sea Islands, has slight hypnotic properties. It promotes relaxation, can be gently stimulating to the genital area, and small amounts may produce a mild euphoria. It is traditionally used by herbalists as a remedy for nervousness and insomnia. A mild diuretic, it helps reduce water retention and relieve cramping due to muscle spasms.

CAUTION: Long-term use can cause liver damage.

144. Licorice

An effective restorer of membrane and tissue function, it is also a hormone balancer, an intestinal secretion stimulant, a respiratory stimulant, and a laxative.

CAUTION: High blood pressure and cardiac arrhythmias are possible side effects of licorice. Additionally, it may cause water retention and should be avoided by women who suffer from PMS. (American manufactured licorice, the sort used in candy, is a synthetic flavoring and does not have these potential side effects—of course, it also doesn't offer any of the benefits.)

145. Evening Primrose Oil

As a dietary supplement, evening primrose oil can help lower blood cholesterol, lower blood pressure, help in weight reduction, relieve premenstrual pain, improve eczema, aid in the treatment of moderate cases of rheumatoid arthritis, slow progression of multiple sclerosis, help hyperactive children, improve acne (when taken with zinc), and help build stronger fingernails.

The active ingredient in evening primrose oil is gamma linoleic acid (GLA), which is needed for the body to produce hormonelike compounds called prostaglandins (PGs), vital for good health. In other words, a deficiency of the former can result in impaired production of the latter and adversely affect your physical well-being.

146. Parsley (seeds and leaves)

A diuretic and gastric stimulant, parsley is used medicinally to treat coughs, asthma, amenorrhea, dysmenorrhea, and conjunctivitis.

147. Pennyroyal

This herb, often referred to as lung mint, is used as an inhalant in treating colds; it's also used as a tea for curing headaches, menstrual cramps, and pain.

CAUTION: Pennyroyal can induce abortion and should therefore NEVER be used during pregnancy.

148. Peppermint (leaves)

An antispasmodic, tonic, and stimulant, peppermint has been used to treat nervousness, insomnia, cramps, dizziness, and coughs. (For headaches, you might want to try a strong cup of peppermint tea, then lie down for 15–20 minutes. It usually works as effectively as aspirin—and there are NO side effects.)

149. Pokeweed

This is a root that's used primarily to treat arthritis pain. It's also an ingredient in creams that help fight fungal infections.

150. Rosemary

Not just a savory spice anymore. Recent research shows that the whole rosemary herb may be an up-and-coming cancer fighter. It has been found to act as an antioxidant and an anti-inflammatory, to prevent carcinogens from binding to DNA, and to stimulate liver detoxification of carcinogens. Used externally in an ointment, rosemary leaves may soothe rheumatism aches, sprains, wounds, bruises, and eczema. Taken internally, in the proper preparation, it can relieve flatulence, colic, and upset stomach.

CAUTION: Rosemary can be toxic in large quantities.

151. Saint John's Wort

Called nature's Prozac™, St. John's wort has been around for centuries to heal wounds. It contains hypericin, a natural mood-booster that also has germicidal and anti-inflammatory properties. Considered a nutraceutical, this herb is also a muscle relaxer used to alleviate menstrual cramps, and is a good expectorant as well. Externally, it is an antiseptic and a painkiller.

As a treatment for depression, St. John's wort may take up to three weeks to produce any mood-elevating effects. There is, however, a new form of St. John's wort with a polyphenol extract, also taken from the plant, that is now available; one tablet per day has been found to produce results in just 2–3 days. It is also available over the counter as dried leaves, flowers, tinctures, extract, oil, ointment, capsules, and prepared tea, but I would not recommend it for long-term use without the supervision of an herbalist or other medical professional.

CAUTION: St. John's wort may cause sensitivity to light and could seriously exacerbate sunburn. (This usually only occurs with high doses.) Do not combine with prescribed antidepressants. (NOTE: Contrary to earlier reports, this herb's antidepressant action is not due to monoamine oxidase [MAO] inhibition, which means it is safe for users to enjoy tyramine-rich foods such as wine, cheese, and chocolate—in moderation, of course. That should perk up spirits right there.)

152. Saw Palmetto (berries)

Saw palmetto berries are helpful in the treatment of chronic cystitis and in the prevention of genitourinary tract infections.

153. Thyme

A natural antiseptic deodorant, thyme—applied externally in compresses—can be an effective liniment for wounds; internally it can act as an antidiarrhetic, relieve gastritis cramps, as well as soothe bronchitis and laryngitis.

154. Valerian

A "natural Valium™" that produces a relaxing effect on the body and is often used to treat anxiety, muscle tension, and insomnia. Unlike prescription drugs, valerian is not addictive and has few unpleasant side effects. It may also relieve gas pains and menstrual cramps.

CAUTION: Extremely high doses may cause weakened heartbeat and paralysis.

155. Wild Yam

A plant source of the female hormone progesterone, wild yam is used for menstrual disorders, threatened miscarriage, as well as to relieve hot flashes, vaginal dryness, and other symptoms of menopause. It also contains saponins that have an anti-inflammatory effect and may help in treating the pain and stiffness of rheumatoid arthritis.

156. Yohimbe Bark

The herb yohimbe is one of the few so-called aphrodisiacs that has been shown to help treat male impotence. Unfortunately, it is also quite dangerous because it contains yohimbine, which is sold by prescription and should only be used under the supervision of a physician. This weaker form, yohimbe bark, is available without prescription, although it is not as effective. (The usual dose is 1–3 capsules daily.)

CAUTION: Yohimbe can lower blood pressure and should not be used by people with hypotension. Because of its potential serious side effects, it should not be used by anyone with a medical problem unless under the supervision of a physician.

157. Dangerous Herbs

The following herbs can be hazardous to your health and should not be brewed in teas or used in other fashion because of their potential toxicity.

NOTE: Since many herbs have several common names, the botanical name of the plant is given in italics.

ARNICA, WOLF'S BANE, LEOPARD'S BANE, MOUNTAIN TOBACCO (*ARNICA MONTANA*)
Arnica, which is helpful in the treatment of bruises, traumas, and pain, is safe to use as directed as a sublingual, homeopathic remedy (which contains only minute amounts of active ingredients in tiny pellets) or as a commercially prepared external salve.

Arnica is an irritant and can produce violent toxic gastroenteritis, intense muscular weakness, nervous disorders, and death.

BELLADONNA, DEADLY NIGHSHADE (*ATROPA BELLADONNA*)

Poisonous. Contains toxic alkaloids.

BITTERSWEET, DULCAMARA, WOODY OR CLIMBING NIGHTSHADE (*SOLANUM DULCAMARA*)

Poisonous.

BLOODROOT, SANGUINARIA, RED PUCCOON (*SANGUINARIS CANADENSIS*)

Contains the poisonous alkaloid sanguinarine, among others.

BROOM-TOPS, SCOPARIUS, SPARTIUM, IRISH BROOM, SCOTCH BROOM, BROOM (*CYTISUS SCOPARIUS*)

Contains toxic sparteine and other harmful alkaloids.

AESCULUS, BUCKEYES, HORSE CHESTNUT (*AESCULUS HIPPOCASTANUM*)

A poisonous plant which contains a toxic coumarin substance.

CALAMUS, SWEET FLAG, SWEET ROOT, SWEET CANE, SWEET CINNAMON (not to be confused with the bark used as a popular spice) (*ACORUS CALAMUS*)

Oil of calamus is a carcinogen (a cancer-causing agent).

HELIOTROPE (*HELIOTROPIUM EUROPAEUM*)

This plant is poisonous and also contains alkaloids that cause liver damage. (It should not be confused with garden heliotrope, whose botanical name is *Valeriana officinalis*, and safe.)

HEMLOCK, CONIUM, SPOTTED HEMLOCK, SPOTTED PARSLEY, ST. BENNET'S HERB, SPOTTED COWBANE, FOOL'S PARSLEY (*CONIUM MACULATUM*)

Contains poisonous alkaloids. It's often mistaken for water hemlock (*Cicuta maculata*) and hemlock spruce (*Tsuga canadensis*).

HENBANE, HYOSCYAMUS, HOG'S BEAN, POISON TOBACCO, DEVIL'S EYE (*HYOSCYAMUS NIGER*)
Poisonous. Contains dangerously toxic alkaloids.

JALAP ROOT, JALAP, TURE JALAP, VERA CRUZ JALAP, HIGH JOHN ROOT, JOHN CONQUEROR, ST. JOHN THE CONQUEROR ROOT (*EXAGONIUM PURGA, IPOMOEA JALAPA, AND IPOMOEA PURGA*)
This is a twining Mexican vine known by many different names, but it can be extremely dangerous. The drug is a potent cathartic, and its extreme purgative action can result in life-threatening excessive bowel movements.

JIMSON WEED, DATURA, STRAMONIUM, APPLE OF PERU, JAMESTOWN WEED, THORNAPPLE, TOLGUACHA (*DATURA STRAMONIUM*)
This is a poisonous plant which contains stropine, hyoscyamine, and scopolamine, drugs that are illegal (for good reason) for nonprescription use.

LOBELIA, INDIAN TOBACCO, WILD TOBACCO, ASTHMA WEED, EMETIC WEED (*LOBELIA INFLATA*)
A poisonous plant that is often unwisely used as an emetic. Overdoses of extracts from the plant's leaves or fruit produce severe vomiting, sweating, paralysis, rapid but feeble pulse, and—more often than not—collapse, coma, and death.

MANDRAKE, MANDRAGORA, EUROPEAN MANDRAKE (*MANDRAGORA OFFICINARUM*)
A poisonous narcotic similar to belladonna.

MAY APPLE, MANDRAKE, PODOPHYLLUM, AMERICAN MANDRAKE, DEVIL'S APPLE, UMBRELLA PLANT, VEGETABLE CALOMEL, WILD LEMON, VEGETABLE MERCUTY (*PODOPHYLLUM PELATUM*)
A poisonous plant with complex toxic constituents.

MISTLETOE, VISCUM, AMERICAN MISTLETOE (*PHORADENDRON FLAVESCENS* AND *VISCUM FLAVESCENS*)
Contains toxic amines. Consider it poisonous.

MISTLETOE, VISCUM, JUNIPER MISTLETOE (*PHOR-ADENDRON JUNIPERINUM*)

This particular mistletoe may or may not be poisonous, but too little is known about it for any wise person to use it for anything but holding up at Christmas time and kissing beneath.

MISTLETOE, VISCUM, EUROPEAN MISTLETOE (*VISCUM ALBUM*)

This branch of mistletoe definitely contains toxic amines and is considered poisonous.

MORNING GLORY (*IPOMOEA PURPUREA*)

The seeds of this particular morning glory do contain amides of lysergic acid, but with a potency much less than that of LSD. Anyone planning to take a "trip" on them will be in for an unpleasant and potentially dangerous surprise, since the seeds also contain a very unhealthy purgative resin.

PERIWINKLE, VINCA, GREATER PERIWINKLE, LESSER PERIWINKLE (*VINCA MAJOR* AND *VINCA MINOR*), CREEPING MYRTLE

Keep these in your garden and out of your system. They contain toxic alkaloids that can cause adverse neurological actions and injure the liver and kidneys.

SASSAFRAS

A "blood purifier" that's carcinogenic and can damage the liver.

SPINDLE TREE (*EUONYMUS EUROPAEUS*)

An extremely violent purgative.

TONKA BEAN, TONCO BEAN, TONQUIN BEAN (*DIPTERYX ODORATA, COUMAROUNA ODORATA, DIPTERYX OPPOSITIFOLIA,* AND *COUMAROUNA OPPOSITIFOLIA*)

The active constituent of these seeds is coumarin, which the FDA has prohibited marketing as a food or food additive, after having been found to cause extensive liver damage, growth retardation, and testicular atrophy when used in the diet of experimental animals. (Check the labels on your OTC medicines!)

WAHOO BARK, EUONYMUS, BURNING BUSH (*EU-ONYMUS ATROPURPUREUS*)
Often used as a laxative, but though its poisonous quali-ties have not been thoroughly identified, it's best to play it safe and keep away from it.

WHITE SNAKEROOT, SNAKEROOT, RICHWEED (*EU-PATORIUM RUGOSUM, E. OGERATOIDES, AND E. URTICAEFOLIUM*)
This poisonous plant contains a toxic, unsaturated alco-hol. It causes "trembles" in livestock and can engender milk sickness in humans who ingest milk, butter, and possibly meat from animals who have eaten this plant.

WORMWOOD, ABSINTHIUM, ABSINTH, MADDER-WORT, WERMUTH, MUGWORT, MINGWORT, WARMOT, MAGENKRAUT, HERBA ABSINTHII (*ARTEMISIA ABSINTHIUM*)
Oil of wormwood is an active narcotic poison. It is used to flavor an alcoholic liqueur—*absinthe*—which is now illegal in America because its use can damage the ner-vous system.

YOHIMBE (*CORYNANTHE YOHIMBI* AND *PAUSINY-STALIA YOHIMBE*)
Not an herb to play around with. It contains the toxic al-kaloid yohimbine.

158. Homeopathy Basics

The key to homeopathy is "The Law of Similars" or that like cures like, a principle often used in conventional medicine for allergy treatments. Symptoms are signs that the body is tying to reestablish its own natural balance. Homeopathic treatment uses the same natural substances that cause certain symptoms if given to a healthy individual in large quantities to stimulate a sick person's body to get better if given in ex-tremely tiny amounts. For example, when you peel an onion, your eyes itch and water and you often get a runny nose, much like when you have a cold. Well, when you have a cold, the homeopathic remedy would be a much diluted, minute dose of red onion (*Allium cepa*) to help the body heal itself.

Homeopathic medicines are prepared from natural plant, mineral, and animal substances. The fact that medically active substances in these medicines are diluted to such infinitesimally small amounts makes them nontoxic, with no known adverse side effects. They're safe for adults and children when taken as directed for self-limiting conditions, such as the flu, minor bruises, allergies, PMS, hot flashes, motion sickness, and the like.

The manufacture of homeopathic medicines is regulated in this country by the FDA, which provides guidelines for their labeling and sales. Available as tablets, liquids, suppositories, and ointments, the most popular form is the tiny beadlike pellet. Most homeopathic medicines are taken sublingually (under the tongue) because the large number of capillaries in the mouth get them into the bloodstream quickly.

THE RIGHT WAY TO TAKE AND HANDLE HOMEOPATHIC MEDICINES

• Keep medicine tightly capped, away from light, in a dry place.
• Do not expose to aromatic substances such as perfumes, camphor, or menthol which can neutralize them.
• Before taking medicine, make sure your mouth is clean of any flavors—especially coffee or mint, which can interfere with the effects of homeopathic remedies. (It's best to avoid mint-flavored toothpaste entirely while on regimen.)
• Do not touch the pellets. Spill the remedy into the cap, then drop it on the tongue and let it dissolve.
• Don't brush your teeth, drink, or eat anything for at least a half hour to give the remedy a chance to work.

COMMON COMPLAINTS AND THEIR
HOMEOPATHIC REMEDIES

Symptom	Remedy
Anxiety	*Argentum nitricum* (Silver nitrate)
Bruises	*Arnica montana* (Mountain daisy)
Burns	*Calcarea sulphurica* (Calcium sulphate)
Colds (with sneezing and watery eyes)	*Allium cepa* (Red onion)
Conjunctivitis	*Euphrasia officinalis* (Eyebright)
Constipation	*Graphites* (Black lead-plumbago)
Cough (bronchitis)	*Antimonium tartaricum* (Tartar emetic)
Cough (dry)	Phosphorus
Diarrhea (with cramps)	*Veratrum album* (White hellebore)
Fever (colds and flu)	*Belladonna* (Deadly nightshade)
Flu (aches and stiffness)	*Eupatorium perfoliatum* (Boneset)
Hangover	*Nux vomica* (Poison nut)
Hemorrhoids	*Hamamelis virginiana* (Witch hazel)
Hot flashes	*Lachesis mutus* (Bushmaster snake)
Insect bites	*Ledum palustre* (Wild rosemary)
Insomnia (stress induced)	*Coffea cruda* (Unroasted coffee)
Joint Pain	*Calcarea fluorica* (Calcium fluoride)
Menstrual cramps	*Caulophyllum thalictroides* (Blue cohosh)

Motion sickness	*Cocculus indicus* (Indian cockle)
Mouth sores	*Borax* (Sodium borate)
Nasal congestion	*Pulsatilla* (Wind flower)
Nausea	*Ipecacuanah* (Ipecac)
PMS	*Sepia* (Cuttlefish ink)
Poison ivy	*Rhus toxicodendron* (Poison ivy)
Sinusitis	*Kali bichromicum* (Potassium bichromate)
Skin eruptions (with itching)	*Sulphur* (Brimstone)
Urinary problems (burning pains/itching)	*Cantharis* (Spanish fly)
Varicose veins	*Calcarea fluorica* (Calcium fluoride)
Warts	*Thuja occidentalis* (Arbor vitae)

159. Aromatherapy and Essential Oils

Aromatherapy is the use of essential oils from plants—and some animal extracts—for psychological and physical well-being. It is a holistic practice that incorporates mind, body, pleasure, and healing, and has been used for centuries throughout the world to treat conditions ranging from minor physical blemishes to near-fatal illness.

Although aromatherapists utilize many different parts of plants (leaves, flower petals, bark, roots), it is the essential oils, the highly concentrated essences derived from these parts, that are used in treatments. These oils contain powerful vitamins and enzymes, and because they are so concentrated, they are used only in tiny doses and work best when diluted. They may be diluted in a humidifier or bath water, inhaled from a bottle, or combined with other oils and applied to directly to the skin.

POSSIBLE HEALTH BENEFITS

Help cure acne	Alleviate arthritis pain
Help retard aging	Relieve migraines
Improve concentration	Draw wastes directly out of the skin
Relieve anxiety	Stimulate the immune system
Repel insects	Alleviate water retention
Improve stamina	Aid in relief of menopausal symptoms
Promote healthy skin, nails, hair	Help cure viral and bacterial infections

Stimulate drainage of the lymph glands to aid in disintegration of cellulite.

COMMON ESSENTIAL OILS AND THEIR USES

Basil—aid in mental alertness

Cinnamon—energy, sexual stimulant

Chamomile—sedative/stress reliever

Geranium—hormonal balance for women

Juniper—diuretic, improve circulation

Lavender—all skin ailments, muscle pain, stress reliever

Neroli—calm anxiety, improve skin

Patchouli—anti-inflammatory for skin

Rosewood—antidepressant

Sandalwood—immune booster, aphrodisiac

Tea Tree—antifungal, antiviral, antiacne

Ylang-Ylang—relaxant, lower blood pressure, stabilize mood swings

CAUTIONS: Essential oils should not be taken internally. Some essential oils should be avoided during pregnancy as well as by individuals with asthma, epilepsy, or other medical health conditions. Check with a naturopath, a reputable holistic physician, or a nutritionally oriented doctor about the safety of each ingredient before using any essential oil.

Keep essential oils away from children; even in small amounts, many oils can be toxic.

Essential oils, as a rule, should not be used undiluted on the skin.

160. Any Questions About Chapter X?

Does dill have any nutritive or health-giving properties?

It does indeed. It can improve appetite and digestion and also act as a diuretic. Furthermore, chewing the seeds can help eliminate bad breath.

Is it true that flaxseed is a laxative?

It can act as one. The seeds are bulk formers. Flaxseed can be eaten raw or cooked (it's great in soups), and one tablespoon daily has been found to prevent constipation in adults. Flaxseed oil is also one of the richest sources of omega-3 fatty acids, helpful in reducing cholesterol and alleviating arthritis pain.

Are there any herbs that are okay under ordinary circumstances, but might be contraindicated during pregnancy or for breast-feeding?

Lots! For example, goldenseal should be avoided during pregnancy and lactation. (Berberine, the alkaloid in goldenseal, is quite similar to morphine.) Also to be avoided are caffeine-containing herbs, such as guarana and kola nuts.

Laxatives, be they natural or manufactured, should not be taken during the first few months of pregnancy, as they could cause miscarriage. (Buckthorn, rhubarb, and senna are natural laxatives.) Strong sedative herbs like skullcap and valerian are not advisable, nor are strong spices such as capsicum and horseradish. Emetics, such as lobelia, can be dangerous early in pregnancy and in the last trimester.

Though garlic and onions are great for many things, it might be wise to avoid them if you're either pregnant or nursing, especially during the latter, as they have been known to pass through the breast milk and produce colic in infants.

My husband has liver problems and hates doctors. I've been told about a plant extract called milk thistle. Can you tell me something about it?

I can tell you that the fruit of milk thistle contains silymarin, which is one of the most potent liver-protecting substances, and that silymarin has been shown to help in the treatment of chronic hepatitis, cirrhosis, and a variety of other liver diseases.

I can also tell you that some of the extracts are based in alcohol and *should be avoided by anyone with liver problems*.

The standard dose, according to Michael T. Murray, author of *PSA Textbook of Natural Medicine* and *The 21st Century Herbal*, is 70–150 mg. three times a day. But before your husband starts a regimen using silymarin, he should definitely consult a nutritionally oriented doctor. (See section 342.)

What are adaptogens? And are they available as supplements?

Adaptogens are a rare group of plants that seem to be able to use their properties within the body—where the body actually needs them—to help protect it from physical, emotional, and environmental stresses (including radiation and chemical poisons).

Among other reported benefits of adaptogens are increased immunity defenses, enhanced energy, accelerated healing from respiratory infections, improved nerve functions, blood-pressure and blood-sugar normalizing effects.

One of the most highly touted for its health benefits

is suma (*Pfaffia paniculata martius kuntze*), often called Brazilian ginseng.

Although unrelated to ginseng, suma (a member of the amaranth family) has been found to contain numerous vitamins, minerals, amino acids, and other healing elements, including germanium (an immune cell activator), allantoin (a wound healer), and sitosterol and stigmasterol (two vegetable hormones that have been found to reduce blood cholesterol and increase—when needed—the body's natural estrogen).

Supplements are available in pill form and as teas.

What is germanium? Is it an herb or a mineral—and what are its natural sources?

Germanium is what is known as a trace element (Ge-132). According to Dr. Parris M. Kidd, director of the Germanium Institute of North America, it has the ability to restore and stimulate immune function, supplement tissue oxygen (important for diets high in unsaturated fats, which—although cholesterol-lowering—deplete oxygen), help inhibit tumor development, and alleviate major diseases.

It is found in trace amounts in garlic, ginseng, sushi, chlorella, pearl barley, and comfrey.

My niece is very much into alternative healing therapies, and she suggests I take an herb called dong quai for my hot flashes, as opposed to a drug. I know nothing about dong quai. What do you think?

I think dong quai (*Angelica sinensis*) is a terrific herb and has been shown to be quite effective in alleviating menopausal hot flashes, as well as vaginal dryness and depression. It potentiates the effectiveness of female (as well as male) sex hormones, and helps the body to maximize utilization of existing hormones. For instance, during menopause, it assists the transition of estrogen production from the ovaries to the adrenal glands.

As to whether it would be better for you than a drug, I

suggest you consult with your doctor or a nutritionally oriented physician. (See section 342.) If you do decide to use it, be aware that it works best in combination with vitamins E, B6, and zinc.

What can you tell me about an herb called Pau D'Arco?

I can tell you that I think its uses in alternative therapies are just beginning. Pau D'Arco (*Tabebuia impetiginosa*) has been found to be quite effective in inhibiting the growth of Candida albicans. (See section 259.) It is also effective in treating allergies where symptoms of bronchial asthma, eczema, and sinus congestion exist. And, last but far from least, it is systemically helpful after long-term antibiotic therapy, immunosuppressant therapy, and steroidal anti-inflammatory therapy.

For best results, Pau D'Arco should be taken in conjunction with vitamins A, C, potassium, magnesium, and digestive enzymes.

Am I better off taking a liquid herbal or a tincture?

Liquids are generally formulated in a weakly acidic solution, allowing the supplement to enter the stomach in a soluble acidic state that can enhance absorption. A tincture, where herbs are usually suspended in alcohol or cider vinegar along with water, provides a weaker but still effective concentration. Both are absorbed quickly by the digestive system. Many people feel that quality tinctures offer more potent herbal concentrates, but it depends on the manufacturer. I'd suggest that you make your choice based on the formulation that most suits your needs.

I've overheard people talking about Ev.Ext-77. What kind of herb is it and what does it do?

It's a patented extract of a subspecies of ginger and it seems to be quite effective in reducing inflammation and may be very helpful in treating joint problems. Available under the trade name Zinaxin™, Ev.Ext-77 inhibits pro-taglandin production (which causes short-term joint prob-lems) and leukotrienes (which can produce long-term joint problems). The recommended dose is one capsule twice daily, with food.

Over one million people develop unhealthy joints each year. Eighty percent of people over the age of fifty already have unhealthy joints. And it is estimated that by the year 2020, more than sixty million Americans will have joint problems! In other words, Ev. Ext-77 is a very welcome sup-plement indeed!

What is this new natural supplement HupA?

It's very exciting. Huperzine A (or HupA) is extracted from club moss, a rare plant grown in China that's been used for centuries to treat various neurological disorders. It's been shown to enhance memory and may help alleviate symptoms associated with Alzheimer's disease. It's avail-able as soft gels and tablets, but should not be taken by preg-nant women or anyone with high blood pressure.

XI

How to Find Out What Vitamins You Really Need

161. What Is a Balanced Diet and Are You Eating It?

A balanced diet is something easily found in books and rarely on the table. Though nutrients are widely scattered all through our food supply, soil depletion, storage, food processing, and cooking destroy many of them. Still, there are enough left to make balancing meals important. After all, supplements cannot work without food, and the better the food you eat, the more effective your supplements will be. Unfortunately, no possible "balanced" diet is likely to meet nutritional needs today.

Nevertheless, to know whether or not you are balancing your meals, you should become familiar with the basic food groups in the Food Guide Pyramid, and the recommended number of portions that should be eaten from them each day. Serving sizes are given—and they are probably less than you think—but they should be individually determined; smaller amounts for less active people, larger amounts for teenagers and people who do physically strenuous work. Keep in mind that as you get older your metabolic rate slows and your energy needs decrease.

Based on the new USDA guidelines, suggested servings per day of grains, breads, cereals, vegetables, and fruits have been significantly increased while servings of dairy and meat products have been decreased. They are now as follows.

GRAIN GROUP

Whole or enriched grains, breads, hot or cold cereals, pasta, rice.
   6–11 servings per day
      1 serving = 1 slice of bread or ½ cup of rice

VEGETABLE GROUP

Dark green, leafy, yellow, or orange vegetables.
   3–5 servings per day
      1 serving = 1 cup raw, leafy vegetables (4 large leaves) or 6 oz. vegetable juice

FRUIT GROUP

Citrus fruits, tomatoes, or others rich in vitamin C.
   2–4 servings per day
      1 serving = 1 medium fruit or 6 oz. fresh fruit juice

DAIRY GROUP

Milk, cheese, yogurt, foods made from milk.
   2–3 servings per day
      1 serving = 1 cup yogurt or milk or 1 oz. cheese

MEAT GROUP

Beef, veal, pork, lamb, fish, poultry, liver, eggs, meat substitutes, dry beans, nuts.
   2–3 servings per day
      1 serving = 3–4 oz. animal protein, roughly the size of a deck of cards, or ¼ cup nuts

FATS, OILS, SWEETS

Use sparingly

The recommended servings, as outlined by the National Research Council, are designed to supply 1,200 calories. You are expected to adjust the size of the servings to suit your own individual growth, weight, and energy needs.

162. How to Test for Deficiencies

If you're wondering whether or not you need vitamin or mineral supplementation, your best bet would be to contact a nutritionally oriented doctor. (See section 342.) Other than that, there are a variety of indicator tests that should tell you enough to point you in the right supplement direction.

Dr. John M. Ellis has devised a quick early-warning test for B6 (pyridoxine) deficiency. Extend your hand, palm up, then try to bend the two joints in your four fingers (not the knuckles of your hand), until your fingertips reach your palm. (This is not a fist, only two joints are bent.) Do this with both hands. If it is difficult, if finger joints don't allow tips to reach your palm, a pyridoxine deficiency is likely.

Betty Lee Morales, the late well-known nutritionist, stated that urine is a fair indicator of the B vitamins in your body. Since B vitamins are water soluble and lost each day through excretion, when your body demands more your urine will be light in color. When the urine is dark, your B demands are less. (NOTE: Many drugs, illnesses, and foods also alter urine color. This should be taken into consideration.)

Hair analyses, where a tablespoon of hair clipped from the back of the neck is sent to a laboratory to check for abnormally high toxic-mineral levels, have recently become a subject of controversy regarding their reliability. Hair analysts say that hair can serve as a permanent record of nutrient consumption and toxic exposure, since substances entering the hair stay there until the hair falls out. Their detractors, on the other hand, say that there are too many factors besides what we eat and drink that can influence the content of hair (dyes, shampoos, colorings, waving lotions, pool chemicals, etc.) to provide a reliable analysis.

As of this writing, the controversy has not been resolved either way. So my advice, once again, is to check with a nutritionally oriented doctor (see section 342) before investing in an analysis on your own.

Probably the best indicator of any vitamin or mineral deficiency is your body—and the way that it's feeling.

163. Possible Warning Signs

A body in need of vitamins usually lets you know about it sooner or later. It's unlikely that any of us will come down with scurvy before realizing we need vitamin C, but more often than not our bodies are giving us clues that we just don't recognize. With the price of medical insurance rising daily, paying attention to your nutritional warning system is about the best and cheapest insurance around. Here are a few common symptoms that you might be ignoring—and shouldn't. Where I've written "Are You Eating Enough?" I'm not implying that you should be downing huge portions of these foods, just suggesting that their absence in your diet could be a good reason to use supplements.

The supplements recommended are not intended as medical advice, only as a guide in working with your doctor.

NOTE: MVP stands for Mindell Vitamin Program (or Most Valuable Player in the nutrition game). It consists of:

• One all-natural high-potency multiple vitamin and amino acid–chelated mineral complex (with digestive enzymes for better absorption)
• One broad-spectrum antioxidant formula (containing alpha- and beta-carotene, lutein, lycopene, vitamin C, vitamin E, selenium, ginkgo biloba, coenzyme-Q10, bilberry, L-glutathione, cysteine, soy isoflavones [genistein and daidzein], grapeseed extract, and green tea extract). Both taken twice daily with food.

POSSIBLE DEFICIENCY   ARE YOU EATING ENOUGH?

SYMPTOM: *Appetite Loss*

Protein	Meat, fish, eggs, dairy products, soybeans, peanuts
Vitamin A	Fish, liver, egg yolks, green leafy or yellow vegetables.
Vitamin B1	Brewer's yeast, whole grains, meat (pork or liver), nuts, legumes, potatoes
Vitamin C	Citrus fruits, tomatoes, potatoes, cabbage, green peppers
Biotin	Brewer's yeast, nuts, beef liver, kidney, unpolished rice
Phosphorus	Milk, cheese, meat, poultry, fish, cereals, nuts, legumes
Sodium	Beef, pork, sardines, cheese, green olives, corn bread, sauerkraut
Zinc	Vegetables, whole grains, wheat bran, wheat germ, pumpkin seeds, sunflower seeds

RECOMMENDED SUPPLEMENT:
1 B complex, 50 mg., taken with each meal
1 B12, 2,100 mcg. (time release) with breakfast
1 organic iron complex tablet (containing vitamin C, copper, liver, manganese, and zinc to help assimilate iron)

SYMPTOM: *Bad Breath*

Niacin	Liver, meat, fish, whole grains, legumes

POSSIBLE DEFICIENCY   ARE YOU EATING ENOUGH?

RECOMMENDED SUPPLEMENT: 1–2 tbsp. acidophilus liquid
                           (flavored) 1–3 times
                           daily
                           1 chlorophyll tablet or
                           capsule 3 times daily
                           1 amino acid–chelated zinc
                           50 mg. tab daily
                           1–2 multiple digestive
                           enzyme tabs 1–3 times
                           daily

SYMPTOM: *Body Odor*

B12   Yeast, liver, beef, eggs, kidney
Zinc   Vegetables, whole grains, wheat bran,
               wheat germ, pumpkin seeds,
               sunflower seeds

RECOMMENDED SUPPLEMENT: 1–2 tbsp. acidophilus liquid
                           (flavored) 1–3 times
                           daily
                           1 chlorophyll tablet or
                           capsule 3 times daily
                           1 chelated zinc 15–50 mg.
                           tab daily
                           1–2 multiple digestive
                           enzyme tabs 1–3 times
                           daily

SYMPTOM: *Bruising Easily* (when slight or minor in-
juries produce bluish, purplish discoloration of skin)

Vitamin C   Citrus fruits, tomatoes, potatoes,
                 cabbage, green peppers
Bioflavonoids   Orange, lemon, lime, tangerine, peas

POSSIBLE DEFICIENCY   ARE YOU EATING ENOUGH?

RECOMMENDED SUPPLEMENT: 1 C complex, 1,000 mg.
(time release) with
bioflavonoids, rutin, and
hesperidin A.M. and P.M.

SYMPTOM: *High Cholesterol*

B complex inositol   Yeast, brewer's yeast, dried lima
beans, raisins, cantaloupe

RECOMMENDED SUPPLEMENT: 1 tbsp. lecithin granules 3
times daily (used on
salads or in soy shake)
1–3 omega fatty acid caps,
1,000 mg. 2–3 times
daily
1 scoop flavored soy
protein blended with 1⅓
cups nonfat soy milk in
place of one meal

SYMPTOM: *Constipation*

B complex   Whole grains, legumes, bran, green
leafy vegetables

RECOMMENDED SUPPLEMENT: 8–10 glasses of water daily
1 tbsp. acidophilus liquid 3
times daily
3 tbsp. bran daily

SYMPTOM: *Diarrhea*

Vitamin K   Yogurt, alfalfa, soybean oil, fish liver
oils, kelp

POSSIBLE DEFICIENCY	ARE YOU EATING ENOUGH?
Niacin	Liver, lean meat, brewer's yeast, wheat germ, peanuts, dried nutritional yeast, white meat of poultry, avocado, fish, legumes, whole grain
Vitamin F	Vegetable oils, peanuts, sunflower seeds, walnuts

RECOMMENDED SUPPLEMENT: 1 g. potassium divided over
         3 meals
         As a preventive 1–2 tbsp.
         acidophilus liquid
         (flavored) 3 times daily

SYMPTOM: *Dizziness*

Manganese	Nuts, green leafy vegetables, peas, beets, egg yolks
B2 (Riboflavin)	Milk, liver, kidney, yeast, cheese, fish, eggs

RECOMMENDED SUPPLEMENT: 50–100 mg. "no-flush"
         niacin 3 times a day
         200 IU dry vitamin E 1–3
         times a day
         60 mg. standardized ginkgo
         biloba tablets 1–3 times
         a day

SYMPTOM: *Ear Noises*

Manganese	Nuts, green leafy vegetables, peas, beets, egg yolks
Potassium	Bananas, watercress, all leafy green vegetables, citrus fruits, sunflower seeds

POSSIBLE DEFICIENCY   ARE YOU EATING ENOUGH?

RECOMMENDED SUPPLEMENT:	50–100 mg. "no-flush" niacin 3 times a day
	400 IU dry vitamin E 1–3 times a day
	50 mg. zinc daily

SYMPTOM: *Eye Problems* (night blindness, inability to adjust to darkness, bloodshot eyes, inflammations, burning sensations, sties)

Vitamin A	Fish, liver, egg yolks, butter, cream, green leafy or yellow vegetables
B2 (Riboflavin)	Milk, liver, kidney, yeast, cheese, fish, eggs

RECOMMENDED SUPPLEMENT:	50 mg. B complex, 1 in A.M. and P.M. with food
	500 mg. vitamin C with bioflavonoids, rutin, and hesperidin, 1 in A.M. and P.M.
	400 IU vitamin E (dry), 1 in A.M. and P.M.
	1 broad-spectrum antioxidant twice daily with food

SYMPTOM: *Fatigue* (lassitude, weakness, no inclination for physical activity)

Zinc	Vegetables, whole grain products, brewer's yeast, wheat bran, wheat germ, pumpkin and sunflower seeds
Carbohydrates	Cellulose

POSSIBLE DEFICIENCY   ARE YOU EATING ENOUGH?

Protein	Meat, fish, eggs, dairy products, soybeans, peanuts
Vitamin A	Fish, liver, egg yolks, butter, cream, green leafy or yellow vegetables
Vitamin B complex PABA	Yeast, brewer's yeast, dried lima beans, raisins, cantaloupe
Iron	Wheat germ, soybean flour, beef, kidney, liver, beans, clams, peaches, and molasses
Iodine	Seafoods, dairy products, kelp
Vitamin C	Citrus fruits, tomatoes, potatoes, cabbage, green peppers
Vitamin D	Fish liver oils, butter, egg yolks, liver, sunshine

RECOMMENDED SUPPLEMENT:

- 1 B complex, 100 mg. 2 times daily
- 1 2,000 mcg. B12 A.M. and P.M.
- 1 DMG (dimethylglycine) 50–100 mg. with meals
- Coenzyme-Q10, 30–100 mg. daily
- MVP, 1 A.M. and P.M. with meals

SYMPTOM: *Gastrointestinal Problems* (gastritis, gastric ulcers, gallbladder, digestive disturbances)

Vitamin B1 (thiamin)	Brewer's yeast, whole grains, meat (pork or liver), nuts, legumes, potatoes
Vitamin B2 (riboflavin)	Milk, liver, kidney, yeast, cheese, fish, eggs

POSSIBLE DEFICIENCY   ARE YOU EATING ENOUGH?

Folic acid (folacin)	Fresh green leafy vegetables, fruit, organ meats, liver, dried nutritional yeast
PABA	Yeast, brewer's yeast, dried lima beans, raisins, cantaloupe
Vitamin C	Citrus fruits, tomatoes, potatoes, cabbage, green peppers
Chlorine	Kelp, rye flour, ripe olives, sea greens
Pantothenic acid	Yeast, brewer's yeast, dried lima beans, raisins, cantaloupe

RECOMMENDED SUPPLEMENT:	10,000 IU beta-carotene 1–2 times daily
	100 mg. B complex, 1 A.M. and P.M.
	Multiple minerals, 1 A.M. and P.M.
	Betaine HC1 500 mg. ½ hour before meals with glass of water
	Multiple digestive enzyme ½ hour after meals with glass of water
	Fresh-squeezed cabbage juice, 1 glass after meals

SYMPTOM: *Hair Problems*
1. DANDRUFF (loose flakes—dry or yellow and greasy—which fall from scalp)

Vitamin B12 (cyanocobalamin)	Liver, beef, pork, organ meats, eggs, milk and milk products

POSSIBLE DEFICIENCY	ARE YOU EATING ENOUGH?
Vitamin F	Vegetable oils, peanuts, sunflower seeds, walnuts
Vitamin B6	Dried nutritional yeast, liver, organ meats, legumes, whole-grain cereals, fish
Selenium	Bran, germ of cereals, broccoli, onions, tomatoes, and tuna

RECOMMENDED SUPPLEMENT: 100 mcg. selenium twice
    daily
1 MVP A.M. and P.M. with
    food
1 omega-3 capsule, 1,000
    mg., with each meal

SYMPTOM: *Hair Problems*
2. DULL, DRY, BRITTLE
OR GRAYING HAIR

Vitamin A complex	Yeast, brewer's yeast, dried lima
PABA	beans, raisins, cantaloupe
Vitamin F	Vegetable oils, peanuts, sunflower seeds, walnuts
Iodine	Seafoods, iodized salt, dairy products

RECOMMENDED SUPPLEMENT: 1 omega-3 capsule, 1,000
    mg. with each meal
3 lecithin caps with each
    meal
1 MVP A.M. and P.M. with
    food

POSSIBLE DEFICIENCY   ARE YOU EATING ENOUGH?

SYMPTOM: *Hair Problems*
3. LOSS OF HAIR

Biotin	Brewer's yeast, nuts, beef liver, kidney, unpolished rice
Inositol	Unrefined molasses and liver, lecithin, unprocessed whole grains, citrus fruits, brewer's yeast
Chlorine	Sodium chloride (table salt)
B complex with C and folic acid	Yeast, brewer's yeast, dried lima beans, raisins, cantaloupe, citrus fruits, green peppers, tomatoes, cabbage, potatoes, fresh green leafy vegetables, fruit, organ meats, liver, dried nutritional yeast

RECOMMENDED SUPPLEMENT: 1,000 mg. choline and
                                                  inositol daily
                                             Cysteine 1 g. daily
                                             Biotin 1000 mcg. daily
                                             B complex 150 mg. A.M.
                                                  and P.M. with meals

---

SYMPTOM: *Heart Palpitation*

Vitamin B12 (cobalamin, cyanocobalamin)	Yeast, liver, beef, eggs, kidney

RECOMMENDED SUPPLEMENT: 1 MVP A.M. and P.M. with
                                                  meals
                                             50 mg. vitamin B complex
                                                  A.M. and P.M. with meals

POSSIBLE DEFICIENCY   ARE YOU EATING ENOUGH?

	500 mg. calcium and 250 mg. magnesium tablet daily

SYMPTOM: *High Blood Pressure*

Choline   Egg yolks, brain, heart, green leafy vegetables, yeast, liver, wheat germ

RECOMMENDED SUPPLEMENT: 1 MVP A.M. and P.M. with meals

Start with 200 IU vitamin E and work up to higher strengths.

Coenzyme-Q10 30 mg. daily

500 mg. calcium and 250 mg. magnesium tab 3 times daily (take one ½ hr. before bedtime)

1 odorless garlic capsule 3 times daily

SYMPTOM: *Infections* (high susceptibility)

Vitamin A (carotene) Fish, liver, egg yolks, butter, cream, green leafy or yellow vegetables

Pantothenic acid   Yeast, brewer's yeast, dried lima beans, raisins, cantaloupe

RECOMMENDED SUPPLEMENT: 1–2 tbsp. acidophilus 3 times daily

Vitamin A up to 10,000 IU every other day for duration of infection

POSSIBLE DEFICIENCY	ARE YOU EATING ENOUGH?
	1 MVP A.M. and P.M. (2–5 g. vitamin C for duration of infection)

SYMPTOM: *Insomnia*

Potassium	Bananas, watercress, all leafy green vegetables, citrus fruits, sunflower seeds
B complex	Yeast, brewer's yeast, dried lima beans, raisins, cantaloupe
Biotin	Brewer's yeast, nuts, beef liver, kidney, unpolished rice
Calcium	Milk and milk products, meat, fish, eggs, cereal products, beans, fruit, vegetables
RECOMMENDED SUPPLEMENT:	1–5 mg. melatonin (sublingual form) ½ hr. before bedtime Vitamin B6 100 mg., niacinamide 100 mg., & chelated calcium & magnesium ½ hr. before bedtime 1 MVP A.M. and P.M.

SYMPTOM: *Loss of Smell*

Vitamin A	Fish, liver, egg yolks, butter, cream, green leafy or yellow vegetables
Zinc	Vegetables, whole grains, wheat bran, wheat germ, pumpkin and sunflower seeds
RECOMMENDED SUPPLEMENT:	50 mg. amino acid–chelated zinc 3 times daily (cut back to 1–2 daily when condition improves)

POSSIBLE DEFICIENCY   ARE YOU EATING ENOUGH?

SYMPTOM: *Memory Loss*

B1 (thiamine)	Brewer's yeast, whole grains, meat (pork or liver), nuts, legumes, potatoes
RECOMMENDED SUPPLEMENT:	L-glutamine, 500 mg. 3 times daily on empty stomach 50 mg. B complex A.M. and P.M. DHA 250 mg. 2–3 times daily Standardized ginkgo biloba tablets, 60 mg. 1–3 times daily

---

SYMPTOM: *Menstrual Problems*

B12	Yeast, liver, beef, eggs, kidney
RECOMMENDED SUPPLEMENT:	7–10 days before period: 1 MVP A.M. and P.M. with meals 100 mg. B6 3 times daily 100 mg. B complex (time release) A.M. and P.M. Evening primrose oil, 500 mg. 3 times daily 500 mg. magnesium & ½ as much calcium once daily

---

SYMPTOM: *Mouth Sores and Cracks*

Vitamin B12 (riboflavin)	Milk, liver, kidney, yeast, cheese, fish, eggs
Vitamin B6	Dried nutritional yeast, liver, organ

POSSIBLE DEFICIENCY   ARE YOU EATING ENOUGH?

(pyridoxine)	meats, legumes, whole-grain cereals, fish

RECOMMENDED SUPPLEMENT: 50 mg. B complex 3 times
daily with meals
1 MVP A.M. and P.M.

SYMPTOM: *Muscle Cramps* (general muscle weakness, tenderness in calf, night cramps, charley horse)

Vitamin B1 (thiamin)	Brewer's yeast, whole grains, meat (pork or liver), nuts, legumes, potatoes
Vitamin B6 (pyridoxine)	Dried nutritional yeast, liver, organ meats, legumes, whole-grain cereals, fish
Biotin	Brewer's yeast, nuts, beef liver, kidney, unpolished rice
Chlorine	Sodium chloride (table salt)
Sodium	Beef, pork, sardines, cheese, green olives, corn bread, sauerkraut
Vitamin D (calciferol)	Fish-liver oils, butter, egg yolks, liver, sunshine

RECOMMENDED SUPPLEMENT: 400 IU vitamin E (dry) 3
times daily
Amino acid–chelated
calcium & magnesium, 3
tabs 3 times daily

SYMPTOM: *Nervousness*

Vitamin B6 (pyridoxine)	Dried nutritional yeast, liver, organ meats, legumes, whole-grain cereals, fish
Vitamin B12 (cyanocobalamin)	Yeast, liver, beef, eggs, kidney

POSSIBLE DEFICIENCY	ARE YOU EATING ENOUGH?
Niacin (nicotinic acid, niacinamide)	Liver, meat, fish, whole grains, legumes
PABA	Yeast, brewer's yeast, dried lima beans, raisins, cantaloupe
Magnesium	Green leafy vegetables, nuts, cereals, grains, seafoods

RECOMMENDED SUPPLEMENT:	B complex 1–3 times daily (50 mg. of all B vitamins)
	Kava kava 250 mg. 1–3 times daily
	1 St. John's wort tablet with polyphenol complex daily
	3 amino acid–chelated calcium and magnesium tabs 3 times daily
	1 MVP A.M. and P.M. with meals

SYMPTOM: *Nosebleeds*

Vitamin C	Citrus fruits, tomatoes, potatoes, cabbage, green peppers
Vitamin K	Yogurt, alfalfa, soybean oil, fish-liver oils, kelp
Bioflavonoids	Orange, lemon, lime, tangerine peels

RECOMMENDED SUPPLEMENT:	1,000 mg. vitamin C with 50 mg. rutin, hesperidin, and 500 mg. bioflavonoids (time release) A.M. and P.M.

POSSIBLE DEFICIENCY   ARE YOU EATING ENOUGH?

SYMPTOM: *Retarded Growth*

Fat	Meat, butter
Protein	Meat, fish, eggs, dairy products, soybeans, peanuts
Vitamin B2 (riboflavin)	Milk, liver, kidney, yeast, cheese, fish, eggs
Folic acid	Fresh green leafy vegetables, fruit, organ meats, liver, dried nutritional yeast
Zinc	Vegetables, whole grains, wheat bran, wheat germ, pumpkin and sunflower seeds
Cobalt	Liver, kidney, pancreas, and spleen (organ meats)

RECOMMENDED SUPPLEMENT: 1 MVP A.M. and P.M. with meals

SYMPTOM: *Skin Problems*
1. ACNE (face blemishes, thickened skin, blackheads, whiteheads, red spots)

Water-solubilized vitamin A	Fish, liver, egg yolks, butter, cream, green leafy or yellow vegetables
Vitamin B complex	Yeast, brewer's yeast, dried lima beans, raisins, cantaloupe

RECOMMENDED SUPPLEMENT: 1 multiple vitamin-mineral (low in iodine) daily
1–2 400 IU vitamin E (dry) daily
10,000 IU beta-carotene, 1–2 tabs daily 6 days a week

POSSIBLE DEFICIENCY	ARE YOU EATING ENOUGH?
	50 mg. amino acid–chelated zinc once daily with food
	1–2 tbsp. acidophilus liquid 3 times daily or 3–6 caps 3 times daily
	(Iodine worsens acne, so eliminate all processed foods—high in iodized salt—from your diet.)
	1 MSM (methylsulfonylmethane) 1,000 mg. tablet 2–3 times daily with food

2. DERMATITIS (skin inflammation)

Vitamin B2 (riboflavin)	Milk, liver, kidney, yeast, cheese, fish, eggs
Vitamin B6 (pyridoxine)	Dried nutritional yeast, liver, organ meats, legumes, whole-grain cereals, fish
Biotin	Brewer's yeast, nuts, beef liver, kidney, unpolished rice
Niacin (nicotinic acid, niacinamide)	Liver, meat, fish, whole grains, legumes
RECOMMENDED SUPPLEMENT:	1 multiple vitamin-mineral (low in iodine) daily
	1–2 400 IU vitamin E (dry) daily
	10,000 IU beta-carotene 1–2 tabs daily 6 days a week

POSSIBLE DEFICIENCY	ARE YOU EATING ENOUGH?
	50 mg. amino acid–chelated zinc once daily with food
	1–2 tbsp. acidophilus liquid 3 times daily or 3–6 caps 3 times daily
	500 mg. evening primrose oil 2–3 times daily
	1 MSM 1,000 mg. tablet 2–3 times daily with food

SYMPTOM: *Skin Problems*
3. ECZEMA (rough, dry, scaly skin, redness and swelling, small blisters)

Fat	Meat, butter
Vitamin A (carotene)	Fish, liver, egg yolks, butter, cream, green leafy or yellow vegetables
Vitamin B complex	Yeast, brewer's yeast, dried lima
Inositol	beans, raisins, cantaloupe
Copper	Organ meats, oysters, nuts, dried legumes, whole-grain cereals
Iodine	Seafoods, iodized salt, dairy products

RECOMMENDED SUPPLEMENT:
    1 multiple vitamin-mineral (low in iodine) daily
    1 MSM 1,000 mg. tablet 2–3 times daily with food
    1–2 400 IU vitamin E (dry) daily
    10,000 IU beta-carotene, 1–2 tabs daily 6 days a week

POSSIBLE DEFICIENCY   ARE YOU EATING ENOUGH?

50 mg. amino acid–chelated
zinc once daily with
food

1–2 tbsp. acidophilus liquid
3 times daily or 3–6 caps
3 times daily

MSM lotion applied
externally 1–3 times
daily

SYMPTOM: *Slow-healing Wounds and Fractures*

Vitamin C   Citrus fruits, tomatoes, potatoes,
                       cabbage, green peppers

RECOMMENDED SUPPLEMENT: 50 mg. zinc once daily
                           400 IU dry vitamin E 3
                           times daily
                           1 MVP A.M. and P.M. with
                           meals

SYMPTOM: *Softening of Bones and Teeth*

Vitamin D   Fish-liver oils, butter, egg yolks, liver,
(calciferol)   sunshine
Calcium   Milk and milk products, meat, fish,
                       eggs, cereal products, beans, fruit,
                       vegetables

RECOMMENDED SUPPLEMENT: 1,000–1,500 mg. calcium,
                           500 mg. magnesium
                           divided over 2 meals
                           daily

SYMPTOM: *Tremors*

Magnesium   Green leafy vegetables, nuts, cereals,
                       grains, seafoods

POSSIBLE DEFICIENCY   ARE YOU EATING ENOUGH?

RECOMMENDED SUPPLEMENT:	B complex and 50 mg. B6 3 times daily
	1,000 mg. calcium, 500 mg. magnesium divided over 3 meals daily
	1 St. John's wort tablet with polyphenol complex daily

SYMPTOM: *Vaginal Itching*

Vitamin B2	Milk, liver, kidney, yeast, cheese, fish, eggs
RECOMMENDED SUPPLEMENT:	2 tbsp. acidophilus 3 times daily or 3–6 caps 3–4 times daily
	(Acidophilus or mild vinegar douche can also help.)

SYMPTOM: *Water Retention*

Vitamin B6	Dried nutritional yeast, liver, organ meats, legumes, whole-grain cereals, fish
RECOMMENDED SUPPLEMENT:	100 mg. B6 3 times daily
	Potassium 99 mg. 3–6 tabs daily

SYMPTOM: *White Spots on Nails*

Zinc	Vegetables, whole grains, wheat bran, wheat germ, pumpkin and sunflower seeds

POSSIBLE DEFICIENCY	ARE YOU EATING ENOUGH?
RECOMMENDED SUPPLEMENT:	15 mg. amino acid–chelated zinc 3 times daily MSM tab, 1,000 mg. twice daily MVP A.M. and P.M. with meals

164. Cravings—What They Might Mean

Cravings, which can sometimes mean allergies, are more often nature's way of letting you know that you're not getting enough of certain vitamins or minerals. Frequently these specific hungers develop because overall diet is inadequate.

Some of the most common cravings are:

Peanut butter   This is definitely among the top ten, and it's not at all surprising. Peanut butter is a rich source of B vitamins. If you find yourself dipping into the jar often, it might be because you're under stress and your ordinary B intake has become insufficient. Since 50 g. of peanut butter—a third of a cup—is 284 calories, you'll find it easier on your waistline to take a B-complex supplement if you do not want to gain weight.

Bananas   When you catch yourself reaching for this fruit again and again, it could be because your body needs potassium. One medium banana has 555 mg. People taking diuretics or cortisone (which rob the body of needed potassium) often crave bananas.

Cheese   If you're more a cheese luster than a cheese lover, there's a good chance that your real hunger is for calcium and phosphorus. (If it's processed cheese that you've been snacking on, you've been getting aluminum and salt, too, without knowing it.) For one thing, you might try eating more broccoli. That's high in calcium and phosphorus, and a lot lower in calories than cheese.

Apples   An apple a day doesn't necessarily keep the doctor away, but it offers a lot of good things that you might be missing in other foods—calcium, magnesium, phosphorus, potassium—and is an excellent source of cholesterol-lowering pectin! If you have a tendency to eat a lot of saturated fat, it could account for your apple cravings.

Butter   Most often vegetarians crave butter because of their own low saturated-fat intake. Salted butter, on the other hand, might be craved for the salt alone.

Cola   The craving for cola is most often a sugar hunger and an addiction to caffeine. (See section 283.) The beverage has no nutritive value.

Nuts   If you're a little nutty about nuts, you probably could use more protein, B vitamins, or fat in your diet. If it's salted nuts you favor, you could be craving the sodium and not the nuts. You'll find that people under stress tend to eat more nuts than relaxed individuals.

Ice cream   High as ice cream is in calcium, most people crave it for its sugar content. Hypoglycemics and diabetics have great hungers for it, as do people asking to recapture the security of childhood.

Pickles   If you're pregnant and want pickles, you're probably after the salt. And if you're not pregnant and crave pickles, the reason is most likely the same. (Pickles also contain a substantial amount of potassium.)

Bacon   Cravings for bacon are usually because of its fat. People on restricted diets are most susceptible to greasy binges. Unfortunately, saturated fat is not bacon's only drawback. Bacon is very high in carcinogenic nitrites. If you do indulge in bacon, be sure you're ingesting enough vitamin C and A, D, and E to counteract the nitrites.

Eggs   Aside from the protein (two eggs give you 13 g.), sulfur, amino acids, and selenium, egg lovers might also be seeking the yolk's fat content or, paradoxically, its cholesterol-and-fat-dissolving choline.

Cantaloupe   Just because you like its taste might not be the only reason you crave this melon. Cantaloupe is high in potassium and vitamin A. In fact, a quarter of a melon has 3,400 IU vitamin A. Since the melon also offers vitamin C, calcium, magnesium, phosphorus, biotin, and inositol, it's not a bad craving to give in to. There's only about 60 calories in half a melon.

Olives   Whether you crave them green or black, you're likely to be after the salt. People with underactive thyroids are most often the first to reach for them.

Salt   No guesswork here, it's the sodium you're after. Cravers quite possibly have a thyroid iodine deficiency or low sodium Addison's disease. Hypertensives often crave salt, and shouldn't.

Onions   Cravings for spicy foods can sometimes indicate problems in the lungs or sinuses.

Chocolate   Definitely one of the foremost cravings, if not *the* foremost. Chocoholics are addicted to the caffeine as well as the sugar. (There are 5–10 mg. of caffeine in a cup of cocoa.) If you want to kick the chocolate habit, try carob instead. (Carob, also called St. John's bread, is made from the edible pods of the Mediterranean carob tree.)

Milk   If you're still craving milk as an adult, you might need a calcium supplement. Then again, it might be the amino acids—such as tryptophan, leucine, and lysine—that your body needs. Nervous people often seek out the tryptophan in milk, since it has a very soothing effect.

Chinese food   Of course it's delicious, but often it's the monosodium glutamate in the food that fosters the craving. People with salt deficiencies usually go all out for Chinese food. (MSG can cause a histamine reaction in some individuals. Headaches and flushing may occur. Most Chinese restaurants will now prepare your food without MSG if you request it.)

Mayonnaise   Since this is a fatty food, it is often craved by vegetarians and people who have eliminated other fats from their diet.

Tart fruits   A persistent craving for tart fruits can often indicate problems with the gallbladder or liver.

Paint and dirt   Children have a tendency to eat paint and dirt. Frequently this is an indication of a calcium or vitamin-D deficiency. A hard reevaluation of your child's diet is essential, and a visit to your pediatrician is recommended. This craving for nonfood items is known as pica. It's a condition also experienced by pregnant women, who should be aware that ingesting such substances can harm fetal development.

165. Getting the Most Vitamins from Your Food

Eating the right foods doesn't necessarily mean that you're getting the vitamins they contain. Food processing, storing, and cooking can easily undermine the best nutritious intentions. To get the most from what you eat (not to mention what you spend) keep the following tips in mind.

• Wash but don't soak fresh vegetables if you hope to benefit from the B vitamins and C they contain.
• Forgo convenience and make your salads when you're ready to eat them. Fruits and vegetables cut up and left to stand lose vitamins.
• Use a sharp knife when cutting or shredding fresh vegetables, because vitamins A and C are diminished when vegetable tissues are bruised.
• If you don't plan to eat your fresh fruit or vegetables for a few days, you're better off buying flash-frozen ones. The vitamin content of good frozen green beans will be higher than those fresh ones you've kept in your refrigerator for a week.
• Store frozen meat at 0 degrees F. or lower immediately after purchase to prevent loss of quality and bacterial growth.
• Outer green leaves of lettuce, though coarser than inner ones, have higher calcium, iron, and vitamin A content.
• Don't thaw your frozen vegetables before cooking.
• Broccoli leaves have a higher vitamin A value than the flower buds or stalks.
• There are more vitamins in converted and parboiled rice than in polished rice, and brown rice is more nutritious than white.

• Frozen foods that you can boil in their bags offer more vitamins than the ordinary kind, and all frozen foods are preferable to canned ones.

• Cooking in copper pots can destroy vitamin C, folic acid, and vitamin E.

• Stainless steel, glass, and enamel are the best utensils for retaining nutrients while cooking. (Iron pots can give you the benefit of that mineral, but they will shortchange you on vitamin C.)

• The shortest cooking time and the smallest amount of water are the least destructive to nutrients.

• Cut longer-cooking vegetables in large pieces for minimum surface exposure to water and heat.

• Rinse canned vegetables to eliminate excess salt.

• Milk in glass containers can lose riboflavin, as well as vitamins A and D, unless kept out of the light. (Breads exposed to light can also lose these nutrients.)

• Well-browned, crusty, or toasted baked goods have less thiamine than others.

• Bake and boil potatoes in their skins to get the most vitamins from them.

• Use cooking water from vegetables to make soups, juices from meats for gravies, and syrups from canned fruits to make desserts.

• Refrain from using any baking soda when cooking vegetables if you want to benefit from their thiamine and vitamin C.

• Store vegetables and fruits in the refrigerator as soon as you bring them home from the market.

BUT DID YOU KNOW: When your grocer sprays water on vegetables to keep them looking fresh, it benefits you as well as him. Broccoli, for instance, when sprayed with a fine mist of water, keeps almost twice as much of its vitamin C as it would if it weren't sprayed. Considering that broccoli is a cruciferous, cancer-fighting vegetable, this is something you'll want to look for when making your selection.

166. Any Questions About Chapter XI?

*I feed my children what I think is a pretty well-balanced diet.
But they're teenagers and when they're out they often have
burgers, hot dogs, shakes, and that sort of junk food. Are
these really bad for them?*

Well, ounce for ounce, munch for munch, and sip for sip,
the bad far outweighs the good. For instance, a fast-food
burger can supply 44 percent of a teenage boy's requirement
for protein. But when you consider that a Big Mac, for example, is also supplying 591 calories, 33 grams of fat, 6
grams of sugar, and 963 mg. of sodium (a Burger King
Whopper has *1,083 mg. of sodium*), you have to admit that's
an awfully high nutritional price to pay for protein. No one
needs all that salt. (See section 310.)

As for hot dogs, there's very little good to say about them.
They're a high-fat, low-protein meat, and usually contain
sodium or potassium nitrite. Nitrites combine with substances called amines, commonly found in foods, and form
nitrosamines, which have been found to be carcinogenic
(cancer-causing).

Shakes, which do contain milk or a milk product, also
contain 8–14 teaspoons of sugar and 276 to 685 mg. of salt.
Your kids could blend one up at home for half the price,
calories, sugar, and salt—and double the nutritional value.
Passing this information along to your children might be a
good way to get them to pass up those fast-food places.

*Very often I experience a sort of hot, burning feeling on my
tongue and lips. It doesn't seem to be related to any foods
I've eaten. Could it indicate a vitamin deficiency?*

It's very possible. The feeling of having a burning tongue
or lips has in many instances been linked to a vitamin B1
(thiamine) deficiency. I'd suggest increasing your intake of
whole wheat, oatmeal, bran, vegetables, and brewer's yeast,

along with taking a balanced vitamin B complex, 50 mg., twice a day with food—and the MVP. (See section 163.)

My mother has a craving for ice. Not just on hot days, but all the time. She chews cubes as if they were candy. Could this sort of craving have anything to do with a dietary deficiency?

If your mother is often tired, her craving for ice might indicate an iron deficiency (which can cause a low-grade anemia). You might try encouraging her to add more iron-rich foods to her diet (liver, dried peaches, red meat, oysters, asparagus, oatmeal) and to take an organic iron supplement, 50–100 mg. daily.

I'm forty-two years old and am developing yellowish growths around my eyes. Is there some vitamin or nutrient that's missing from my diet that could be causing this?

More likely those growths are cholesterol deposits, which can occur when the body is trying to rid itself of excess cholesterol. This sort of condition tends to run in families and could possibly indicate that you're in the high-risk heart disease percentile. See section 92 for how to reduce cholesterol. Also, increase your intake of vitamin B, chromium, and zinc, in foods and supplements.

How long does orange juice retain its vitamin C?

For commercial orange juice, the vitamin C life span is about one week from the time you've opened the container. For fresh-squeezed juice kept refrigerated in a sealed container, the life span of vitamin C is about three weeks.

Do you lose more or fewer nutrients by microwaving food?

As a rule, fewer. Microwaving requires minimum cooking time and minimum water.

XII

Read the Label

167. The Importance of Understanding What's on Labels

All too often people buy supplements and never even look at the labels. They ask a clerk for a multivitamin and take what they are given, not realizing that they might be getting shortchanged on the vitamin content. All multivitamins differ in amounts included, and the most expensive tablet is not necessarily the best. The only way to be sure you're getting the B6, folacin, or C that you need is to read the small print on the label. Also, if you have any allergies, it's wise to check what else you're getting with your supplement. (See section 23.)

If there are words on the label that you don't understand, ask the pharmacist or vitamin clerk to explain them. If she can't, buy your supplements where someone can. And above all, remember to check the dosage you're getting. If you've been instructed to take vitamin E 4 times a day, it's unlikely that you want 400 IU. Vitamins and minerals come in different strengths. Be sure you're getting what you ask for—and need. Not understanding labels can often negate a lot of vitamin benefits.

The U.S. Food and Drug Administration (FDA) rules for the new millennium (effective as of March 1999) should make understanding labels a lot easier. They require vitamins, minerals, herbs, and amino acids be labeled as dietary supplements. As such, these products must feature a Supplement Facts panel with information similar to the Nutrition Facts panels that appear on processed foods.

The Supplement Facts panel must include an appropriate serving/dosage size and information about 14 nutrients when present at significant levels, including vitamins A and C, sodium, calcium, and iron. Dietary ingredients that have no RDI/RDA must also be listed. In the case of herb supplements, the part of the plant used to make the product must also be identified.

But you still have to *read* the label. For example, the term high potency may be used for any single-ingredient dietary supplement that contains at least 100 percent of the daily value, which in most cases is regrettably low. In multi-ingredient products, the term high potency can be used if two-thirds of the daily value nutrients are present at 100 percent or more of their daily value. In other words, if you want to get the most from your vitamins read the label not the hype.

168. How Does That Measure Up?

> IU, RE, MG, MCG—a little can mean a lot.

The terminology for measuring vitamin activity is not as confusing as you might think. Fat-soluble vitamins (A, E, D, and K) are usually measured in International Units (IU). But a few years ago, an expert committee of the Food and Agriculture Organization/World Health Organization (FAO/WHO) decided to change this order of measurement for vitamin A. Instead of using International Units, they proposed that vitamin A be evaluated in terms of retinol equivalents (RE), that is, the equivalent weight of retinol (vitamin A1, alcohol) *actually absorbed and converted.*

Retinol equivalents come out to about five times less than International Units (IU). Recommended allowances of

5,000 IU for a male between the ages of twenty-three and fifty would only be 1,000 RE; 4,000 IU for similarly aged females would only be 800 RE.

Most other vitamins and minerals are measured in milligrams (mg.) and micrograms (mcg.). If you know that 1 g. equals .035 ounce, that it takes 28.35 g. to equal 1 ounce (and 1 fluid ounce equals 2 tablespoons), you'll have a better idea of just how much—or rather, how little—it takes for vitamins and minerals to do their job. The following table is a handy guide to refer to:

WHAT'S WHAT IN WEIGHTS AND MEASURES

Metric Measure

1 kilogram equals 1,000 grams
1 gram equals 1,000 milligrams
1 milligram equals 1/1,000th part of a gram
1 microgram equals 1/1,000th part of a milligram
1 gamma equals 1 microgram

Avoirdupois Weight

16 ounces equal 1 pound
7,000 grains equal 1 pound
453.6 grams equal 1 pound
1 ounce av. equals 437.5 grains
1 ounce av. equals 28.35 grams

Conversion Factors

1 gram equals 15.4 grains
1 grain equals 0.085 grams (85 milligrams)
1 ounce apothecary equals 31.1 grams
1 fluid ounce equals 29.8 cc.
1 fluid ounce equals 480 minims

Liquid Measure

1 drop equals 1 minim

1 minim equals 0.06 cc.
15 minims equal 1.0 cc.
4 cc. equal 1 fluid dram
30 cc. equal 1 fluid ounce

Household Measure

1 teaspoon equals 4 cc. equals 1 fluid dram
1 tablespoon equals 15 cc. equals ½ fluid ounce
½ pint equals 240 cc. equals 8 fluid ounces

Abbreviations

AMDR	Adult Minimum Daily Requirement
USP Unit	United States Pharmacopeia
IU	International Unit
MDR	Minimum Daily Requirement
mg.	milligram
mcg.	microgram
g.	gram
gr.	grain

169. Breaking the RDA Code

Many people are bewildered by the variances between vitamin standards listed as RDA, U.S. RDA, RDI, and DV. It becomes much less confusing when you understand that they are not the same thing.

RDA (Recommended Dietary Allowances) came into being in 1941, when the Food and Nutrition Board of the National Research Council of the Academy of Sciences was established by the government to safeguard public health. The RDA are not formulated to cover the needs of those who are ill—they are not therapeutic and are meant strictly for healthy individuals—nor do they take into account nutrient losses that occur during processing and preparation. They are *estimates* of nutritional needs necessary to ensure satisfactory growth of children and the prevention of nutrient depletion in adults. *They are not meant to be optimal intakes, nor are they recommendations for an ideal diet.* They are not average requirements but recommendations intended to meet the needs of those *healthy* people with the highest requirements.

U.S. RDA (U.S. Recommended Daily Allowances) were formulated by the Food and Drug Administration (FDA) to be used as the *legal* standards for food labeling in regard to nutrient content. (The RDA were used as the basis for the U.S. RDA). Serving size, number of servings per container, calories, and ten nutrients—protein, carbohydrate, fat, vitamin A, vitamin C, thiamin, riboflavin, niacin, calcium, and iron—had to be listed on food labels. (Today, unless a food is fortified or a manufacturer claims that it is a good source of vitamin B, levels of B vitamins are excluded.) Information about sodium, cholesterol, and saturated and unsaturated fat was formerly optional, but is now mandatory. (U.S. RDA percentages for vitamins D, E, B6, phosphorus, iodine, magnesium, zinc, copper, biotin, and pantothenic acid remain optional.)

RDI (Reference Daily Intakes) and DV (Daily Values) are what the FDA now wants to use to replace both the RDA and the U.S. RDA. The RDI are subdivided into the Daily Value (DV), based on both the RDI for vitamins and minerals and the Daily Reference Values (DRV), for protein, fat, and carbohydrates. Unfortunately, despite updated Recommended Dietary Allowances, all are still based on the old 1968 edition of the RDA.

Stress and illness, past or present, affect everyone's nutritional requirements differently. Just because a product claims to provide 100 percent of the U.S. RDA or DV for a nutrient, doesn't necessarily mean that *you* are getting it, or that it's a sufficient amount for *your* individual needs. As far as I and many other leading nutritionists are concerned, the proposed RDI as well as the RDA and the U.S. RDA are woefully inadequate. Nonetheless, you will find them listed in sections 28 through 71 in the facts section for each vitamin and mineral.

170. What to Look For

When buying minerals, look for *amino acid–chelated* on the label. Only 10 percent of ordinary minerals will be assimilated by the body, but when combined with amino acids in chelation, the assimilation is three to five times more efficient.

Hydrolyzed means water dispersible. *Hydrolyzed protein-chelate* means the supplement is in its most easily assimilated form.

Predigested protein is protein that has already been broken down and can go straight to the bloodstream.

Cold pressed is important to look for when buying oil or oil capsules. It means vitamins haven't been destroyed by heat and that the oil, extracted by cold-pressed methods, remains polyunsaturated.

171. Any Questions About Chapter XII?

What are emulsifiers?

Emulsifiers are used to homogenize ingredients which do not normally mix well. Lecithin and pectin, which are natural and safe, are commonly used, but unfortunately they're not used exclusively. Polysorbate 60 (which the FDA still has under investigation), locust bean (on the FDA list of additives requiring further study for mutagenic, reproductive, and teratogenic effects), and carrageenan (another being studied all too slowly by the FDA), among others, are still being used. Though these are at present generally recognized as safe (GRAS) I personally prefer and recommend products without them.

Are the dyes used in vitamin coatings natural or artificial, and how can I tell?

Regrettably, a lot of synthetic vitamins use coal-tar dyes in their coatings—and keep it a secret. (Look for FD&C dye # listings.) These dyes are not necessarily harmful, but they can cause allergic reactions. My advice is to play it safe and buy natural vitamins that have no artificial adulterants—and *say so!*

Are calories counted differently in foreign countries?

Most foreign countries use the metric system, and the energy value of food is measured in units called joules, our kilocalories, better known as calories. Four of our calories are the equivalent of 17 joules. In other words, a joule is slightly less than ¼ calorie.

When dealing with vitamin A, how do you convert IUs into mgs. or mcgs.?

There are no rigid conversions, but 1 IU vitamin A = 0.3 mcg. retinol and 1 IU beta-carotene = 0.1 mcg. retinol.

XIII

Your Special Vitamin Needs

172. Selecting Your Regimen

We all know that not everyone has the same metabolism, but we often forget that this also means that not everyone requires the same vitamins. In the following sections I have outlined a number of personalized regimens for a variety of specialized needs. Look them all over and see which ones best fit your own special situation. If you fall under more than one category, adjust the combined regimens so that you are not double-dosing yourself, only adding the additional supplements.

You will notice that in most cases I advise what I call an MVP, a Mindell Vitamin Program (which can make you an MVP—a Most Valuable Player in the nutrition game). This simple, potent pair—taken with meals—is my foundation for general good health.

MVP MINDELL VITAMIN PROGRAM

• An all-natural, high-potency multiple vitamin and amino acid–chelated mineral complex (containing no preservatives or artificial colors and digestive enzymes for better absorption)

AND

• A broad-spectrum antioxidant formula (containing alpha- and beta-carotene, lutein, lycopene, vitamin C, vitamin E, selenium, ginkgo biloba, coenzyme-Q10, bilberry, L-gluta-thione, soy isoflavones [genistein and daidzein], grapeseed extract, and green tea extract)

Take each of these twice daily, A.M. and P.M. with meals. (Dosage is suitable for individuals over twelve years of age.)

WHAT TO LOOK FOR IN RECOMMENDED COMBINATION SUPPLEMENTS

Coenzyme-Q10 complex (look for vitamin E, garlic, cayenne, and hawthorn extract)

Calcium and magnesium (look for amino acid chelation—even better, glycinated amino acid chelation—and a balance of twice as much calcium as magnesium; in a complex, look for vitamin D, boron, and soy isoflavonoids)

Ginkgo biloba complex (look for Dimethylaminoethanol [DMAE], club moss, phosphatidylcholine [PC], phos-phatidylserine [PS], and phosphatidylisoleucine [PI]

St. John's wort (look for a polyphenol combination)

MSM (methylsulfonylmethane) tablets (look for pharma-ceutical grade with vitamin C and bioflavonoids)

I recommend that all powder supplements be mixed with filtered water or fruit juice—fresh or frozen (not from con-centrate). SUPPLEMENTS SHOULD BE TAKEN WITH FOOD UNLESS OTHERWISE NOTED.

IMPORTANT NOTE: Before starting any program, you should check "Cautions" (see section 334) and with a nu-tritionally oriented doctor. *The regimens in this book are not prescriptive nor are they intended as medical advice.*

---

173. Women

12–18   MVP (see section 172)
                     Amino acid–chelated calcium 250 mg.
                        and magnesium 125 mg. twice daily

19–50	MVP (see section 172)
	Amino acid–chelated calcium 500 mg. and magnesium 250 mg. twice daily
	Vitamin E, 400 IU (dry form)
Also:	Organic iron, 15–50 mg. daily, if needed
	B complex 50 mg. A.M. and P.M. if stress conditions exist
50+	MVP (see section 172)
	Vitamin E, 400 IU (dry form)
	Coenzyme-Q10, 100 mg. complex 1 cap 1–2 times daily

174. Men

| 11–18 | MVP (see section 172) |

19–50	MVP (see section 172)
	Zinc, 15–50 mg. daily
	Lecithin granules, 2 tbsp. or 9 capsules daily (Add 2 tbsp. lecithin granules to 1 scoop of soy food protein and blend in 1–1¼ cups of soy milk with ice cubes, and fruit if desired; use as breakfast or other meal replacement)
	Chelated calcium 500 mg. and magnesium 250 mg. daily
	B complex 50 mg. A.M. and P.M. if needed
50+	MVP (see section 172)
	Coenzyme-Q10 100 mg. complex; 1 cap daily
	Ginkgo biloba 60 mg. twice daily

175. Infants

| 1–4 | One good-tasting chewable multiple vitamin daily (check label to see that all the primary vitamins are included); there should be no artificial color, |

flavors, or sugar (sucrose) added.
(Liquid vitamins are available for very
young children. Remember to check
with your pediatrician before making
any supplement choice.)

176. Children

4–12   Growing children need a stronger
                multiple vitamin containing minerals,
                especially calcium and iron, for normal
                growth. The tablet should also be high
                in B complex and vitamin C (50
                percent of American children do not
                even get the RDA for vitamin C). One
                daily is sufficient (check label to be
                sure there is no artificial color, flavor,
                or sugar—sucrose—added).

177. Pregnant Women

The right vitamins are essential at this time:

MVP (see section 172)
Folic acid, 800 mcg. daily
Chelated calcium 500 mg. and magnesium 250 mg. 1 tablet
    3 times daily
Ginger extract, 1 capsule 1–3 times daily if needed for
    morning sickness

178. Nursing Mothers

The same supplements recommended for pregnant women
plus additional vitamins B6, B12, and C. Your body and
your baby need the best nourishment you can give them.

179. Runners

During the first 15–20 minutes of running, you burn up almost only glucose. The body then comes in with fats (lipids) for energy (in utilizing lipids for energy, a compound called acegyl-coenzyme-A is formed). If there are only animal fats present, the compound forms slowly and energy is insufficient. If polyunsaturates are present, on the other hand, the compound forms quickly. Increase your intake of polyunsaturates—seeds, peanuts—and antioxidants, such as vitamins C, E, and selenium, to avoid free-radical reactions.

A good supplement program would be:

MVP (see section 172)

B complex, 50 mg. A.M. and P.M.

Soy shake: 1 scoop soy food protein blended in 1–1½ cups soy milk with ice cubes, and fruit if desired, for breakfast (meal replacement)

Two tablespoons MSM powder mixed with filtered water or juice. Drink one glass before, during, or after workout to decrease lactic acid buildup.

180. Joggers

The nutritional needs of joggers are the same as those for runners.

181. Executives

With tension and stress an accepted part of your daily life, and energy a necessity, you need a vitamin regimen that won't let you down. Many high-level executives I know use this one:

MVP (see section 172)

B complex, 50 mg. A.M. and P.M.

Standardized ginkgo biloba, 60 mg. complex with DMAE and club moss, 1 tablet twice daily

Chelated calcium 500 mg. and magnesium 250 mg. 1–2
   times daily

If you're in a hurry in the morning, you might want to try
my high-energy breakfast drink:

RECIPE:

2 tbsp. soy food protein	3–4 ice cubes
powder	2 tbsp. fresh or frozen fruit,
1 tbsp. whey	or 1 banana
2 tbsp. lecithin granules	1½ cups soy milk

Mix in blender at high speed for one minute.

182. Students

Eating on the run, skipping breakfast, and not getting
enough rest is a way of life for most students. And as if this
isn't bad enough for good health, student diets usually consists of mostly starches and carbohydrates. If you're in this
category, be aware that these factors, as well as your constant stress situations at school, are taking their toll. A good
daily supplement program would be:

MVP (see section 172)
Standardized ginkgo biloba, 60 mg. complex, 2–3 times
   daily

183. Computer Users

If you're spending most of your days—and nights—in front
of a computer screen, click on this: the eye lens is dependent
on adequate levels of antioxidants to prevent damage by free
radicals. My advice is to get on line nutritionally with supplements that alleviate eyestrain and protect against oxidative damage. And if you're stressed out from surfing the
web, you'll need something for your strained nerves, too.

MVP (see section 172)
B complex, 50 mg. A.M. and P.M.

Calcium 500 mg. and magnesium 250 mg. twice daily (and one at bedtime if needed)
Standardized ginkgo biloba, 60 mg. twice daily
Coenzyme-Q10 and vitamin E complex, 1 capsule daily
St. John's wort polyphenol combination, 1 daily.

184. Senior Citizens

The nutritional needs of senior citizens may vary widely, depending on the individual. As a general rule, however, if you're over sixty-five, you need extra minerals, especially calcium and magnesium, as well as extra vitamins such as B complex and C. Vitamin E can help alleviate poor circulation, which is often responsible for leg cramps. And don't forget about fiber. If chewing is a problem, high-fiber foods can be ground to convenient sizes and textures and are just as effective. Also, sweets should be discouraged; there is a high incidence of sugar diabetes among older people.

A good supplement regimen would be:

MVP (see section 172)
Vitamin E 200–400 IU
Calcium 500 mg. and magnesium 250 mg. twice daily
Standardized ginkgo biloba, 60 mg., complex with DMAE 2–3 times daily
Coenzyme-Q10 100 mg. complex; 1 capsule 2–3 times daily
(See section 293 for drug, food, and nutrient interactions that can cause malabsorption and other problems.)

185. Athletes

Athletes have very demanding nutritional needs. The prime nutritional requirement for performance is energy, and high-energy—as opposed to quick-energy foods—should be eaten. If you're involved in action sports, you need a diet with more complex carbohydrates and protein than someone involved in a low-energy sport. Then again, even golf can become a high-energy game when carried on intensively for a long time. Keep in mind that excess amounts of glucose, sugar, honey, or hard candy tend to draw fluid into the gastrointestinal tract. This can add to dehydration problems in endurance performance. A thirst-quenching tart drink of frozen or fresh fruit juice is the best quick-energy beverage.

For supplements, I recommend:

MVP (see section 172)
B complex, 50 mg., twice daily
Coenzyme-Q10, 30–100 mg. daily
Octacosanol, 1,000 mcg. 3 times daily
Creatine monohydrate, 1 tbsp. (5,000 mg.) in juice (not from concentrate) or water daily
OPTIONAL: Branched chain amino acids (see Bodybuilders)
MSM powder, 1–2 spoonfuls dissolved in 8 oz. water; drink before, during, or after workout.

186. Bodybuilders

If you work out with weights, being on the right diet is as important as your warm-ups and cool-downs. In fact, without combining them, you may wind up with bulging muscles that will be layered with fat and won't do much for your overall shape.

While it's true that protein builds and repairs muscles, it is complex carbohydrates that supply energy for the continuous and repeated muscular contractions that occur during prolonged exercise. For best results, I'd advise getting 80–90 percent of your calories from complex carbohydrates and no more than 10 percent from meat protein. You might also want to try branched chain amino acids (see section 86) which are natural anabolic muscle builders.

My supplement suggestion:

• MVP (see section 172)
• B complex, 50 mg. twice daily
• Octacosanol, 1,000 mcg. 1–3 times daily
• Creatine monohydrate, 1 tbsp. (5,000 mg.) in juice (not from concentrate) or water daily

- Arginine, 1–3 g. with lysine (on empty stomach one hour before bedtime)
- Soy shake (see section 181 recipe) for breakfast and between meals if desired
- MSM powder 1–2 spoonfuls dissolved in 8 oz. water after workout to decrease lactic-acid buildup

OPTIONAL: Branched chain amino acids (BCAA) 600 mg.
For heavy workout 4–6, taken a half hour before workout
For moderate workout 3–4, taken a half hour before workout
For light workout 1–2, taken a half hour before workout

187. Night Workers

The Center for Research on Stress and Health at the Stanford Research Institute has found that "the rotating shift exacts a heavy physical and emotional toll from workers." When eating and sleeping patterns are disrupted, so are the body's biological rhythms, and it takes "three to four weeks for the circadian rhythms to become synchronized." If you change from day to night shifts, often your body is under much stress, your chances of illness are greater, and your risk of ulcers is high. I feel that supplements are essential:

MVP (see section 172)
1 vitamin D, 400 IU with largest meal
If you switch to regular hours on the weekend, take calcium 500 mg. And magnesium 250 mg. 1–2 tablets half an hour before bedtime. Or take 1 mg. melatonin, sublingually (allow to dissolve under the tongue) 15 minutes before bedtime.

188. Truck Drivers

Tension, stress, and a diet that is all too often high in greasy foods are important reasons for considering the following supplements:

MVP (see section 172)
B complex, 50 mg. A.M. and P.M.
St. John's wort polyphenol complex, 1 daily

189. Dancers

Dancers have energy requirements that rank with those of athletes, but because of weight restrictions they cannot consume the same amount of carbohydrates. Good supplements are indispensable, as most dancers will tell you. I suggest:

MVP (see section 172)
Calcium-magnesium complex (with soy isoflavonoids), 2 tabs A.M. and P.M.
Coenzyme-Q10, 30–100 mg. daily
Octocosanol, 1,000 mcg. daily

190. Construction Workers

One out of every four workers is exposed to substances considered hazardous, according to the National Institute for Occupational Safety and Health (NIOSH). Construction workers are particularly vulnerable. Depending upon the sort of construction you're doing and where you're doing it, you're exposed to a variety of harmful conditions from general pollution to inhaling lead oxide, which can happen if you're soldering scrap metal or plastics. In any event, a diet rich in antioxidants such as vitamins A, C, and E will help detoxify your body. The following supplements are recommended:

MVP (see section 172)
B complex, 50 mg. twice daily
Coenzyme-Q10 30–100 mg. daily
Octocosanol, 1,000 mcg. daily.

191. Gamblers

If you're a gambler, I don't have to tell you about your stress, sleep, and dietary needs. I'm sure you're aware that all three are higher than average. What you might not realize, though, is that you could be in need of vitamin-D supplementation because of lack of sunlight. For best performance at any table, I suggest the following supplements:

MVP (see section 172)
Coenzyme-Q10 complex, 30–100 mg. daily
Calcium-magnesium complex, A.M. and P.M.

192. Salespersons

The daily grind of having to deal with the public cannot be underestimated. Whether you're selling automobiles, books, exercise machines, or food, doing it on the road or from behind a counter, the emotional and physical stress on your body is great. And because appearances are often as important as products in your line of work, you'd be wise to pack the right supplements along with your samples. You'll be happily surprised with the results.

MVP (see section 172)
B complex, 50 mg. A.M. and P.M.
Calcium 500 mg. and magnesium 250 mg. A.M. and P.M.
Coenzyme-Q10 complex, 30–100 mg. daily
Ginkgo biloba, 60 mg. A.M. and P.M.
St. John's wort polyphenol combination, 1 daily

193. Actors—Stage, Screen, Radio, and TV Performers

There's not an actor I know who doesn't need a B-vitamin supplement. The stress and tension of performing is an occupational given. And if you're like most theatrical performers, dieting is the only form of eating you know, too often denying you necessary vitamins. A helpful supplement scenario would be:

MVP (see section 172)
B complex, 50 mg. A.M. and P.M.
Coenzyme-Q10 complex with vitamin E, 1 daily
Calcium 500 mg. and magnesium 250 mg., A.M. and P.M.
St. John's wort polyphenol complex, 1 daily

194. Singers

Like actors, singers are also under high levels of stress, whether performing or rehearsing. If you worry about laryngitis, or other throat infections, it's advisable to keep your vitamin-C levels high at all times. Time-release vitamin C is your best choice.

MVP (see section 172)
Additional vitamin C, 1,000 mg. A.M. and P.M. when necessary

195. Doctors and Nurses

If you work with illness, you need all the protection you can get. Long hours, stress, and germs themselves, all contribute to your need for vitamin and mineral supplementation.

MVP (see section 172)
B complex, 50 mg. A.M. and P.M.
Extra vitamin C to ward off infections.
Calcium 500 mg. and magnesium 250 mg. complex A.M. and P.M.

196. Manicurists and Hair Colorists

You may be in the beauty business, but your daily exposure to chemical fumes creates destructive free radicals, and healthwise that's not a pretty picture. As free-radical levels rise, so does your body's need for additional antioxidants to disable them.

MVP (see section 172)
B complex, 50 mg. A.M. and P.M.
Extra vitamin C, 500 mg. 1–2 times daily
Ginkgo biloba complex, 60 mg. A.M. and P.M.
Coenzyme-Q10 vitamin E complex, 1–2 daily

197. Bicyclists

Cycling is great aerobic conditioning. But if you're on the road taking in the scenery, you're also taking in pollution and ultraviolet radiation from the sun. And since the intensity of your exercise is already generating unwanted free radicals, your natural antioxidants need nutritional backup.

MVP (see section 172)
Coenzyme-Q10 vitamin E complex, 1 daily
Calcium and magnesium complex, 1–3 times daily
Octocosanol, 1,000 mcg. 1–3 times daily
MSM powder, 1–2 tbsp. in 8 oz water or juice before, during, or after cycling.

198. Swimmers

If you take the plunge regularly, you're giving your entire body a fine all-over workout. But you are also subjecting it to stress and generating extra free radicals. A high-antioxidant diet along with supplements will keep you in the swim.

MVP (see section 172)
B complex, 50 mg. A.M. and P.M.
Coenzyme-Q10, 30–100 mg. daily
MSM powder, 1–2 tbsp. dissolved in 8 oz. water or juice, before or after swimming.

199. Handicapped

If you're disabled, your needs for vitamins are usually increased. More often than not, if one part of your body is not

functioning properly, another part is working twice as hard—
and needs nourishment. Helpful basic supplements would be:

MVP (see section 172)
B complex, 50 mg. A.M. and P.M.
Calcium 500 mg. and magnesium 250 mg. complex A.M.
  and P.M.
St. John's wort polyphenol complex, 1 daily

200. Golfers

As much as you enjoy it, golfing takes a lot out of you. The
stress and tension of the game can use up B vitamins at a
rapid clip. The right supplements might not get you down
into the seventies, but they can help you stay energetic
throughout the game.

MVP (see section 172)
B complex, 50 mg. A.M. and P.M.
Zinc, 15–50 mg. daily
Calcium 500 mg. and magnesium 250 mg. complex A.M.
  and P.M.

201. Tennis Players

If you play tennis often, you might look good on the outside,
but be a nutritional mess inside. I've found that far too many
tennis buffs skip meals, or eat only protein—both bad
habits. A demanding game like tennis requires that you serve
yourself all the vitamins you need.

MVP (see section 172)
B complex, 50 mg. A.M. and P.M.
Calcium 500 mg. and magnesium 250 mg. complex A.M.
  and P.M.
MSM powder, 1–2 tbsp. dissolved in 8 oz. water or juice;
  drink after match to decrease lactic-acid buildup
Coenzyme-Q10 complex with vitamin E, 1 daily
Octocosanol, 1,000 mcg. 1–3 times daily
Soy shake (see section 181)

202. Racquetball Players

Few sports require as intense physical stamina as racquetball, so if you intend to play it on a regular basis (or even on an occasional lunch hour), you'd better be prepared not only to meet your opponent, but the nutritional challenge as well.

MVP (see section 172)
Octocosanol, 1,000 mcg. 1–3 times daily
Coenzyme-Q10 complex with vitamin E, 1 daily
B complex, 50 mg., A.M. and P.M.
MSM powder, 1–2 tbsp. dissolved in 8 oz. water or juice; drink before, during, or after game.

203. Teachers

School days are as stressful for teachers as they are for students, if not more so. To keep your energy and spirits up, a good vitamin program is important.

MVP (see section 172)
B complex, 50 mg. A.M. and P.M.
Calcium 500 mg. and magnesium 250 mg. A.M. and P.M.
Coenzyme-Q10 complex with vitamin E, 1 daily
St. John's wort polyphenol complex, 1 daily

204. Smokers

Every cigarette you smoke destroys about 25–100 mg. of vitamin C. Also, lung cancer risks aside, you're more prone to cardiovascular and pulmonary disorders than nonsmokers. Without going into the long list of deleterious effects cigarettes can have, I feel confident in telling smokers that they need all the nutritional help they can get, especially from antioxidants such as vitamins A, C, E, and selenium.

MVP (see section 172)
Vitamin C, 500 mg. A.M. and P.M.
Ginkgo biloba complex, 60 mg. A.M. and P.M.
Selenium, 200 mcg. daily

205. Drinkers

Alcoholism is the chief cause of vitamin deficiency among civilized people with ample food supplies. If you're a heavy drinker, the alcohol you consume usually takes the place of needed protein, or, in some cases, prevents absorption or proper storage of ingested vitamins.

MVP (see section 172)
B complex, 100 mg. twice daily (especially needed are B1, B6, and folic acid)
Calcium 500 mg. and magnesium 250 mg. 2–3 times daily
Silymarin (milk thistle), 1 capsule 3 times daily for liver rejuvenation.
Kudzu, 500 mg. 1–3 capsules before or after drinking alcohol.

206. Excessive TV Watchers

Just because you spend a lot of time relaxing in front of your set doesn't mean you're not in need of extra vitamins. For the eyestrain it's more than likely that you need additional vitamin A. And if you rarely get to see the light of day, you might need vitamin D also.

MVP (see section 172)
Beta-carotene, 10,000 IU with breakfast (take for 5 days, stop for 2)
Vitamin D, 400 IU 5 days a week if necessary

207. Travelers on the Go

The stresses of travel, though they often go unnoticed, can be significant. If you're heading to warm or tropical places, be sure that the vitamins you take are in opaque containers and that you keep them in a cool place, not out in the sun. If you're headed for chillier environs, be sure to bring along plenty of vitamin C and take it with all your meals, not just breakfast and dinner. And if you're traveling to foreign ports, keep in mind that acidophilus (3 capsules or 2 table-spoons liquid) 3 times a day is a good diarrhea preventive.

MVP (see section 172)
Coenzyme-Q10 complex with vitamin E, 1–2 daily
B complex, 50 mg. A.M. and P.M.
If you're having trouble sleeping in a new time zone take:
Calcium 500 mg. and magnesium 250 mg., 2 tablets before
   bedtime or 1 mg. melatonin sublingual (let dissolve under
   your tongue) 15 minutes before bedtime.

208. Any Questions About Chapter XIII?

Are foreign vitamins different?

Vitamins the world over are the same, only dosages vary. The metric system is used internationally for measurement, and nutrients are measured by weight. (See section 168 for a better understanding of what equals what.)

My obstetrician doesn't say too much to me, except "Take your vitamins." Since you're a pharmacist as well as a nutritionist, could you tell me what drugs or medicines could be dangerous to me and my baby?

I'd feel safest in saying all of them—unless specifically prescribed by your doctor. No drug—whether it's OTC (over-the-counter) or prescription, alcohol, nicotine, or caffeine—should be considered safe during pregnancy. Most drugs can cross the placenta and thus affect fetus as well as mother. Considering that the major stages in an embryo's development occur during life's first few weeks, if you're even *thinking* about being a mother, check with your doctor before taking any medication.

Are older people subject to any specific nutrient deficiencies?

As a general rule, they are. Aside from the fact that they consume more drugs than any other age group, they usually suffer from subclinical nutritional deficiencies because of their lifestyle and marginal intakes of key nutrients owing to malabsorption, poor teeth, loneliness, and other social problems.

Their most common nutrient deficiencies are folic acid, calcium, vitamin B12, vitamin D, and vitamin C. Also, because older people have a tendency to take stimulant laxatives on a regular basis, they lose large amounts of vitamins A, D, E, and K as well as calcium and potassium. (See section 293 for other drug-related vitamin deficiencies.)

I'm a thirty-five-year-old woman and I work out daily. And I mean WORK OUT—weights, Nautilus, the whole nine yards. I know I must need more of certain nutrients than ordinary people do. But what are they?

They are vitamin A, vitamin B6, vitamin C; calcium (for optimal protein utilization), magnesium (lost through workout sweating and essential for muscle relaxation), and branched chain amino acids (for repair and reconstruction). For extended energy to keep you going through workouts, some nutrients and foods are better than others. For instance: soybeans would be better for you than peas; whole-wheat spaghetti better than white; beets preferable to carrots; grapefruit better than oranges, apples, or bananas.

XIV

The Right Vitamin at the Right Time

209. Special Situation Supplements

Your body's vitamin needs are not always the same, and special situations require special food regimens and supplements. What follows is a list of such situations, most of them temporary, with supplement suggestions. (For foods that offer specific vitamins and minerals, see sections 28 through 70. Once again, this information is not prescriptive. (See section 172 for MVP.)

210. Acne

This scourge of teenage years has been treated in a variety of ways, from X rays to tetracycline, with only varying degrees of success. I encourage more natural treatment of the condition, and have been delighted by the results.

MVP (see section 172)
Vitamin E (dry form), 400 IU daily
Beta-carotene, 10,000 IU daily
Zinc, 15–50 mg. chelated, 1 tablet daily with a meal
Acidolphilus liquid, 1–2 tbsp. 3 times daily, or 3–6 capsules
   3 times daily.

Cysteine, 1 g. daily half an hour before meals with vitamin
  C, 1,000 mg. 3 times daily
MSM, 1,000 mg., 1 tab daily
MSM lotion, apply 3 times daily
Eliminate all processed foods. They are usually high in salt
  that has been iodized. (CAUTION: If you are taking a
  prescription medication for acne, do NOT take extra vita-
  min A unless advised by your doctor.)

211. Athlete's Foot

Vitamin-C powder or crystals applied directly to the affected
areas seems to help this fungus infection. Keep your feet
dry, and out of shoes as much as possible, until the infection
clears. Tea tree oil applied to the affected area can help as
well.

212. Bad Breath

Along with proper brushing and flossing, you might try:

MVP (see section 172)
1 chlorophyll tablet or capsule 1–3 times daily
3 acidophilus capsules 3 times daily, or 1–2 tbsp. flavored
  acidophilus
Zinc, 50 mg. daily

213. Baldness or Falling Hair

There are no guarantees, but many people report a definite
diminution of hair loss with this regimen:

B complex, 50 mg. twice daily
Choline and inositol, 1,000 mg. of each daily
Daily jojoba oil scalp massage and shampoo
Calcium, 500 mg. and magnesium 250 mg. 1 daily
Cysteine, 1,000 mg. daily
Vitamin C, 500 mg. A.M. and P.M.

214. Bee Stings

The best thing to do about bee stings is try to avoid them. Vitamin B1 (thiamine) has been shown to be a fairly good insect repellant. Taken three times daily, 100 mg. B1 creates a smell at the level of your skin that insects do not like. If you're too late with the B1 and do get stung, 1,000 mg. vitamin C could help ease allergic reactions. Also, 1 MSM tablet, 1,000 mg., taken 3 times daily for a week is a good idea.

215. Bleeding Gums

The most effective vitamin therapy for bleeding gums is 1,000 mg. vitamin C complex, with bioflavonoids, rutin, and hesperidin, taken 3 times a day.

216. Broken Bones

If you've ever broken a bone, you know how frustrating it is waiting for it to mend. That feeling can be alleviated, and bone-healing accelerated, by increasing your calcium and vitamin-D intakes. Daily doses of 1,000 mg. calcium and 500 mg. magnesium in a complex with vitamin D are recommended 2–3 times daily.

217. Bruises

Vitamin C complex, 1,000 mg. with bioflavonoids, rutin, and hesperidin, taken three times daily will help prevent capillary fragility, those black-and-blue marks that occur when the tiny blood vessels beneath the skin rupture.

218. Burns

The most important thing to do with a burn is to put cold water on it immediately. To effectively stimulate wound-healing, 50 mg. zinc daily has been found useful and is worth trying. Vitamin C complex, 1,000 mg. with bioflavonoids, taken in the morning and evening is recommended to prevent infections. Vitamin E, 1,000 IU used orally and topically can help prevent scarring. MSM lotion applied 3 times daily and 1 MSM tablet, 1,000 mg. taken 3 times daily are advised for a month.

219. Chemotherapy

A complete antioxidant formula can enhance the effectiveness of chemo in reducing cancerous tumors while at the same time protecting healthy tissue and fortifying your immune system. Ginger aids in alleviating some of the unwanted side effects such as nausea and vomiting. I'd suggest taking one Ev.Ext-33 capsule (which is a patented herbal extract of a unique subspecies of ginger) twice daily along with my MVP. (See section 172.)

CAUTION: If you are undergoing chemotherapy, be sure to check with your doctor before adding any new supplements.

220. Cold Feet

If you're embarrassed by wearing socks to bed all the time, you could try a good multimineral supplement with iodine twice a day, along with kelp tablets. The cold feet could be due to the fact that your thyroid glands are not producing enough thyroxin. Niacin and vitamin E can also help circulation. I also suggest ginkgo biloba, 60 mg. 1–3 times daily.

221. Cold Sores and Herpes Simplex

Few things are more annoying than cold sores. The best supplement remedy I've discovered is:

Lactobacillus acidophilus, 3 capsules 3 times a day
Vitamin-E oil, 28,000 IU applied directly to affected area
Lysine, 3 g. (3,000 mg.) daily (in divided doses) between
    meals (with water or juice—no protein)

As a preventive: Lysine, 500 mg. daily (with water or juice
—no protein)
Vitamin C, 1,000 mg. A.M. and P.M.

222. Constipation

Everyone is bothered by constipation at some time or other.
Usually this is due to a lack of bulk in the diet or because of
certain medications, such as codeine. Harsh laxatives can
rob the body of nutrients, as well as cause rebound constipation and laxative dependency, so natural remedies should
be your first choice.

1 rounded teaspoon psyllium fiber (if not allergic to it) in
    juice or nonfat milk works wonders
1 tbsp. acidophilus liquid 3 times daily
A vegetable laxative and sugar-free stool softener for a short
    time if necessary
8–10 glasses of water daily (and a little exercise wouldn't
    hurt)

223. Cuts

Vitamin C complex, 1,000 mg. with bioflavonoids twice
daily, along with 50 mg. zinc and 400 IU vitamin E.

224. Dry Skin

Vitamin-E (dry form) oil seems to work wonders when applied to dry skin, as do oils rich in vitamins A and D. As a
dietary supplement, I recommend 200–400 IU vitamin E
daily and 10,000 IU vitamin A (take for 5 days and stop for
2). I also recommend an MVP (see section 172) and omega-
3 fatty acids, 1–3 capsules three times a day. (See section 94
for the complete lowdown on omega-3 fatty acids.)

If you don't want to take fish oils (omega-3 fatty acids are
marketed primarily as EPA [eicosapentaenoic and docosahexaenoic acid]), other natural sources of omega-3 fatty acids
are flaxseed oil, pumpkin oil, canola oil, and soy oil (1–2

teaspoons added to a salad dressing should help). Significant amounts are also found in English walnuts, navy beans, kidney beans, soybeans, and Great Northern beans.

225. Hangovers

To prevent them, take 1 B complex, 100 mg., before going out, 1 again while you're drinking, and another right before going to bed. (Alcohol destroys B complex.) Cysteine, 500 mg. with vitamin C, 1,500 mg., can help, too. (See section 205.)

226. Hay Fever

Stress can cause hay fever attacks to worsen. If you're one of the many who suffer, you might find relief with 1 B complex twice daily, pantothenic acid 1,000 mg. 3 times daily, and the same dose of vitamin C, which has evidenced effective antihistamine properties. Also, MSM tablets, 1,000 mg., three times daily may help you through the sneeze season.

227. Headaches

A surprisingly effective vitamin-mineral regimen for headaches is:

100 mg. niacin 3 times daily
100 mg. B complex (time release) twice daily
Calcium and magnesium (twice as much calcium as magnesium is the proper ratio), which are nature's tranquilizers
For migraines try:
White willow bark or feverfew capsules 3 times daily
Ginkgo biloba, 60 mg. A.M. and P.M. may help prevent migraines

228. Heartburn

Over-the-counter antacids, such as Gelusil™, Kolantyl™, Maalox™, Di-Gel™, Rolaids™, contain aluminum, which disturbs calcium and phosphorus metabolism. You'll probably be better off taking one MSM 1,000 mg. tablet 3 times daily to decrease the acid (or two calcium 250 mg. and magnesium 125 mg. tablets 3 times daily), multiple digestive enzymes 1–3 times daily, chewable papaya, drinking fluids before or after meals, *not* during, and eating more slowly.

229. Hemorrhoids

Just about half the people over fifty are afflicted by hemorrhoids. Improper diet, lack of exercise, and straining at stool are all contributing factors. And coffee, chocolate, cola, and cocoa are accessories to the discomfort by promoting anal itching. If you're bothered by hemorrhoids, 1 tablespoon of unprocessed bran 3 times a day is helpful, along with 1,000 mg. vitamin C complex twice a day for healing membranes, and 3 acidophilus capsules 3 times a day (or 1–2 tablespoons of acidophilus liquid one to 3 times a day). Vitamin-E oil, 28,000 IU per ounce, can be applied to affected area with a cotton swab.

230. Impotence

If you have trouble maintaining an erection adequate for satisfactory sexual performance, you might want to try some natural remedies before you go for a Viagra™ prescription. I suggest ginkgo biloba, 60 mg. three times daily; 2–4 saw palmetto, zinc, pumpkin seed oil combination capsules daily; and arginine, 4–5 grams, taken 45 minutes before sex. If you are over fifty years of age, I also recommend one 25–50 mg. DHEA tablet daily. (DHEA should *not* be taken by anyone under forty unless blood level of that hormone is low. Men over fifty can take 50 mg. daily, women 25 mg. daily.)

231. Insomnia

Can't sleep? Maybe you need a more naturally effective anti-insomnia program:

1 chelated calcium 250 mg. and magnesium 125 mg. tablet 3 times daily—and 3 tablets a half hour before bedtime.

Vitamin B6, 100 mg., and niacinamide 100 mg. work together to produce the brain chemical serotonin, which is essential for restful REM sleep.

Turkey is a good source of tryptophan. Therefore, an open-face turkey sandwich and a cup of herbal tea (chamomile, valerian, skullcap) before bedtime could be the sleep remedy of your life.

For more difficult insomnia, try 1 mg. of melatonin sublingually (dissolved under the tongue) 15 minutes before bedtime.

232. Itching

As an antihistamine, one 1,000 mg. vitamin-C tablet, plus a 1,000 mg. MSM tablet, in the morning and in the evening, with food, might be helpful. I would also recommend 1,000 mg. pantothenic acid 1–3 times daily, and vitamin-E cream (20,000 IU per ounce) applied to afflicted area three times daily.

233. Jet Lag

So your plane from London lands at 9 A.M. and you're supposed to be at a meeting at 10 A.M. No problem, except for the fact that as far as your body is concerned, it's still only 4 A.M. and you should be asleep. Your best bet is to help your system catch up with your schedule by giving it the vitamins it needs.

B complex, 50 mg. A.M. and P.M. (start while still on the plane).

MVP with food, twice during flights of 5 or more hours (see section 172).

Melatonin, 1 mg., sublingual form can be used for 6–12 hour flights. After 2–3 hours in the air, dissolve one or two under your tongue for a refreshing sleep.

If you're feeling run-down, as well as tired, be sure to take additional vitamin C.

NOTE: Intestinal gas expands at high altitudes, so pass on the beans and other gas-inducing foods right before and during the flight if you want to feel fit on arrival. Also, keep in mind that alcohol destroys vitamin B complex, which is one of the best jet-lag fighters around. And be sure to drink water every hour on the plane; the pressurized cabin causes your body to dehydrate faster.

234. Leg Pains

Increase your calcium. Try 1 chelated calcium and magnesium tablet with breakfast and dinner. Vitamin E has been reported quite helpful in cases of charley horse. The most common doses for it are 400–1,000 IU vitamin E 1–3 times daily. And ginkgo biloba, 60 mg. 1–3 times daily can also help the circulation to your legs.

235. Menopause

Because of the risks that have recently been brought to light about estrogens, many women have been seeking other ways to relieve the discomforts of menopause. A good number of menopausal women have found that 200–400 IU vitamin E (mixed tocopherols) with selenium 1–3 times a day does indeed alleviate hot flashes. If you're at that time of life, MVP and a 50 mg. B complex twice a day also seem to help. Chelated calcium (250 mg.) and magnesium (125 mg.) can be taken with a soy isoflavonoid complex (containing daidzein, genistein, vitamin D, and boron) twice daily. And for a soothing, mood-elevating and muscle-relaxing aid, try a St. John's wort polyphenol combination in the morning.

236. Menstruation

Between the cramps and the bloating, menstruation is for most women a monthly annoyance. But this annoyance can dwindle down to a mere distraction once the discomfort is alleviated.

MVP (see section 172)
Vitamin B6, 50 mg. 3 times daily (most effective as a natural diuretic)
B complex, 50 mg. A.M. and P.M.
Evening primrose oil, 500 mg., 3 times daily

237. Motion Sickness

This is one condition where remedies are most effective if taken beforehand. Vitamins B1 and B6 are the nutrients of choice (in fact, many prenatal antinausea preparations contain vitamin B6). Taking 50 mg. B complex the night before you leave and the morning of your trip has been found to be effective by many queasy travelers.

Ginger extract capsules taken 3 times daily work also!

238. Muscle Soreness

For that ache-all-over feeling after a workout, or just general muscle soreness, I've seen many people find relief with vitamin E, 400–800 IU taken one to three times daily. A chelated calcium and magnesium tablet in the morning and at night also has helped.

239. The Pill

If you take oral contraceptives, not only are you more vulnerable than other women to blood clots, strokes, and heart attacks, but you're also more likely to be deficient in zinc, folic acid, vitamins C, B6, and B12 (which accounts for much nervousness and depression among pill-takers).
    Supplements are important:

MVP (see section 172)
Zinc, 15 mg. chelated, 1 tablet daily
Folic acid, 800 mcg. daily
B6, 50–100 mg. daily

240. Poison Ivy/Poison Oak

MSM lotion, vitamin-E oil, or aloe vera gel applied externally 3 times daily can help healing. 1,000 mg. vitamin-C
tablet taken A.M. and P.M. should alleviate the itching.

241. Polyps

These small annoying growths should definitely be seen by
a doctor, and in most instances surgical removal is necessary. But as far as supplements go, Dr. Jerome J. DeCosse,
professor and chairman of surgery at the Medical College of
Wisconsin, used 3,000 mg. vitamin C daily on patients with
polyps, and had noteworthy success with the treatment.

242. Postoperative Healing

After surgery, your body needs all the nutritional support it
can get.

MVP (see section 172) take 3 times daily, with meals
2 vitamin C complex, 1,000 mg. with bioflavonoids, hes-
    peridin, and rutin A.M. and P.M.
This regimen can be used for 2 weeks before and 2 weeks to
    4 weeks after surgery.
FOR POST–PLASTIC SURGERY ADD:
Arnica, 4 pellets sublingually (under tongue) on an empty
    stomach, before meals, 3–4 times daily. (For bruising)
Bromelain, 500 mg., 1–2 tablets daily. (To reduce swelling)

CAUTION: Do not take large doses of vitamin E for 2
weeks before or after surgery.

243. Prickly Heat

Much like itching, prickly heat seems to respond to the antihistamine properties of vitamin C. (See section 232 for
regimen.)

244. Prostate Problems

Chronic prostatitis, where inflammation of the gland is often combined with infection, has been found to respond to treatment with zinc. (The prostate gland normally contains about 10 times more zinc than any other organ in the body.) In many cases, symptoms have completely disappeared, especially with supplements that also contain pygeum and saw palmetto.

MVP (see section 172)
Combination saw palmetto, pygeum, pumpkin seed oil, stinging nettle, and zinc tablet, 1–2 times daily.

245. Psoriasis

Though many jokes have been made about this disease, it is no laughing matter to the millions who suffer from it. No one treatment has been found to be totally effective, but the following has met with much success:

MVP (see section 172)
Beta-carotene, 10,000 IU daily
B complex, 50 mg. A.M. and P.M.
Rose hips vitamin C, 500 mg. A.M. and P.M.
Vitamin E (dry form), 200–400 IU twice daily
Evening primrose, borage, or flaxseed oil capsules, 500 mg. 3 times daily
Selenium, 100–200 mcg. daily.

246. Stopping Smoking

It's no mean feat to stop smoking, and your body knows it. Those withdrawal symptoms are real. For the irritability that occurs, take 1 St. John's wort polyphenol complex, a chelated calcium (250 mg.) and magnesium (125 mg.) tablet, and a B complex, 50 mg. in the morning with food. Between meals take 1,000 mg. cysteine. With the evening meal, take another calcium and magnesium tablet and a 50 mg. B complex. And don't forget your MVP (see section 172).

CAUTION: If you are using a nicotine gum to help you quit smoking, be aware that consuming coffee, cola, or acidic drinks before chewing nicotine gum *significantly inhibits its absorption.*

247. Sunburn

A good sunscreening preparation should always be used before exposing yourself to the sun's ultraviolet rays for any length of time. What most people don't realize is that the sun actually burns the skin, and bad burns can break the skin and leave it vulnerable to infection.

If it's too late for preventives, try this:

Aloe vera gel applied 3–4 times daily
An MSM lotion or vitamin-E cream (20,000 IU) also applied 3–4 times daily
MVP (see section 172)
Additional vitamin C, 500 mg. A.M. and P.M. until burn heals

248. Teeth Grinding

People are usually unaware of grinding their teeth. It occurs more often in children than adults, and most often during sleep. To get out of the "grind," try: MVP (see section 172); B complex, 50 mg. A.M. and P.M.; 1 St. John's wort polyphenol complex daily; and chelated calcium (250 mg.) and magnesium (125 mg.) taken at bedtime.

249. Varicose Veins

Age, lack of exercise, and chronic constipation are contributing factors to varicose veins. Watching your diet and exercising regularly can do a lot toward preventing them. MVP with an extra 500 mg. vitamin C complex twice daily has been found to help, along with 400–800 IU vitamin E.

I'd also suggest ginkgo biloba, 60 mg., 2–3 times daily for improved circulation.

250. Vasectomy

Men with vasectomies are more susceptible to infections and would be wise to take an additional 1,000 mg. vitamin C complex daily, along with regular MVP diet supplementation. Extra zinc, 15–50 mg. every day, is also a good idea.

251. Warts

They don't come from handling frogs, but they do seem to effectively disappear when treated with vitamin-E oil. The most successful regimen appears to be 28,000 IU vitamin E applied externally 1–2 times daily and 400 IU vitamin E (dry form) taken internally 3 times a day. Vitamin C complex, 1,000–2,000 mg. daily, can help build up the body's immunity and possibly prevent warts from occurring at all.

252. Any Questions About Chapter XIV?

You talk about digestive enzymes being helpful for heartburn. What are they and what do they do?

Enzymes, which can be purchased as supplements, can help your own digestive system assimilate the foods you eat. *Bromelain,* for instance, is a digestive enzyme from pineapple. *Cellulose* is an aid to digesting vegetable matter and breaking down food fiber. *Hydrochloric acid (HCl)* works in the stomach on tough foods, such as fibrous meats, vegetables, and poultry. (Betaine HCl is the best form available.) *Lipase* assists in fat digestion and *mylase* dissolves thousands of times its own weight in starches so you can more easily assimilate them. *Papain* is a protein-digesting enzyme (from papaya), and *prolase* is a concentrated protein-digesting enzyme derived from papain. (See section 228.)

Is there a specific reason for your recommending a soy isoflavonoid complex in the treatment of menopause?

Definitely. Since estrogen replacement began in the 1960s, it has been linked to a 35 percent increase in uterine cancer. Soy isoflavones, particularly genistein and daidzein, are estrogen-like compounds that can not only help relieve the symptoms of menopause, such as hot flashes, irritability, and vaginal dryness, they can help protect against cancer as well. In fact, the combination of soy isoflavones, plus calcium, magnesium, vitamin D, and boron, has also been found helpful in preventing osteoporosis!

XV
Getting Well and Staying That Way

253. Why You Need Supplements During Illness

During illness the body is under stress. Cells are destroyed, exhausted adrenal glands deprived of nutrients are unable to function properly, and the body's stress-fighting team of vitamin C, B6, folic acid, and pantothenic acid is severely depleted, zinc and vitamin C are also needed in greater amounts.

Because we require these vitamins to utilize effectively other nutrients and to keep our metabolism functioning all the time, our need for them is obviously increased when we're ill. And since we know that fever and stress rob our body of its most essential nutrients, the importance of supplements is self-evident. Keep in mind that all supplements should be taken with food, unless otherwise indicated.

Again, the following regimens are not intended as medical advice, only as a guide in working with your doctor.

254. Allergies

Allergies come in all shapes and sizes, with all sorts of symptoms, and you can contract them for just about anything. Nonetheless they take their nutritional toll, and supplements can help.

MVP (see section 172) A.M. and P.M.
Vitamin B complex, 50 mg. 2 times daily
Pantothenic acid, 500 mg. A.M. and P.M.
MSM 1,000 mg. with vitamin C complex, 1–3 times daily

If you have an allergy, it would be a good idea to take a hard look at your present diet. Many allergies are caused by MSG, food coloring, additives, and preservatives.

255. Arthritis

Thousands of people suffer from this painful chronic condition. Because it puts so much stress on the body, vitamin-mineral supplementation is really essential.

MVP (see section 172)
Extra vitamin C, 500 mg. 1–2 times a day (if you're taking lots of aspirin, you're losing vitamin C)
Pantothenic acid, 100 mg. 3 times daily
2 omega-3 capsules 2–3 times daily
Copper, 2 mg. daily
1 Zinaxin™ capsule, twice daily
St. John's wort polyphenol complex, 1 daily
Increase your consumption of fatty fish, such as cod, salmon, halibut. They are a great source of omega-3 fatty acids which have anti-inflammatory properties. I'd also suggest you eliminate the nightshades, such as potatoes, tomatoes, and eggplant, from your diet as they may aggravate your condition.

256. Asthma

Asthma is a chronic allergic condition that affects the bronchial tubes. When an attack occurs, the muscle tissue of the tubes constricts spasmodically, squeezing the air passages and causing labored breathing and a feeling of suffocation. Allergies, heredity, and emotional stress have all been implicated as contributing factors to asthmatic conditions, but many nutrients have been found to provide remarkable natural relief.

MVP (see section 172) A.M. and P.M.

Extra vitamin C, 500 mg. A.M. and P.M.

2 Evening primrose oil capsules, 500 mg., 3 times daily for 3–4 months; then 1 capsule 3 times daily.

(If you are taking steroids, you won't benefit from EPO, because steroids interfere with EPO's action.)

Vitamin B15, 50 mg., 1 tablet daily for 1 month, then twice daily for the second month, and 3 times daily in the third month.

(Severe cases may require two 50 mg. tablets 3 times daily with food. Decrease dosage when positive reaction occurs.)

Dimethylglycine, 50 mg., 3 times daily with meals

Beta-carotene, 10,000 IU daily

Vitamin B complex, 50 mg. twice daily

Ginkgo biloba, 60 mg., 2–3 times daily

1 Zinaxin capsule twice daily

257. Blood Pressure—High and Low

HIGH

Over eighty million Americans have high blood pressure, which has been intimately linked to heart attacks and strokes. The importance of keeping your blood pressure down cannot be overestimated, and there are a number of natural ways that can help.

• Talk slower (fast talkers often don't breathe properly, and this can result in elevated blood pressure).

• Reduce, if you are overweight, (controlled, sensible dieting can significantly lower blood pressure in overweight individuals).

• Decrease sodium and increase potassium in your diet (see section 311 on hidden salt in foods).
• Decrease your sugar intake (see section 309).
• Eliminate caffeine (see section 284).
• Eat more onions and garlic.
• Stop smoking.
• Avoid stress or anxiety-provoking situations (jangling everyday noises, even loud televisions, can cause stress and elevate blood pressure.
• Exercise regularly (brisk walking) and get adequate rest.

Regimen

Potassium may be necessary if you are taking an antihypertensive, but check with your doctor to be sure it's not contraindicated for your particular medication.

MVP (see section 172)
Calcium 1,000 mg. daily
Magnesium 500 mg. daily
Coenzyme-Q10 complex with vitamin E, 2–3 times daily

LOW

Low blood pressure, unless extreme, is a far better condition to have than its alternative. Nonetheless, hypotensives often suffer from dizziness and occasional fainting spells and blackouts.

Regimen

1–3 kelp tablets daily
(If you're taking thyroid medication, check with your doctor, as kelp might decrease the need for the amount you're currently taking.)
MVP (see section 172)

258. Bronchitis

This inflammation of the bronchial tube lining is quite common and extremely enervating. The stress it puts on the body is high, and even antibiotics are the bad guys as far as nutrients are concerned (see section 293).

Beta-carotene 10,000 IU daily
Rose hips vitamin C, 1,000 mg. A.M. and P.M.
MVP (see section 172)
Vitamin E (dry form) 400 IU 1–3 times daily
Water, 6–8 glasses daily
3 acidophilus caps 3 times daily, or 1–2 tbsp. liquid 3 times
  daily

259. Candida Albicans

This yeast infection takes advantage of circumstances in the body that are conducive to its growth, and there are many. For example: antibiotics, birth control pills, cortisone, diabetes mellitus, nutritional deficiencies, chronic constipation or diarrhea, and physical or emotional stress.

Symptoms can range from all those associated with vaginitis (discharge, itching, bladder infection, menstrual irregularities and cramps) to severe depression, acne, anxiety, fatigue, nervousness, and mental confusion.

The first step in treating Candida albicans is to deprive the body of all yeast-containing foods. For example: cheese, leavened breads, sour cream, buttermilk, beer, wine, cider, mushrooms, soy sauce, tofu, vinegar, dried fruits, melons, and frozen or canned juices.

If your doctor has not yet put you on a yeast fungus-killing drug, such as nystatin, there are many natural and surprisingly effective dietary combatants. Among them are garlic, broccoli, cabbage, onions, plain yogurt, turnips and other vegetables.

And an effective supplement regimen would be:

MVP (see section 172)
MSM, 1,000 mg. 3 times daily
Vitamin E (dry form) 200–400 IU daily
Caprylic acid supplement, 1–3 times daily
Acidophilus (yeast free) 1 capsule 3 times daily

260. Chicken Pox

This childhood staple is caused by a virus closely related to that of shingles. The fever and itching deplete a good amount of nutrients. Many mothers have found their children up and about faster by adding the following supplements to their diets.

Rose hips vitamin C, 500 mg. 3 times daily
Vitamin E (dry form), 100–200 IU 1–3 times daily
Beta-carotene, 10,000 IU daily (check pediatrician for proper dosage according to age and weight)
All-natural chewable vitamin and mineral MVP if child is over twelve years of age

261. Chronic Fatigue Syndrome

It's known by different names in different countries, but the common symptoms are: sudden onset, extreme fatigue, chills or low-grade fever, sore throat, tender lymph nodes, muscle pain, headaches, joint pain (without swelling), confusion, memory loss, visual disturbances, and sleep disorders, among others.

Two to five million Americans have been stricken with this illness. The British and Canadians know it as ME (myalgic encephalomyelitis) and the Japanese refer to it as low natural killer cell syndrome. In this country it's referred to as chronic fatigue immune dysfunction syndrome (CFIDS) or chronic fatigue syndrome (CFS).

Originally thought to be caused by the Epstein-Barr virus (the herpes virus that causes infectious mononucleosis), it is now known that CFS victims develop high amounts of antibodies to numerous other bugs.

According to a report in *Newsweek* magazine, Dr. Jay Goldstein, a Southern California physician, has theorized that the illness begins "when an unknown chemical or contagion damages the immune system . . . enabling viruses ordinarily held in check to start running amok. The immune system's helper T cells then start churning out tougher chemicals called 'cytokines,' which can themselves cause CFS symptoms." And the normal killer T cells that should attack anything foreign become mysteriously underactive (or, in some cases, unhealthily overactive).

There's no "silver bullet" treatment for CFS, but the body's immune system can use all the nutritional help it can get.

MVP (see section 172) A.M. and P.M.
Beta-carotene, 10,000 IU daily, 5 days a week (stop for 2 days)
Vitamin C, 1,000 mg. 1–3 times daily
Vitamin E (dry form), 200–400 IU, 1–3 times daily
Cysteine, 1 daily with vitamin C (3 times as much vitamin C as cysteine)
Selenium, 200 mcg. daily
Zinc, chelated, 15–50 mg., daily
Evening primrose oil, 500 mg., 1–3 times daily
MSM, 1,000 mg., 3 times daily

MY ADVICE:

Because the herpes virus is implicated, I'd suggest avoiding arginine-rich foods (see section 82). I'd also advise steering clear of refined carbohydrates, caffeine, alcohol, highly allergenic foods, and foods containing artificial flavors, colors, and other additives that can stress the immune system.

262. Colds

No one pays too much attention to a cold, except the body—it pays plenty.

MVP (see section 172)

Rose hips vitamin C, 1,000 mg. 3–6 times daily for 2 days

Beta-carotene, 10,000 IU 1–3 times daily (take for 5 days and stop for 2)

Water, 6–8 glasses daily

3 acidophilus capsules 3 times daily, or 1–2 tbsp. liquid 3 times daily

Zinc lozenge (let dissolve in mouth) 3–4 times daily

Echinacea and American feverfew extract, 3–5 daily at onset of symptoms, for 2–3 days.

263. Colitis

As a rule this illness is more common in women than men and often is triggered by emotional upset. Alternating diarrhea and constipation, as well as abdominal pain, are its distressing hallmarks. Diet is of prime importance and vitamins are recommended.

MVP (see section 172)

Potassium, 99 mg. (elemental) 1–3 times daily

Raw cabbage juice (vitamin U), 1 glass 3 times daily

Water, 6–8 glasses daily

Aloe vera juice (for internal use), 1 tbsp. 3 times daily or 1–3 capsules 3 times daily

3–6 acidophilus caps 3 times daily or 2 tbsp. liquid 3 times daily

1 tbsp. bran flakes 3 times daily or 3–6 bran tablets

MSM, 1000 mg. 3 times daily

264. Diabetes

What happens in diabetes, primarily, is that the pancreas fails to produce adequate insulin and the blood sugar rises uncontrollably. In mild cases diet alone can control the condition. (Beware of hidden sugars. See section 309.) In severe cases, replacement insulin is necessary. In all cases, the care of a physician is essential.

Supplements that have aided diabetics are:

MVP (see section 172)
Chromium picolinate 200 mcg.
Potassium, 99 mg. 3 times daily
Chelated zinc, 50 mg. 1–3 times daily
Water, 6–8 glasses daily

265. Eye Problems

From simple inflammations to refraction difficulties to serious diseases, eye problems should never be ignored, nor should visits to the ophthalmologist be postponed. There are, however, generally beneficial supplements you can take.

MVP (see section 172)
Beta-carotene, 10,000 IU daily
Vitamin C complex, 500 mg. A.M. and P.M.
Vitamin E (dry form) 400 IU daily
Lutein 20 mg. daily

266. Heart Conditions

With any heart condition, you should be under a doctor's care. Though the following supplements have been found to be quite safe and helpful, you should check with your physician to make sure they are not contraindicated in your particular case. (Vitamin E can increase the imbalance between the two sides of the heart for some people with rheumatic hearts.)

MVP (see section 172)
Coenzyme-Q10 complex 2–3 times daily
Vitamin B, 100 mg. A.M. and P.M.
Soy isoflavonoid complex twice daily
EPA and DHA, 1–3 capsules daily (fish oil or flaxseed oil)

HEART ATTACK *PREVENTION* TACTICS

• Decrease sugar and salt consumption.
• Stop smoking.

- Exercise regularly.
- Watch your weight.
- Practice relaxation techniques such as meditation and biofeedback to reduce stress.
- Decrease intake of saturated fats, hydrogenated oils, and cholesterol.
- Eat more garlic, fresh fruit, and fish.
- Increase your soy protein intake (use in place of animal protein whenever possible).
- Get enough calcium and magnesium in your diet (supplements of 1,000 mg. calcium and 500 mg. magnesium daily are recommended).
- Be sure you're getting enough vitamins C, B6, and E.
- Supplement lecithin in your diet.
- Laughter is great medicine (not only does it release pent-up emotions and stress . . . it's fun and feels good, too).

267. HIV (AIDS)

When human immunodeficiency virus (HIV), the virus that causes AIDS, attacks disease-fighting T cells and multiplies, it brings about the breakdown in the body's immune system. Anyone with HIV or AIDS needs higher amounts of nutrients because malabsorption is a common problem. My best advice is to contact a nutritionally oriented practitioner (see section 342) who can personalize a regimen that will be most effective for you. The internet, also, has some solid HIV and AIDS web sites with the latest in alternative as well as traditional treatments that are worth checking out: **www.hivinsite.ucsf.edu** and **www.tpan.com.** For a general immune system–boosting regimen, though, I suggest the following:

MVP (see section 172)
Selenium 200 mcg. daily
Vitamin C (buffered) 500 mg. 1–3 times daily
Acidophilus caps, 2, taken three times daily ½ hour before or
    after meals

Coenzyme-Q10 complex 1–3 times daily
1 standardized maitake mushroom extract tablet daily
Beta-1,3 Glucan, 2.5 mg. capsule, 1 daily ½ hour before a
    meal or 2 hours after eating
Cat's claw (una de gato), 500 mg., 1–3 capsules daily

CAUTION: If you are currently taking any medication, be
sure to check with your physician before adding any supplements to your diet. (See section 340 for more immune
system boosters at a glance.)

268. Hypoglycemia

Though an estimated 20–40 million Americans have it, this
disease is one of the most often undiagnosed. It is a condition of low blood sugar, and, like diabetes, presents a situation where the body is unable to metabolize carbohydrates
normally. Since a hypoglycemic's system overreacts to sugar,
producing too much insulin, the key to raising blood sugar
levels is not by eating rapidly metabolized refined carbohydrates but by eating more complex carbohydrates and protein.

Recommended supplements:

Beta-carotene and vitamin-D capsules, (500 and 400 IU)
    daily
Vitamin C, 500 mg. with or after each meal
B complex, 50 mg. 3 times daily
Fish oil capsules, 1,000 mg. 3 times daily
Digestive enzymes if necessary
GTF chromium or chromium picolinate, 200 mcg. 3 times
    daily
St. John's wort polyphenol complex, 1 daily
Soy food shake for breakfast (see section 181)

269. Impetigo

Caused by germs similar to those that cause boils—staphylococcus or streptococcus—it occurs more in children than

adults, but no one is immune. It often results from scratching and infecting insect bites, allowing the germs to get into broken skin.

Vitamin A and D capsules (10,000 and 400 IU) daily (reduce dose for child) for 5 days, then stop for 2
Vitamin E (dry form), 100–400 IU once a day
Rose hips vitamin C, 500 mg. A.M. and P.M.
MSM, 1,000 mg. A.M. and P.M.
MSM lotion applied 3 times daily

270. Measles

You can get measles at any age, though it's more common among children. It is the most contagious of the communicable diseases. There is now a preventive vaccine for it, but the virus still manages to get a large number of the unprotected each year. The disease and rash can be mild, or severe with a heavy cough. Your body needs vitamins to help fight and recover from it.

Beta-carotene, 10,000 IU (reduce dose for child) 1–3 times daily
Rose hips vitamin C, 500–1,000 mg. A.M. and P.M.
Vitamin E (dry form), 200–400 IU A.M. *or* P.M.

271. Mononucleosis

Commonly contracted by adolescents and young adults, mono (glandular fever) or "the kissing disease" as it is often called, can happen to anyone and can deplete the body of massive amounts of nutrients.

Diet is important and supplements are generally considered essential during the long convalescence.

MVP (see section 172) A.M. and P.M. with food
Extra vitamin C, 1,000 mg. A.M. and P.M. for 3 months
Potassium, 99 mg. 3 times daily

B complex, 50 mg. A.M. and P.M.
Zinc, chelated, 15–50 mg. daily
Echinacea and American feverfew extract capsules, 1–2,
A.M. and P.M. for 1 month

272. Mumps

A vaccine for mumps exists, but the disease is still quite
common and just as nutritionally debilitating. The virus
can spread through the patient's entire system, involving
not only the salivary glands but the testicles or ovaries,
the pancreas, the nervous system, and sometimes even the
heart.

Beta-carotene, 10,000 IU (reduce dose for children) 1–3
times daily for 5 days, then stop for 2
Rose hips vitamin C, 500–1,000 mg. twice daily
Vitamin E, 200–400 IU (dry form) daily

273. PMS (Premenstrual Syndrome)

For two to ten days before the onset of menstruation, millions of women are affected by a wide range of physical discomforts and mood disorders—from bloating, depression,
and insomnia to severe pains, uncontrolled rages, crying
spells, and even suicidal depression. This is known as PMS,
premenstrual syndrome.

FOODS AND BEVERAGES TO AVOID

• Salt and salty foods (see section 312)
• Licorice (it stimulates the production of aldosterone
which causes further retention of sodium and water)
• Cold foods and beverages (these adversely affect abdominal circulation and worsen cramping)
• Caffeine in all forms (see section 284). Caffeine increases
the craving for sugar, wastes B vitamins, washes out potas-

sium and zinc, and increases hydrochloric acid (HCl) secretions which can cause abdominal irritation
• Astringent dark teas (tannin binds important minerals and prevents absorption in the digestive tract)
• Alcohol (adversely affects blood sugar, depletes magnesium levels, and can interfere with proper liver function, which can aggravate PMS)
• Spinach, beet greens, and other oxalate-containing vegetables (oxalates make minerals nonassimilable, difficult to be properly absorbed)

FOODS AND BEVERAGES TO INCREASE

• Strawberries, watermelon (eat seeds), artichokes, asparagus, parsley, and watercress (these are natural diuretics)
• Raw sunflower seeds, dates, figs, peaches, bananas, potatoes, peanuts, and tomatoes (rich in potassium)
• Try dong quai, it's an herb known as the female ginseng and can improve circulation, regulate liver function, and help remove excess water from the system.

Suggested supplements
Vitamin B6, 50–300 mg. daily (work up from 50 mg. gradually)
MVP (see section 172)
Magnesium, 500 mg. and calcium 250 mg. daily
(Yes, with PMS it is twice as much magnesium as calcium, because a magnesium deficiency causes many of the PMS symptoms.)
Vitamin E (dry form), 100–400 IU daily
Pantothenic acid (vitamin B5), 1,000 mg. (1 g.) daily
Evening primrose oil, 500 mg., 1–3 times daily
St. John's wort polyphenol complex, 1 daily
And exercise! Aside from the fact that this will improve abdominal circulation, perspiration helps remove excess fluids.
Brisk walking for 30 minutes twice daily and/or swimming are highly recommended.

274. Shingles

Shingles (herpes zoster) is caused by a virus much like the one that causes chicken pox. But where chicken pox causes a general skin eruption, shingles usually erupts along a nerve path. Differences aside, the nutritional deficit caused by both diseases is high.

Beta-carotene, 10,000 IU daily
Vitamin B complex, 50 mg. A.M. and P.M.
Rose hips vitamin C with bioflavonoids, 1,000–2,000 mg. A.M. and P.M.
Vitamin D, 400 IU daily for 5 days, then stop for 2
Lysine, 1,000 mg., twice daily between meals on an empty stomach

275. Tonsillitis

An inflammation of the tonsils that can afflict any age group, though it is more common in children. Good nutrition and supplements have been effective in preventing it as well as recovering from it.

MVP (see section 172) A.M. and P.M. with food
Beta-carotene, 10,000 IU (reduce dose for children) 1–3 times daily
Extra vitamin C complex, 1,000 mg A.M. and P.M.
Vitamin E (dry form) 200–400 IU daily
3 acidophilus caps or 1–2 tbsp. 3 times daily
Water, 6–8 glasses daily

276. Ulcers

There are two types of peptic ulcer, one in the stomach and the other in the duodenum, usually associated with excessive acidity in the stomach juices (see section 9). For both of these conditions, supplements have been found helpful.

Beta-carotene, 10,000 IU daily
Vitamin B complex, 100 mg. A.M. and P.M.

Vitamin C complex, 1,000 mg. (time release) A.M. and P.M.
Aloe vera gel, 1–3 capsules or 1–3 tbsp. liquid daily

277. Venereal Disease

Syphilis and gonorrhea are still among the most widespread venereal diseases, and though sulfa drugs, penicillin, tetracycline, erythromycin, and newer antibiotics are the most effective treatments for them, these remedies cause almost as much need for supplements as the diseases themselves.

MVP (see section 172)
3 acidophilus capsules or 1–2 tbsp. liquid 3 times daily
Extra vitamin C 1,000 mg. A.M. and P.M.
Vitamin K, 100 mcg. daily if on an extended antibiotic program

Genital herpes, America's #1 venereal disease of the '80s, has, unfortunately, made it to the '90s. Like herpes simplex type I, which causes cold sores (see section 221), type II herpes, which causes genital infection, also seems to respond well to lysine-rich foods. As a preventative, it wouldn't be a bad idea to increase your intake of cottage cheese, flounder, tuna fish, peanuts, raw chickpeas (garbanzos), and soybeans. Valtrex and Famuir™ are drugs that—at this writing—seem to be effective in blocking herpes replication, but the final results are not yet in. Meanwhile, I'd suggest a preventative supplement of lysine, 500 mg. daily (with water or juice—no protein) and vitamin C, 1,000 mg. A.M. and P.M. If you already have the virus: lysine, 3 g. (3,000 mg.) 3 times daily—in divided doses—between meals.

CAUTION: If you have symptoms of herpes virus simplex I or II, avoid supplementation of arginine and arginine-rich foods (see section 82).

278. Any Questions About Chapter XV?

When you talk about blood pressure, what's normal and what's high?

You are considered within the normal range if your higher (systolic) pressure is between 100 and 140, and your lower (diastolic) pressure is in the range of 60 to 90. For a healthy young adult, a reading 120/80 is considered normal.

I work at a loom all day and I think I'm developing carpal tunnel syndrome. Are there any supplements you could recommend?

Well, your occupation does put you at risk for developing it. Repetitive stress injury, which is another name for carpal tunnel syndrome, is brought on by overuse of the muscles and tendons of the fingers, hands, arms, and shoulders. I'd suggest a vitamin B complex with B6, 50 mg. 3 times daily; MSM, 1000 mg. with a vitamin C complex A.M. and P.M.; 1 Ev.Ext-33 capsule twice daily; and a daily St. John's wort polyphenol combination supplement until symptoms subside.

My father is on the mend after his stroke, but he'd like to speed up the process. Any supplement suggestions?

Ginkgo biloba and DMAE have both been found to help improve mental function and memory by boosting blood circulation to brain cells. I'd recommend your dad take an MVP (see section 172) with breakfast and dinner, along with a ginkgo biloba, 60 mg. combination capsule (one that contains club moss and DMAE) 3 times daily.

I get cystitis a lot. Are there supplements that can help prevent a recurrence?

Because cystitis is an inflammatory condition of the bladder, usually caused by some type of bacteria, supplements that produce an antibacterial effect and make the urine more acid have been found to provide relief and may help to prevent a recurrence.

Cranberry juice helps to keep problem bacteria from clinging to the wall of the urinary tract. (Cranberry also contains compounds called *anthocyanosides*, which are natural antibiotics.) If you find the juice too tart, you can get the benefit—without added sugar—by taking 1 to 2 cranberry concentrate capsules 1–3 times a day. Drink at least 6–8 glasses of water daily, and avoid caffeine, refined carbohydrates, and alcohol. Increase the natural diuretics in your diet (parsley, celery, asparagus, watercress) and decrease citrus fruits, which produce alkaline urine that can encourage bacterial growth. Along with an MVP (see section 172) you might need a potassium supplement of 95 mg. daily to replenish the potassium lost when you lose fluid.

Are there any herbs that you would recommend for chronic fatigue syndrome?

At this writing there have been no controlled trials with botanicals, but many patients have found that St. John's wort helps enormously in alleviating depression and in improving decreased appetite. Shiitake mushrooms and lemon balm also may help fight CFS by stimulating the body's production of interferon and inhibiting viral replication. And for long-term support of the adrenal glands, Siberian ginseng and Asian ginseng have been recommended as effective adaptogens—that is, herbs that enhance the body's reaction to stress and improve resistance against infection.

There's so much being written about osteoporosis these days that I am now totally confused. Could you explain, simply, how I can tell if I'm at risk (I'm an active forty-eight-year-old woman), and what supplements I should be taking?

It's not all that complicated, but it is important that you know the facts. Osteoporosis is a progressive decrease in bone density that weakens them and makes them more likely to fracture. Up until the age of about thirty—with adequate nutrition, calcium, and vitamin D—our bones increase in density. After age thirty, bones decrease in density—especially if the body is not able to absorb the needed nutrients. And because estrogen is the main female hormone which helps regulate the incorporation of calcium into bone, osteoporosis occurs most frequently in postmenopausal women.

FACTORS THAT INCREASE A WOMAN'S RISK OF OSTEOPOROSIS

- Family history of osteoporosis
- Thin build
- Smoking
- Drinking alcohol
- Early menopause
- No pregnancies
- Insufficient calcium in diet
- Lack of weight-bearing exercise
- Overactive thyroid
- Excessive caffeine intake
- Excessive intake of carbonated beverages that contain phosphorus (which in high amounts can deplete calcium from the body).

Be aware that only weight-bearing exercises (walking, stair climbing, jogging, tennis) increase bone density. Swimming, for instance, does not. As for supplements you should be taking daily, I suggest:

Vitamin C with bioflavonoids, 1,000 mg.
Vitamin D, 400 IU
Vitamin E, 400–800 IU (dry form)
Vitamin K, 100–200 mcg.
Vitamin B12, 500 mcg. sublingual form
Boron, 1–3 mg. (Sodium borate)
Soy isoflavone complex (with 10 mg. daidzein and genistein)
Calcium, 1,000 mg. and magnesium, 500 mg. complex

I've read about a supplement called hydroxyapatite for os-teoporosis. What's in it?

Hydroxyapatite is made from ground-up bovine bone. It may not sound appealing, but it is an effective calcium supplement—and one of the few that is well absorbed by the body. It contains calcium that is identical to the calcium found in our bone, along with other minerals essential for strong bones, including magnesium, fluoride, sodium, and potassium.

Several supplements containing hydroxyapatite are available. Be sure to look for one that provides at least 1,000 mg. of calcium. You can make up the other 200–500 mg. with food. (See section 52.) If you're a vegetarian, calcium citrate is also highly absorbable by the body.

XVI

It's Not All in Your Mind

279. How Vitamins and Minerals Affect Your Moods

The first scientifically documented discovery to relate mental illness to diet occurred when it was found that pellagra (with its depression, diarrhea, and dementia) could be cured with niacin. After that, it was shown that supplementation with the whole B complex produced greater benefits than niacin alone.

Evidence of biochemical causes for mental disturbances continues to mount. Experiments have shown that symptoms of mental illness can be switched off and on by altering vitamin levels in the body.

> Even normal, happy people can become depressed when made deficient in niacin or folic acid.

Dr. R. Shulman, reporting in the *British Journal of Psychiatry,* found that forty-eight out of fifty-nine psychiatric patients had folic-acid deficiencies. Other research has shown that the majority of the mentally and emotionally ill are deficient in one or more of the B-complex vitamins or vitamin C. And even normal, happy people have been found to become depressed and experience other symptoms of emotional disturbance when made niacin or folic-acid deficient.

280. Nutrients That Combat Depression, Anxiety, and Stress

Vitamin B1 (thiamine)	Above-average amounts can help alleviate depression and anxiety attacks.
Vitamin B6 (pyridoxine)	Aids in the proper production of natural antidepressants such as dopamine and norepinephrine.
Pantothenic acid	A natural tension-reliever.
Vitamin C (ascorbic acid)	Essential for combating stress.
Vitamin B12 (cobalamin)	Helps relieve irritability, improve concentration, increase energy, and maintain a healthy nervous system.
Choline	Sends nerve impulses to brain and produces a soothing effect.
Vitamin E (dry form) (alpha-tocopherol)	Aids brain cells in getting needed oxygen.
Folic acid (folacin)	Deficiencies have been found to be contributing factors in mental illness.
Zinc	Promotes mental alertness and aids in proper brain function.

Magnesium	The antistress mineral, necessary for proper nerve functioning.
Manganese	Helps reduce nervous irritability.
Niacin	Vital to the proper function of the nervous system.
Calcium	Alleviates tension, irritability, and promotes relaxation.
Tyrosine	Helps increase the rate at which brain neurons produce the antidepressants dopamine and norepinephrine.
Tryptophan	Works with vitamin B6, niacin, and magnesium to synthesize the brain chemical serotonin, a natural tranquilizer.
Phenylalanine	Necessary for the brain's release of the antidepressants dopamine and norepinephrine.

281. Other Drugs Can Add to Your Problem

Alcohol is a nerve depressant. If you take tranquilizers and a drink, the combination of the two can cause a severe depression—or even death.

If you're on the pill and depressed,
it's not surprising.

If you take a sedative with an antihistamine (such as any found in over-the-counter cold preparations) you might find yourself experiencing tremors and mental confusion.

Oral contraceptives deplete the body of B6, B12, folic acid, and vitamin C. If you're on the pill and depressed, it is not surprising. Your need for B6, necessary for normal tryptophan metabolism, is fifty to a hundred times a non-pill-user's requirement.

DRUGS AND MEDICATIONS THAT YOU MIGHT NOT THINK WOULD CAUSE DEPRESSION—BUT CAN

The following list is not all-inclusive, but all mentioned deplete the body—in varying degrees—of important mood-regulating nutrients. (See section 293.) So if you're taking medication to get well and feeling down, there's a good chance that it's not all in your mind!

- Adrenocorticoids
- Arthritis medicines
- Antihistamines
- Antihypertensives
- Baclofen
- Barbiturates
- Beta-blockers (Inderal™)
- Diuretics
- Estrogens
- Fluorides
- Indomethacin (Indocin™)
- Isoniazid (INH, Nydrazid™)
- Laxatives, lubricants
- Meprednisone (Betapar™)
- Methotrexate (Mexate®)
- Nitrofurantoin (Furadantin®, Macrodantin®)
- Oral contraceptives
- Penicillamine (Cuprimine™)
- Penicillin (all forms)
- Phenytoin (Dilantin™)

- Potassium supplements
- Prednisone
- Procainamide
- Propoxyphene (Darvon™)
- Pyrimethamine (Daraprim™)
- Tetracyclines
- Trimethobenzamide (Tigan®)

282. Any Questions About Chapter XVI?

As the producer of a daily television show, I live in Stress City. I eat sporadically, so I'd like to know if there are some foods that would be better for me than others.

There are. Whether it's a power breakfast or an on-the-set lunch, go for the complex carbohydrates instead of the protein. In other words, take the pasta, rice, or cereal instead of the steak and eggs. Complex carbohydrates help boost your brain levels of the chemical *serotonin,* making you calmer and less stressed—but no less alert.

Every once in a while I find myself depressed when there's really nothing in my life to be depressed about. I'm a twenty-nine-year-old male, happily married, and I don't know why I got into these depressions. Could there be a dietary reason?

Absolutely! Especially if you're consoling yourself with sugar-rich foods. Sugar, be it in refined carbohydrates, alcohol, or whatever, can deplete your body of B vitamins, especially vitamin B1, which can bring on depression. Amino acids (see section, 77, 79) such as tyrosine and phenylalanine can all be used as antidepressants. Check with your doctor, but I'd recommend 500–2,000 mg. (2 g.) of a combination of these amino acids, taken at bedtime or in the morning, with water or juice (no protein). Also, you might want to try a St. John's wort polyphenol combination tablet, 1 daily in the morning.

XVII
Drugs and You

283. Let's Start with Caffeine

There are no doubts about it, caffeine is a powerful drug. That's right, *drug*. Chances are you're not just enjoying your daily coffees or colas, you're addicted to them.

> Caffeine is the most psychoactive
> drug in the world.

Caffeine acts directly upon the central nervous system. It brings about an almost immediate sense of clearer thought and lessens fatigue. It also stimulates the release of stored sugar from the liver, which accounts for the "lift" coffee, cola, and chocolate (the caffeine big three) give. But these benefits may be far outweighed by the side effects:

• The release of stored sugar places heavy stress on the endocrine system. (Eventually, adrenal exhaustion can occur, resulting in hypoglycemia.)
• Heavy coffee drinkers often develop nervousness or become jittery.
• Daily intake adds up over a year, and a lot of caffeine accumulates in the body's fat tissue—and is not easily eliminated.

• Coffee-drinking housewives demonstrated symptoms typical of drug withdrawal when switched to a decaffeinated beverage.

• Dr. John Minton, professor of surgery at Ohio State University and specialist in cancer oncology, has found that excessive intake of methylxanthines (active chemicals in caffeine) can cause benign breast disease and prostate problems.

• Caffeine can rob the body of B vitamins, especially inositol, as well as vitamin C, zinc, potassium, and other minerals.

• Coffee increases the acidity in your gastrointestinal tract and can cause rectal itching.

• Many doctors consider caffeine a culprit in hypertensive heart disease.

• The British medical journal *The Lancet* reported a strong relationship between coffee consumption and cancer of the bladder and the lower urinary tract.

• People who drink five cups of coffee daily have a 50 percent greater chance of having heart attacks than non–coffee drinkers.

• The *Journal of the American Medical Association* reports a disease called caffeinism, with symptoms of appetite loss, weight loss, irritability, insomnia, feelings of flushing, chills, and sometimes a low fever.

• Caffeine has been shown to interfere with DNA replication.

• The Center for Science in the Public Interest advises pregnant women to stay away from caffeine, since studies have shown that the amount contained in about four cups of coffee per day causes birth defects in test animals.

• High doses of caffeine will cause laboratory animals to go into convulsions and then die.

• Can dangerously increase heart rate and blood pressure when taken with decongestants or pulmonary bronchodilators such as the inhalers Proventil™, Ventolin™, Bronkaid®, and Primatine™.

Caffeine can be highly toxic (the lethal dose is estimated to be around 10 g.). New research shows that one quart of coffee consumed in three hours can destroy much of the body's thiamine.

284. You're Getting More Than You Think

The following table shows the amount of caffeine (in milligrams) consumed in specific beverages and drugs:

BEVERAGE	12-OUNCE CAN OR BOTTLE
Coca-Cola™	64.7 mg.
Dr Pepper™	60.9 mg.
Mountain Dew™	54.7 mg.
Diet Dr Pepper™	54.2 mg.
Tab™	49.4 mg.
Pepsi-Cola™	43.1 mg.
RC Cola™	33.7 mg.
Diet RC Cola™	33.0 mg.
Diet-Rite™	0.0 mg.
Coffee	*Per Serving*
Instant	66.0 mg.
Percolated	110.0 mg.
Dripolated	146.0 mg.
Tea Bags	
Black 5-minute brew	46.0 mg.
Black 1-minute brew	28.0 mg.
Loose Tea	
Black 5-minute brew	40.0 mg.
Green 5-minute brew	35.0 mg.
Cocoa	13.0 mg.
Chocolate	
Milk chocolate, 1 oz.	6.0 mg.
Dark semisweet chocolate, 1 oz.	20.0 mg.

DRUGS	PER PILL
Anacin™ (also available without caffeine)	32.0 mg.
Bio Slim T capsules	140.0 mg.
Cafergot™	100.0 mg.
Dexatrim™ (also available without caffeine)	200.0 mg.
Empirin™	32.0 mg.
Emprazil™	30.0 mg.
Excedrin™	65.0 mg.
(Excedrin P.M.™ has no caffeine, but does have an antihistamine.)	
Fiorinal™	130.0 mg.
Midol™	32.4 mg.
No-Doz™	100.0 mg.
Soma CMPD	32.0 mg.
Triaminicin™	30.0 mg.
Vanquish™	33.0 mg.
Vivarin™	200.0 mg.

285. Caffeine Alternatives

Decaffeinated coffee is *not* the best solution to the caffeine problem. Trichlorethylene, which was first used to remove caffeine, was found to cause a high incidence of cancer in test animals. Though the manufacturers have switched to methylene chloride, which is safer, it, too, introduces the same carbon-to-chloride bond into the body that is characteristic of so many toxic insecticides.

> Ginseng can give you a
> real lift.

Regular tea is not the answer either, since that has nearly as much caffeine. But herb teas can be quite invigorating, and most natural-food stores have a wide variety to choose from. Then, too, ginseng can give you a real lift, much like the one you get from caffeine, without the side effects.

Colas, diet or regular, have become as popular as coffee for those who enjoy the caffeine boost. Try substituting club soda or mineral water, or even a flavored soda if you must. You won't get the caffeine lift, but you'll be doing your body a big favor.

286. What Alcohol Does to Your Body

Alcohol is the most widely used drug in our society, and because it is so available, most people don't think of it as a drug. But it is; and if misused, it can cause a lot of damage to your body.

• Alcohol is not a stimulant, but actually a sedative-depressant of the central nervous system.
• It is capable of rupturing veins.
• It does not warm you up, but causes you to feel colder by increasing perspiration and body heat loss.
• It destroys brain cells by causing the withdrawal of necessary water from them.
• It can deplete the body of vitamins B1, B2, B6, B12, folic acid, vitamin C, vitamin K, zinc, magnesium, and potassium.
• Four drinks a day are capable of causing organ damage.
• It can hamper the liver's ability to process fat.

287. What You Drink and When You Drink It

Just because the alcohol content varies in different beverages, don't be fooled. It is true that beer has only about 4 percent alcohol, wine about 12 percent, and whiskey up to 50 percent; but a can of beer, a glass of wine, and a shot of whiskey all have virtually the identical inebriation potential. In other words, 4 cans of beer can get you just as tipsy as 4 shots of tequila.

> A Bloody Mary at breakfast is
> more harmful than a whiskey
> sour at dinner.

Surprisingly, what you drink doesn't matter nearly as much as *when* you drink it. Dr. John D. Palmer, of the University of Massachusetts, reports that the length of time alcohol remains in circulation in your blood varies throughout the day. Which means, of course, the more time the alcohol spends in your blood, the more time it has to act on your brain cells. Between 2 A.M. and noon are the most vulnerable hours, while late afternoon to early evening are the least. A cocktail at dinner will be burned away 25 percent faster than a Bloody Mary at breakfast, and the last drink of a party, consumed after midnight, is metabolized relatively more slowly than the ones that preceded it, producing a more lasting rise in blood alcohol.

288. Vitamins to Decrease Your Taste for Alcohol

> Heavy drinkers can break
> the habit.

Research at the University of Texas has shown that if alcoholic mice are fed nutritious, vitamin-enriched diets, they quickly lose their interest in alcohol. This seems to hold true for people, since heavy drinkers have been able to break the habit—and even lose interest—with the right diet and proper nutritional supplements. Vitamins A, D, E, C, and all the B vitamins—especially B12, B6, and B1—along with calcium and magnesium, choline, inositol, niacin, and a very high-protein diet have brought about the best results. Dr. H. L. Newbold, of New York, who has worked with alcoholics, recommends building up to 5 glutamine capsules

(200 mg.)—not glutamic acid—3 times a day to control drinking, and working with a good nutritionally oriented doctor for the best all-around regimen. (See section 342.)

Recently, the ancient Chinese herb kudzu, which has been used as an antidote for hangovers, is being used to help break alcohol addiction. This is not really surprising since Asian herbalists have used a tea brewed from the kudzu root to treat alcoholism for the past 2,000 years. Kudzu contains two phytochemicals, daidzin and daidzein, which help reduce blood alcohol levels. It is available as a supplement in 500 mg. capsules. For best results, take one 3 times daily, before or after drinking alcohol.

289. The Lowdown on Marijuana and Hashish

Marijuana and hashish come from the hemp plant *Cannabis sativa*. The marijuana consists of the chopped leaves and stems of the plant, while the hashish is formed from the resin scraped from the flowering tops.

Both of these drugs can be either smoked or eaten. If smoked, the effects usually last from 1 to 3 hours. If eaten, they can last from 4 to 10 hours, though it takes longer for the user to feel them.

Unlike other illicit drugs, marijuana and hashish have the unusual property of "reverse tolerance," meaning that seasoned users need less of the drug to get high than first-timers. Essentially, these drugs act as intoxicants, relaxants, tranquilizers, appetite stimulants, and mild hallucinogens, though effects vary with the individual.

The smoking of one joint can cause a rise in blood pressure, an increased heartbeat, a lowering of body temperature and vitamin-C levels in the blood. It has been found, too, that smoking marijuana during pregnancy can cause low birth weight in newborns and increase the risk of lung cancer.

CAUTION: Toxic psychosis can occur if *Cannabis* is eaten and the user hasn't been able to judge the amount ingested.

Supplements and foods that can help users
Increase your intake of citrus fruits and green leafy vegetables. (Those "munchies" usually give you more than your share of refined sugars and carbohydrates, meaning that you've deprived yourself of necessary B vitamins.)
Vitamin C, 1,000 mg. A.M. and P.M.
Vitamin E, 100–400 IU 1–3 times daily to protect your lungs

290. Cocaine Costs a Lot More Than You Think—in More Ways Than One

Cocaine is a vasoconstrictor, a stimulant of the central nervous system, and potentiates the effects of nerve stimulation. Applied externally, it blocks nerve impulses and produces a numbing sensation.

The wrong "cut" can kill.

What users get—no matter how much they pay—is rarely more than 60 percent pure cocaine. The rest is the "cut," which is used by dealers to dilute or enhance the drug for more profit. Some cuts are relatively harmless: lactose, dextrose, inositol (a B vitamin), and mannitol. Other nondrug cuts, such as cornstarch, talcum powder, and flour, can be dangerous because they are basically insoluble in blood and can clot up in the body. *Benzocaine,* which is pharmacologically active, can also cause blood clots and serious complications when used as a cut for cocaine.

Because the drug is absorbed rapidly through the mucous membranes, nasal inhalation is the most popular form of taking cocaine, though it is also often applied locally under the tongue and eyelids, and on the genital region. It can also be injected intravenously or smoked in a process called "freebasing," or as crack, which is cocaine, baking soda, and water distilled into an instantly smokable "rock."

The short-lived effects of coke (about a half hour) are usually euphoria, feelings of psychic energy and self-confidence, but then more of the drug is necessary to recapture the high. Dependence is intense.

Aside from causing nosebleeds, rapid heartbeat, cold sweats, appetite loss, and in some cases the feeling that gnats or bugs are crawling on you, cocaine can cause convulsions, vomiting, anaphylactic shock, and death. Its toxicity is unpredictable. Even small doses with the wrong cut or taken by susceptible individuals can be lethal.

Supplements and foods to help users
MVP (see section 172)
Chelated calcium (500 mg.) and magnesium (250 mg.) tablets, twice daily—one at bedtime
A kava kava capsule may be taken at bedtime for restless sleep
Vitamin C, 1,000 mg., vitamin E, 200–400 IU, and vitamin B complex, 100 mg., all 1–3 times daily

291. Help for Coming Down or Kicking the Cocaine Habit

Tyrosine, an amino acid that's usually found in meat and wheat (see section 85), has been found to alleviate the depression, fatigue, and irritability that make quitting cocaine so difficult. At Fair Oaks Hospital in Summit, New Jersey, addicts took the amino acid in their orange juice for 12 days. They also took vitamin C, the B vitamins (thiamine, niacin, and riboflavin), and tyrosine hydroxylase, the enzyme that helps the body use tyrosine. The results were remarkably effective. One St. John's wort polyphenol complex tablet taken in the morning is also effective in alleviating depression.

292. Whether Rx or Over-the-Counter, There Are Alternatives to Drugs

Americans consume over 1.5 million pounds of tranquilizers and well over 4 million pounds of antibiotics a year. Are all these drugs necessary? Probably not; but when people pay for a visit to their doctor, they expect to walk away with a prescription.

But there are alternatives, which orthomolecular physicians and nutritionally minded individuals are trying before resorting to drugs.

> Inositol and pantothenic acid
> instead of sleeping pills

Dr. Robert C. Atkins, author of *Dr. Atkins' New Diet Revolution,* has had patients try pantothenic acid and about 2,000 mg. of inositol as sleep-inducers, instead of Seconal™, Nembutal™, Butisol™, or other barbiturate sleeping pills. He also had success using B15 to control blood sugar, and B13 (orotic acid) to lower high blood pressure.

So before you pop that next pill, you might want to consider some natural alternatives.

DRUG	NATURAL ALTERNATIVES
Antacids	Deglycyrrizinated licorice extract (DGL), papaya, lukewarm herbal teas such as fenugreek, slippery elm, comfrey, and meadowsweet (no lemon), MSM (methylsulfonylmethane).
Antibiotics and antihistamines	Garlic, vitamin C, and (yep, it's true) chicken soup have amazing antibiotic and antihistamine properties. Other fine infection-fighters and histamine-hinderers are vitamin A, zinc, selenium, grapefruit seed extract, echinacea, pantothenic acid, quercetin, and green tea.
Antidepressants	Kava kava, St. John's wort, calcium and magnesium;

	vitamins B1, B6, and B12, tyrosine and phenylalanine (do not take in conjunction with MAO inhibitors).
Antihypertensives	Omega-3 fatty acids, magnesium, calcium; cruciferous vegetables (broccoli, cabbage, kale), celery; vitamin C, potassium (not for anyone with a kidney disorder); dong quai, Siberian ginseng.
Antidiarrhesis	Rice, bananas, and *lactobacillus acidophilus* yogurt for diarrhea caused by antibiotics.
Antinauseants	Vitamins B1 and B6 can help alleviate nausea due to motion or morning sickness; ginger root capsules; Ev.Ext-33. Niacin, bioflavonoids, and standardized ginkgo biloba can help in the treatment of dizziness and queasiness due to diseases of the inner ear.
Decongestants	Vitamins A and C; quercetin, echinacea, goldenseal, and bayberry herbal teas; potassium.
Diuretics (water pills)	Alfalfa, asparagus, celery, dandelion leaves, and vitamin B6 can work as natural diuretics.
Laxatives	Vitamin C, vitamins B1, B2, B6, and B12, potassium, magnesium, acidophilus, alfalfa, hawthorn berry, gotu kola, skullcap, bran, and water.
Tranquilizers (sedatives, relaxants, etc.)	Valerian, melatonin, choline, niacin, vitamins B1, B6, B12, calcium, and magnesium; manganese, zinc, pantothenic

> acid, and inositol; kava kava, St.
> John's wort; phenylalanine and
> tyrosine.

CAUTION: If you are already on a medication, do not go off it suddenly to switch to a natural alternative. Work with an experienced, nutritionally oriented professional (see section 342) so you can adjust dosages properly while you wean yourself from drugs.

293. The Great Medicine Rip-Off

More than ever before, Americans are gulping down drugs. What most people don't realize is that a lot of these medications—prescription as well as over-the-counter—are taking as much as they're giving, at least nutritionally. All too often the drugs either stop the absorption of nutrients or interfere with the cells' ability to use them.

A recent study showed that ingredients found in common over-the-counter cold, pain, and allergy remedies actually lowered the blood level of vitamin A. Since vitamin A protects and strengthens the mucous membranes lining the nose, throat, and lungs, a deficiency could give bacteria a cozy home to multiply in, prolonging the illness the drug was meant to alleviate.

> Aspirin can *triple* the excretion
> rate of vitamin C.

Aspirin, the household wonder drug, the most common ingredient in pain-relievers, cold and sinus remedies, is a vitamin-C thief. Even a small amount can *triple* the excretion rate of vitamin C from the body. It can also lead to a deficiency of folic acid and vitamin B, which could cause anemia as well as digestive disturbances.

Corticosteroids (cortisone, prednisone), used for easing arthritis pain, skin problems, blood and eye disorders, and asthma, have been found to be related to lowered zinc levels.

According to a study that appeared in the *Postgraduate Medical Journal,* a significant number of people who take barbiturates have low calcium levels.

Laxatives and antacids, taken by millions, have been found to disturb the body's calcium and phosphorus metabolism. And any laxative taken to excess can deplete large amounts of potassium as well as vitamins A, D, E, and K.

Diuretics, commonly prescribed for high blood pressure, and antibiotics are also potassium thieves.

The following is a list of commonly prescribed drugs that can induce nutrient deficiencies and the nutrients they deplete. Look it over before you take your next medicine.

THIEVING DRUG	NUTRIENTS DEPLETED
Alcohol (including alcohol-containing cough syrups, elixirs, and OTC medications such as Nyquil™)	Vitamins A, B1, B2, biotin, choline, niacin, vitamin B15, folic acid, and magnesium
Ammonium Chloride (e.g., Ambenyl™, expectorant, Triaminicol™, decongestant cough syrup, P.V. Tussin syrup)	Vitamin C
Antacids (e.g., Maalox™, Mylanta™, Di-Gel™ liquid)	Calcium, phosphate, copper, iron, magnesium, potassium, zinc, protein
Antibiotics (e.g., Amoxil™, Ceclor™, Keflex™, Augmentin™, PenVee K™)	B complex; vitamins C, K, acidophilus
Anticoagulants (e.g., Coumadin™, dicumarol, Panwarfin™)	Vitamins A & K
Antihistamines (e.g.,	Vitamin C

Chlor-Trimeton™,
Pyrabenzamine™)

Aspirin (and remember, APC drugs contain *aspirin*)	Vitamins A, B complex, C; calcium, potassium
Barbiturates (e.g., pheno-barbital, Seconal™, Nembutal™, Butisol™, Tuinal™)	Vitamins A, D, folic acid, & C
Beta Blockers (e.g., Inderal™, Lopressor™, Sectral™)	Coenzyme-Q10
Caffeine (present in all APC medicines)	B1, inositol & biotin; potassium, zinc, can also inhibit calcium & iron assimilation Vitamin K & niacin
Chemotherapy drugs	Most nutrients
Cholesterol-lowering drugs (e.g., Cholestid™, Questran™, Locholest™)	Vitamins A, D, E, K, B12, beta-carotene, folic acid, iron & fat
Clofibrate (Atromid-s™)	Vitamin K
Colchicine (Colbenemid™)	B12, A, and potassium
Corticosteroids (e.g., cortisone, hydrocortisone)	Calcium, vitamin D, Potassium, selenium, zinc
Diethylstilbestrol (DES)	Vitamin B6
Diuretics (e.g., Diuril™ Hydrodiuril™, SER-AP-ES, Lasix™)	B complex, potassium, magnesium, zinc, & coenzyme-Q10
Estrogen replacement (e.g., Premarin™, Menest™)	Vitamin B6
Fluorides	Vitamin C
Glutethimide	Folic acid

(Doriden™)

Gout medications (e.g., Zyloprim™)	Beta-carotene, vitamin B12, sodium, potassium
Isoniazid (INH, Nydrazid™)	B6
Kanamycin (Kantrex™)	Vitamins K & B12
Laxatives, lubricant (e.g., castor oil, mineral oil)	Vitamins A, D, E, K, calcium & phosphorus
Meprednisone (Betapar™)	Vitamins B6, C, zinc, & potassium
Methotrexate (Mexate®)	Folic acid
Nitrofurantoin (e.g., Furadantin®, Macrodantin®)	Folic acid
NSAIDs (e.g., Anaprox™, Dolobid™, Indocin™)	Vitamins B1, C & folic acid
Oral contraceptives (e.g., Brevicon™, Demulen™, Enovid™, Lo/Ovral™, Tri Norinyl™, Ovral™)	Folic acid, vitamins C, B2, B6, B12, & E
Penicillamine (Cuprimine™)	Vitamin B6
Penicillin (in all its forms)	Vitamins B6, niacin, & K
Phenylbutazone (e.g., Azolid™, Butazolidin™)	Folic acid
Phenytoin (Dilantin™)	Vitamin B12, D, folic acid, & calcium
Prednisone (e.g., Meticorten, Prednisolone™, Orasone™)	Vitamins B6, D, C, zinc, & potassium
Propantheline (Pro-Banthine™)	Vitamin K

Proton pump inhibitors (e.g., Prevacid™, Prilosec™)	Vitamin B12, protein
Pyrimethamine (Daraprim™)	Folic acid
Sulfonamides, systemic (e.g., Bactrim™, Gantanol™, Tantrisin™, Septra™)	Folic acid, vitamins K & B12
Sulfonamides and topical steroids (e.g., Aerosporin™, Cortisporin™, Neosporin™, Polysporin™)	Vitamins K, B12, & folic acid
Tetracyclines (e.g., Achromycin-V™, Sumycin™, Tetracyn™)	Vitamin K, calcium, magnesium, & iron
Tobacco	Vitamins C, B1, and folic acid; calcium
Tranquilizers (e.g., Clorazil™, Haldol™, Moban™, Loxitane™)	Vitamin B2, coenzyme-Q10
Tricyclic antidepressants (e.g., Elavil™, Tofranil™, Norpramin™)	Vitamin B2, coenzyme-Q10
Trifluoperazine (Stelazine™)	Vitamin B12
Triamterene (Dyrenium)	Folic acid
Tuberculosis drugs	Vitamins B6, D, E, niacin, & calcium
Ulcer medications (e.g., Tagamet™, Pepcid™, Axid™, Zantac™)	Vitamin D, B12, folic acid & zinc

294. Any Questions About Chapter XVII?

I know that coffee can give you the jitters, but I've switched to drinking decaffeinated, and still find myself getting moody and uptight. Can such a small amount of caffeine do this?

Caffeine isn't the only substance in coffee that has an effect on behavior. There is, though not yet identified, another substance in both regular and decaffeinated coffee (but not in tea) which blocks the normal activity of brain opiates (endorphins), which act as painkillers and mood elevators.

Some prescription medications that I take are specifically labeled: "Do not drink alcoholic beverages while taking this medication." If there is no label, does that mean it's safe to have a drink while on them?

Only if you think that Russian roulette is safe. Alcohol can interact adversely with almost all drugs. In fact, any drug that's available in time-release or spansule form can become dangerous if taken in conjunction with alcohol. The coating that's supposed to allow the drug to be released slowly over an extended time period (usually 8–12 hours) can dissolve rapidly in alcohol and give you an uncomfortable and potentially toxic dose of the medication. My advice is get well first, then celebrate afterward.

XVIII
Losing It—Diets by the Pound

295. The Atkins Diet

This diet (*Dr. Atkins' Diet Revolution, Dr. Atkins' Superenergy Diet, Dr. Atkins' New Diet Revolution*), ignores calorie content and focuses on carbohydrate restriction; but unlike other low-carbohydrate programs, Dr. Atkins calls for almost *no* carbohydrates (at least for the first week). By doing this, the body begins to throw off ketones (tiny carbon fragments that are by-products of incompletely burned fat) in amounts sufficient to account for substantial weight loss. According to Dr. Atkins, because carbohydrates are the first fuel your body burns for energy, if none are taken in then the body will draw upon stored fat for fuel, and as ketones are excreted, hunger as well as weight will disappear.

The pros and cons are many (especially since the diet also encourages high fat consumption despite its inherent health hazard), but if you are on this diet, Dr. Atkins does recommend a high-potency vitamin supplement. I would suggest following the MVP program outlined in section 172, and taking an additional 1,000 mg. vitamin C with bioflavonoids if you've cut out all citrus fruit. Also at least 50 mg. B complex with morning and evening meal, 1 g. potassium divided over three meals, and 400–800 mcg. folic acid daily.

296. The Zone Diet

The "zone" is an expression often used by athletes to describe a near-euphoric state where the body and mind work at peak efficiency. In *Mastering the Zone,* Barry Sears, Ph.D. presents a dietary approach to reaching this state by tightly controlling portions of protein, carbohydrates, and fat in an equal number of "blocks" at every meal. Three "blocks" for women, four for men. (1 protein block = 7 g. protein; 1 carbohydrate block = 9 grams of carbohydrate; 1 fat block = 1.5 grams of fat.) Essentially, the zone diet obtains 30 percent of calories from protein, 40 percent from carbohydrates, and the remaining 30 percent from fat. Sears believes that getting 55–60 percent of your daily calories from carbohydrates, which is what the Food Guide Pyramid recommends, is too much. His diet restricts foods with a high glycemic index (see section 96), but not just refined carbs. Sears also advises avoiding carrots, bananas, brown rice, and whole-grain breads—which I don't agree with.

Essential fatty acids are necessary for reaching the "zone," which is good. Gamma-linolenic acid (GLA) of the omega-6 fatty acids is, according to Sears, the most important. But too much GLA—through supplements or foods—can negate zone benefits unless the GLA is properly balanced with enough eicospentaenoic acid (EPA), which can be tricky to figure out.

The diet advocates healthy foods, but rigid quantities at prescribed times—even if you're not hungry. Whether you're successful at reaching the "zone" or not, I suggest covering your nutritional bases with an MVP (see section 172).

297. Weight Watchers

This is a long-term regimen that advocates three meals a day with measured portions of protein, carbohydrates, and fat.

Though the program is nutritionally well-rounded, most Weight Watchers that I've met agree that supplements have helped them keep up their energy levels while their calorie intake goes down. The MVP in section 172 should fill the bill.

298. Liquid Protein Diets

These diets are dangerous and potentially lethal. In fact, the Food and Drug Administration has issued a ruling that all protein supplements (liquid or powder) used in reducing diets must carry the following label:

Warning—Very low-calorie protein diets (below 800 calories per day) may cause serious illness or death. Do not use for weight reduction without medical supervision. Use with particular care if you are taking medication. Not for use by infants, children, or pregnant or nursing women.

Radical diets, such as these, can cause disastrous effects on the body, not the least of which being abnormal heart function and severe deficiencies in vital minerals due to extremely rapid weight loss. I couldn't in good conscience offer supplement suggestions, since I firmly believe that these diets should not be undertaken without strict medical supervision.

299. Zen Macrobiotic Diet

Contrary to popular belief, this diet is not connected with the Zen Buddhists, but is the creation of a Japanese man named George Ohsawa. Though it has gained many adherents, it is nutritionally dangerous when strictly followed.

There are ten stages to the diet, and milk is prohibited. You start by giving up dessert and eating nothing but grains, preferably brown rice. The diet, based on the oriental yin-yang philosophy, restricts fluid intake, which is dangerous as is the lack of nutrients provided in meals consisting of nothing but brown rice. Followers believe that if your thoughts are right you can produce vitamins, minerals, and proteins within your own body, and actually change one element to another.

Just in case your thoughts aren't always right, it would be advisable if you are on this diet, or just a strict vegetarian one, to take supplements. A high-potency vegetarian multiple-vitamin and mineral tablet twice daily along with a good B complex with folic acid is recommended. Also vitamin B12, 100 mcg. 1–3 times a day.

300. Kelp, Lecithin, Vinegar, B6 Diet

This low-profile, word-of-mouth diet has been around for more than two decades and is still popular. The basic components of the diet can be obtained in one tablet that contains kelp, lecithin, apple-cider vinegar, and vitamin B6. There are two potencies available: single and double strength. (With the single strength you take two tablets with each meal and with the double strength you take one.)

As with any diet that cuts down caloric intake, an MVP with breakfast and dinner is recommended. Also a B complex and 500 mg. vitamin C twice daily.

301. Mindell Dieting Tips

• Before starting any diet, check with your physician. If you don't feel that your family doctor understands your dieting needs, contact a bariatrician, who specializes in the field. For the name of one in your area, write to the American Society of Bariatric Physicians, Suite 300, 5200 South Quebec, Englewood, Colorado 80111. (Enclose a stamped self-addressed envelope.)

• If you're on a low- or no-carbohydrate diet, beware of artificially sweetened "sugarless" or "dietetic" gum or candy that has sorbitols, mannitols, or hexitols. These ingredients are metabolized in the system as carbohydrates, *only more slowly!*

• If you're on a diet that allows alcohol, a glass of wine before dinner stimulates the gastric juices and aids in proper digestion.

• If you do have wine, remember that dry white has fewer calories than red.

• If you're eating popcorn as a low-calorie snack, be aware that movie-theater popcorn has twice the calories per cup as "light" microwave—and two and a half times that of air-popped.

• When a recipe calls for a cup of sour cream, substitute low-fat yogurt and you'll save over 300 calories.

• Remember that the body's natural response to a decreased food intake is to burn *fewer* calories—which is why diets without exercise don't work in the long run.

• Watch out for such diet fallacies as:

Gelatin dessert is nonfattening.
Grapefruit causes you to lose weight.
Fruits have no calories.
High-protein foods have no calories.
A pound of steak is not as fattening as a potato.
Toast has many fewer calories than bread.

• Whatever you're eating, sit down to eat it, and eat it slowly. (You might expend more calories standing than sitting, but you tend to eat more that way, too.) Also, don't read or watch TV until you finish your meal.

• When selecting fruit, remember that all fruits are not equal, that an apple, a banana, or a pear has more calories and carbohydrates than a half cantaloupe, a cup of raw strawberries, or a fresh tangerine.

• When choosing your vegetable, take green beans instead of peas (you save 40 calories on a half-cup serving), spinach instead of mixed vegetables (you save 35 calories), and mashed potatoes—if you must—instead of hash browns (you save 139 calories).

• Carbohydrate watchers, don't underestimate onions; one cup of cooked onions has 18 g.

• If you're counting every calorie, realize that 1 tablespoon of lecithin granules contains 50 calories and a lecithin capsule about 8.

• Try a one-day-a-week water fast (the ancient Greeks did it). Limit yourself to cold filtered tap or bottled (not iced) or herb tea with lemon or lime juice. Nothing else. This should pep you up, too.

302. Mindell Vitamin-Balanced Diet to Lose and Live By

I know your mother told it to you, but it is true anyway—breakfast *is* the most important meal of the day. It comes after the longest period of time that you've been without food, and you cannot catch up nutritionally by eating a good lunch or dinner later.

If you're dieting, it is especially important to perk up your energy level at the start of the day.

BREAKFAST

8 oz. nonfat or low-fat soy milk (or juice)
A flavored low-calorie soy food protein powder
4 ice cubes
Mix well in blender for 60 seconds. Calories, approximately: 150

This mixture can be frozen and used as a dessert for dinner or a pick-me-up snack if your calorie quotient allows.

Lunch is a tricky meal. Fast-food restaurants are seductively convenient, and nothing blows a diet faster than "a few french fries" and a "tiny milkshake." If you really want to lose weight, think more along these lines:

LUNCH

A modest portion (3–5 ounces) of water-packed canned or fresh fish, skinless chicken or white meat turkey, a raw vegetable salad (with lemon or vinegar dressing), and a piece of fruit.

OR

A low-cal turkey sandwich (3 oz. turkey, 1 tsp. mayo, 2 slices whole-wheat bread, lettuce, thin-slice tomato), small carrot, ½ cup unsweetened applesauce, mixed with ½ cup nonfat yogurt.

OR

A diet pizza (2 oz. sliced low-fat mozzarella cheese, ½ whole-wheat muffin, small sliced tomato, 1 tsp. olive oil with oregano sprinkled on top), ¼ cantaloupe or 1 cup frozen melon balls.

(Vary lunches from day to day.)

Dinner is usually a dieter's downfall, but it doesn't have to be that way:

DINNER

Five nights a week you should have fish (sole, trout, salmon, halibut, etc.) or poultry broiled, boiled, or roasted (remove skin before eating—but leave on for cooking); and two nights a week you can have meat, once again broiled, boiled, or roasted; a cooked vegetable; a large salad (no more than 1 teaspoon oil in the dressing); a small boiled or baked potato once or twice a week; and a fresh fruit for dessert. Substituting tofu for meat or poultry is a great way to cut calories and fat.

BEVERAGES

For best results (and improved health) stay away from alcohol—try sparkling mineral water with lime instead. Also be sure to drink at least six 8-ounce glasses of water daily. Herb teas, hot or iced, are recommended alternatives to diet sodas—especially those that contain caffeine. (See section 284.)

SUPPLEMENTS

MVP (see section 172)
Calcium (500 mg.) or magnesium (250 mg.) 1 twice daily
    for men, 2 twice daily for women
Chromium picolinate complex, 200 mcg. 1–3 times daily

303. Supplements for Eating More and Gaining Less

The amino acids arginine and ornithine (see section 84) have been found to stimulate the pituitary gland to continue to produce growth hormone, which can rejuvenate your metabolism. While some hormones encourage the body to store fat, growth hormone acts as a mobilizer of fat, helping you to look trimmer and have more energy as well.

> You can rejuvenate your metabolism
> while you sleep.

Best of all, you can rejuvenate your metabolism while you sleep because that's when growth hormone is secreted! Supplements are available in tablets or powder and work best when taken on an empty stomach with water or juice (no protein). For reducing benefits, take 2 grams (2,000 mg.) immediately before retiring.

CAUTION: Arginine is contraindicated for growing children, persons with schizophrenic conditions, and anyone who has a herpes virus infection. Doses exceeding 20 grams can be dangerous.

304. More Natural Alternatives to Diet Drugs

Because of the dangers of diet drugs, many people are seeking safer alternatives to weight loss. The following is a list of natural alternatives you might want to consider using along with your diet and exercise regimen if you'd like to be in better shape than the shape you're in.

Chitosan: This is an effective fat blocker that enhances weight loss by preventing the absorption of fat. As it passes through the digestive tract it can absorb 4–6 times its weight in fat, flushing it out of the body before it can be metabolized and stored as excess pounds. Unfortunately, chitosan can also rob you of important fat-soluble vitamins, such as vitamins E, A, D, and K. It should only be used occasionally, and not for more than two weeks at a time. If you take it, you *must* supplement your diet with fat-soluble vitamins and essential fatty acids. Take 1–3 250 mg. tablets daily with meals. Be sure to drink 8 ounces of filtered water with each tablet.

CAUTION: Do not use chitosan if you have an allergy to shellfish. This supplement (or any other fat blocker) should not be used by pregnant or lactating women or by children.

Coenzyme-Q10 (Co-Q10): This great antioxidant, which also facilitates the production of energy, may make it easier for body to burn fat for fuel. (See section 110.)

Conjugated Linoleic Acid (CLA): Helps reduce the amount of body fat while increasing muscle. Since muscle burns excess calories, the more muscle you have, the less likely you are to become overweight. (CLA may also protect against many forms of cancer.) As a diet aid, I suggest three 600–1,200 mg. capsules before meals.

DHAP: This is a combination of pyruvate and its precursor, dihydroxyacetone, and referred to as DHAP. Available as a supplement, it increases athletic stamina and the amount of fat lost during exercise. Even at rest, it helps the body burn fat for fuel. The recommended dosage is 2–5 grams taken twice daily with meals. It is not recommended for children or pregnant women.

DL-Phenylalanine, tyrosine, and 5-HTP: This amino acid combination, soon to be available as a patented formula supplement, has been found to help curb sugar and carbohydrate cravings that are the downfall of binge dieters. (Recommended dosages for individual amino acids can be found in Chapter V.)

Ephedra (Ma huang) and St. John's wort: A potent combination that can help suppress appetite and boost metabolism.

CAUTION: Ephedra can cause dangerous side effects and should not be taken by anyone who has a history of heart disease or who is taking a prescription antidepressant. I recommend consulting a nutritionally oriented practitioner before using ephedra in any diet regimen.

Hydrocitric Acid (HCA): This is the active ingredient extracted from the sour Indian fruit garcinia cambogia, which Ayurvedic healers have used as a natural appetite suppressant for centuries. Marketed under the tradenames of Citrin™ and Citrimax™, as well as HCA, it is non–habit forming. Some studies suggest it can reduce caloric intake by as much as 10 percent. For best results, take three 500–750 mg. capsules daily, half an hour before meals—in conjunction with a sensible diet and exercise regimen.

L-Carnitine: This vitamin-like nutrient can help increase physical stamina and promote weight loss. (It can also lower high blood cholesterol while raising levels of good HDL cholesterol.) I suggest 1–3 capsules (250–500 mg. strength) taken half an hour before meals.

Pyruvate: Can increase stamina and help you burn fat for fuel—even *without* exercise. Pyruvate is naturally found in the body as a by-product of normal metabolism; it triggers the release of adenosine triphosphate (ATP), the fuel that runs the body. It also helps lower cholesterol and blood pressure. Pyruvate enthusiasts report that doses as low as 5 grams daily have produced good results. There are few side effects, except for occasional stomach upset, but it is not recommended for pregnant women or children.

305. Any Questions About Chapter XVIII?

I know that no more than 30 percent of my daily calories should come from fat. But I'm not good at figuring out percentages. I read labels, but I'm still confused. Is there an easy way to determine how much I'm getting?

As a matter of fact, a newsletter called *Alternatives* has come up with one. Always keep in mind that 1 gram of fat equals about 9 calories. Therefore, to keep your fat intake below 30 percent daily, when you check food labels be sure that for every 100 calories there are no more than 3 grams of fat.

What is a setpoint? And what does it have to do with losing weight?

The setpoint theory is one of the most widely accepted on weight gain and loss. It holds that fatness is caused by the setting of an area in the hypothalamus (part of the brain), sometimes called an appestat, which controls your appetite for food. Needless to say, everyone's appestat is not on the same setting.

Glycerol, which is bound and released according to the fat content of a cell, along with the blood level of insulin, informs the brain of the body's fat reserves and sets your appestat accordingly. Unfortunately, external influences—such as the aroma and taste of delectable food—can *raise* your appestat.

But you can reset your setpoint by exercising regularly. In other words, you'll reduce your appetite by lowering the point at which you feel full.

To reset for weight loss, the minimum requirement is half an hour of aerobic exercise 3 times a week. A simple and effective way to do this is by walking 2 miles in half an hour 3 times a week (or 1 mile in 15 minutes 6 times a week.)

Does grapefruit really help you lose weight?

If you eat it instead of chocolate cake it does. Grapefruit, which has been touted as a miracle diet food, is little more than a fine source of vitamin C, and other nutrients in lesser amounts. Despite its being sold in pill form, it's still just grapefruit. On the bright side, half a grapefruit only has 58 calories.

I've heard that you're likely to be more successful dieting in warm weather. Is this true?

If this were completely true, dieters would be moving to Florida and Southern California in droves. What has been purported by Susan Perry and Jim Dawson in *The Secrets Our Body Clocks Reveal* (Rawson Associates) is that we are genetically disposed to have extra fat layers in fall and winter. Therefore, when days start getting longer, in spring, it's allegedly easier for us to lose weight. The question is, easier than what?

What real dangers are there in liquid dieting—aside from running the risk of gaining the weight back?

Extremely real dangers. Many people who go on very-low-calorie diets (VLCD) do so without proper medical supervision. They are unaware that a VLCD is designed for people who are at least 30 percent over their ideal weight (as determined by a physician—not a fashion model). Once on a VLCD, a dieter must be medically monitored (receiving regular blood tests, electrocardiograms, and blood pressure checks).

If you are less than 30 percent over your ideal weight, and you go on one of the over-the-counter (OTC) liquid diets, substituting it for all meals (instead of the recommended one or two for a limited period), you risk losing too much muscle, bone, and lean body mass in proportion to fat—causing possible heart arrhythmia, permanently slowed metabolism, fatigue, and, in extreme cases, even death.

I've replaced virtually all my fatty foods with fat-free or fake fat substitutes and I'm gaining weight. What gives?

My guess is that you're eating more. Fat substitutes don't slow down digestion the way real fats do. They fool your taste buds, but your not your stomach. They're a fast fix and you'll find yourself hungrier sooner after eating them. Studies have shown that people who replaced 20 percent of their fat with fat substitutes (see section 94) were not only wildly hungry by the end of the day, they wound up eating almost twice their normal amount of fat-filled foods the next day. Forget those substitutes and find filling, low-fat alternatives. And keep in mind that low-fat and no-fat do not mean no calories!

Can I gain weight if I just chew on fatty things and then spit them out?

You might not gain weight, but you could be doing something more harmful to your body. Merely tasting fatty foods has been found to raise the amount of fat in your blood. A study done at Purdue University showed that people who chewed and spit out full-fat cream cheese on crackers almost doubled their levels of potentially heart-damaging triglycerides!

Which has less fat, something marked extra lean or low fat?

Foods marked extra lean have less than 5 g. total fat, less than 2 g. saturated fat, and less than 95 mg. cholesterol per 100 g. serving. Low-fat foods have 3 g. or less per serving.

Can you explain this body-mass index (BMI) thing? My old doctor told me I was okay at 5'5" and 150 pounds—and now my new doctor tells me I'm overweight. What's it all about?

Let me first tell you that you're not alone. There are about 29 million Americans who have just discovered that they are overweight. The old male-female height and weight statistics that have been around since the '50s have been replaced by a new measurement system, created by the National Heart, Lung, and Blood Institute. The BMI (body-mass index) is a single number that represents height and weight without regard to age or sex.

To figure out your BMI, you multiply your weight in pounds by 703 and then divide it by your height in inches squared. The number you end up with is your BMI. (It's your weight in kilograms divided by the square of your height in meters.)

BMI's of 22–24 are considered healthy. BMI's above 27 are considered dangerously overweight. Your BMI is 25, and anywhere between 25–26 is now considered overweight. But not by everyone. In fact, the National Center for Health Statistics still feels that you're not overweight unless you're above 27. Let me put it this way: if you're exercising, eating properly, and keeping to a low-fat, high-fiber diet—and you're happy with the way you look and feel—relax and go back to your old doctor.

For those of you who would like to know what your BMI is—without doing the math—the following chart from the National Center for Health Statistics should give you a pretty good idea.

BMI—	23	24	25	26	27	28
5'	118	123	128	133	138	143
5'1"	122	127	132	137	143	148
5'3"	130	135	141	146	152	158
5'5"	138	144	150	156	162	168
5'7"	146	153	159	166	172	178
5'9"	155	162	169	176	182	189
5'11"	165	172	179	186	193	200
6'1"	174	182	189	197	204	212
6'3"	184	192	200	208	216	224

XIX

So You Think You Don't Eat Much Sugar and Salt

306. Kinds of Sugars

More than a hundred substances that qualify as sweet can be called sugars. The ones we come in contact with most often are *fructose,* a natural sugar found in fruit and honey; *glucose,* the body's blood sugar and the simplest form of sugar in which a carbohydrate is assimilated; *dextrose,* made from cornstarch and chemically identical to glucose; *lactose,* milk sugar; *maltose,* the sugar formed from the starch by the action of yeast; and *sucrose,* the sugar that is obtained from sugar cane or beets and refined to the product that reaches us as granules.

> Brown sugar is merely sugar crystals
> coated with molasses syrup.

Brown sugar, which many people assume to be healthier than white sugar, is merely sugar crystals coated with molasses syrup. (In the United States most brown sugar is made by simply spraying refined white sugar with the molasses syrup.) Raw sugar is banned in the United States because it contains contaminants. When it's partially refined and cleaned up, it can be sold as turbinado sugar. *Honey* is a blend of fructose and glucose.

307. Other Sweeteners

Sorbitol, mannitol, and *xylitol* are naturally occurring sugar alcohols that are absorbed more slowly into the blood than glucose or sucrose. The biggest misconception about these sweeteners is that they have no calories. The fact is, they have as many calories as sugar—and in some instances, products using them as sweeteners contain *more* calories than they would if made with regular sugar. In other words, these are not low- or no-calorie sugar substitutes, even though products containing them are often sold in the dietetic section of food markets. Always check labels. Products using these sweeteners must reveal that they are not a reduced calorie food or be marked not for weight control.

> Just because a product is marked sugarless
> doesn't mean it's low-calorie!

Aspartame (Equal™, Nutrasweet™) is a combination of amino acids phenylalanine and aspartic acid (see sections 79 and 85) and has no calories. *Acesulfame K* (Sunette™, Sweet One™) looks like sugar, but is derived from acetoacetic acid and has no calories. And *saccharin* (Sweet 'n low™, Sweet* 10™), a noncaloric petroleum derivative estimated to be 300–500 times sweeter than sugar, and chemically similar to acesulfame K, is absorbed but not modified by the body, and is excreted unchanged in the urine.

CAUTION: If you have diabetes or hypoglycemia, be sure to check with your doctor or a nutritionally oriented dietician before adding any products containing alternative sweeteners to your diet.

308. Dangers of Too Much Sugar

> Ketchup has 8 percent more sugar
> than ice cream.

The big problem with sugar is that we eat too much of it (over 154 pounds) and often don't even know it. All carbohydrate sweeteners qualify as sugar, even though they may be called by other names; and when sucrose is the number-three ingredient on a box of cereal, corn syrup number five, and honey number seven, you don't realize it but you're eating something that is 50 percent sugar!

The consumer today is hooked on sugar right from the start. Baby formulas are often sweetened with sugar, as are many baby foods (check labels). Because sugar also acts as a preservative, retains and absorbs moisture, it's often in products we never think of as containing it, products such as salt, peanut butter, canned vegetables, bouillon cubes, and more. Would you believe that the ketchup you put on your hamburger has just less than 8 percent more sugar than ice cream? That cream substitute for coffee is 65 percent sugar compared to 51 percent for a chocolate bar?

The fact is, we're eating too much sugar for our health. It is beyond argument that sugar is a prime factor in tooth decay. Also, one-third of our population is overweight, and obesity increases the possibility of heart disease, diabetes, hypertension, gallstones, back problems, and arthritis. Not that sugar alone is the cause, but its presence in foods induces you to eat more, and if you cut your calorie count without cutting your sugar intake, you'll lose nutrients faster than pounds. Sugar is also the villain where hypoglycemia is concerned, and, though there have been arguments pro and con, directly or indirectly a factor in diabetes and heart disease.

309. How Sweet It Is

Hidden sugars are where you least expect them. (Would you believe that Canada Dry™ tonic water has approximately 18¼ teaspoons of sugar in a 12 oz. serving?) If you want to be a sugar detective, my advice is to check labels. Look for sucrose substitutes such as corn syrup or corn sugar, and watch out for words ending in *-ose*, which indicates the presence of sugar. A sugar by any name is still a sugar. And remember that not even medicines are immune from added sweeteners!

MEDICINES	SUGAR PER TABLESPOON
Alternagel™ liquid	2,000 mg.
Basaljel™ extra-strength liquid	375 mg.
Gaviscon™ liquid	1,500 mg.
Gaviscon-2™ tablets	2,400 mg.
Maalox™ plus tablets	575 mg.
Mylanta™ liquid	2,000 mg.
Riopan Plus™ chew tablets	610 mg.

(When in doubt about sugar or saccharin content of any medication—ask your pharmacist.)

310. Dangers of Too Much Salt

Taking things with a grain of salt is all well and good, but eating things with it might be a different story. The normal intake of sodium chloride (table salt) is 6 to 18 g. daily, but the American Heart Association recommends an intake of no more than 3 g. (3,000 mg.) daily. An intake over 14 g. is considered excessive. And too many of us are being excessive. The average American consumes about 15 pounds (a bowling ball) of salt each year!

Too much salt can cause hypertension (high blood pressure), which increases the chances of heart disease, and has recently been cited as one of the causes for migraine headaches. It causes abnormal fluid retention, which can result in dizziness and swelling of the legs. Also it may cause potassium to be lost in the urine and interfere with the proper utilization of protein foods. In addition, recent studies have linked excess sodium in the diet and low potassium to sodium ratios as high risk factors for colorectal cancer—particularly in men.

311. High-Salt Traps

Just because you stay away from pretzels and snack foods and don't pour on the table salt doesn't mean you're not getting more salt than you should. Salt traps are as hidden from view as sugar ones.

If you want to keep your salt intake down:

• Hold back on beer. (There's 25 mg. sodium in every 12 ounces.)
• Avoid the use of baking soda, monosodium glutamate (MSG, Accent™), and baking powder in food preparation.
• Stay away from laxatives, most of which contain sodium.
• Do not drink or cook with water treated by a home water softener; it adds sodium to the water.
• Look for the words salt, sodium, or the chemical symbol *Na* when reading food labels.
• Watch out for tomato juice. It's low in calories, but very high in sodium.
• Don't eat cured meat such as ham, bacon, corned beef, or frankfurters, sausage, shellfish, any canned or frozen meat, poultry, or fish to which sodium has been added.
• When dining out, ask for an inside cut of meat, or chops or steaks without added salt.
• Watch out for diet sodas—the calories might be low, but in many the sodium content is still *high!*
• Be aware that 2 slices of most processed breads (even if "lite" or whole wheat) contain approximately 230 mg. of salt.

312. How Salty Is It?

APPROXIMATE SODIUM CONTENTS OF COMMON FOODS

Item	Amount	Salt (mg.)
Pickle, dill	1 large	1,928
Frozen turkey three-course dinner (Swanson™)	1 (17 oz.)	1,735
Soy sauce	1 tbsp.	1,320
Pancakes (Hungry Jack Complete™)	3 pancakes 4 in. each	1,150
Chicken noodle soup (Campbell's™)	10 oz.	1,050
Tomato soup (Campbell's™)	10 oz.	950
Green beans, canned (Del Monte™)	1 cup	925
Cheese, pasteurized, processed American (Kraft®)	2 oz.	890
Baked red kidney beans (B and M™)	1 cup	810
Pizza, frozen (Celeste™)	4 oz.	656
V8™ vegetable juice	6 oz.	654
Danish cinnamon rolls w/raisins (Pillsbury™)	1 serving	630
Pudding, instant chocolate (Jell-O®)	½ cup	486
Bologna (Oscar Mayer™)	2 slices	450
Tuna, in oil	3 oz.	430
Frankfurter, beef (Oscar Mayer™)	1	425

313. Any Questions About Chapter XIX?

Isn't it true that in very hot weather you need salt supplements, especially if you do exercise and perspire heavily?

No! This is not only a myth, but one that could result in dangerous consequences. The truth is that salt tablets have a dehydrating effect, and are never indicated. When you exercise, your body uses mechanisms to conserve salt—and since the average American eats somewhere around 60 or more times the salt than is needed by the body, salt depletion is highly unlikely. In fact, too much salt under those conditions can contribute to heat exhaustion and heat stroke. (In the very, *very* rare case where a salt deficiency might occur, replacement should be administered with a 0.1% solution of salt administered in drinking water—and a doctor should be consulted.)

I've been told that eating a candy bar before running is not good for you. I don't understand why a quick energy fix would be bad. Can you explain?

Eating sugar or drinking a sugar drink within half an hour before exercise has been shown to stimulate the release of insulin, causing a drop in blood sugar (and, therefore, needed energy). Research done at the Human Performance Lab at Ball State University in Muncie, Indiana, found that once exercise starts, the insulin response is inhibited, which is why athletes can then drink beverages, such as Gatorade™, that contain sugar in a glucose form that won't cause bloating.

Does sugarless chewing gum really help prevent cavities?

The claim for sugarless gum is that it doesn't *promote* cavities. There is no claim that it actually has a prophylactic effect. In fact, sugarless gum, or candy, that contains sorbitol or mannitol can increase your chances of tooth decay!

No, sorbitol and mannitol don't actually promote cavities, but both of them nourish and increase the type of bacteria in your mouth—namely, *Streptococcus mutans*—that do. According to Dr. Paul Keyes, founder of the International Dental Health Foundation, *Streptococcus mutans* have the mechanism to stick to teeth but will remain harmless until you eat something containing sugar or sucrose, with which they then quickly combine to cause decay. Because the sorbitol and mannitol have swelled the ranks of these bacteria, there are more of them available to use passing sugars to attack your teeth.

Rinsing your mouth with water within 15 minutes after eating or drinking anything containing sucrose is the best preventive.

XX

Staying Beautiful—Staying Handsome

314. Vitamins for Healthy Skin

What you look like on the outside depends a lot on what you do for yourself on the inside. And as far as your skin is concerned, vitamins and proper nutrition are essential.

To look your best, make sure that you drink eight glasses of water daily (herbal teas can count for a few of them) and keep your milk and yogurt consumption restricted to the nonfat variety. Keep away from chocolates, nuts, dried fruits, fried foods, cola drinks, coffee, alcohol, cigarettes, and excessive salt. Also, do not use sugar. Small amounts of honey will sweeten just as well and you'll look better for it.

A good start toward healthy, glowing skin is a daily soy-food protein drink. It can be taken in place of any meal, but it makes an especially good breakfast.

PROTEIN DRINK

2 tbsp. soy-food protein powder
1 tbsp. whey
2 tbsp. lecithin granules
1½ cups soy milk
2 tbsp. fresh or frozen fruit, or 1 banana
3–4 ice cubes
Mix in blender at high speed for one minute.

SUPPLEMENTS
(Take with meals unless otherwise indicated.)

• An all-natural, high-potency multiple vitamin and amino acid–chelated mineral complex (containing vitamin A, beta-carotene or carotenoids, vitamins B1, B2, B3, B5, B6, B12, biotin, choline, folic acid, inositol, vitamin C, vitamin D, vitamin E, boron, calcium, chromium, copper, magnesium, manganese, selenium, vanadium, and zinc)—1 twice daily, A.M. and P.M.

Essential for skin tone and nerve health.

• A broad-spectrum antioxidant formula (containing alpha- and beta-carotene, lutein, lycopene, vitamin C, vitamin E, selenium, ginkgo biloba, coenzyme-Q10, bilberry, L-gluta-thione, soy isoflavones [genistein and daidzein], grapeseed extract, and green tea extract)—1 twice daily, A.M. and P.M.

Helps replenish antioxidants that protect skin and keep it healthy and young-looking.

If your multivitamin-mineral complex and antioxidant formula do not contain the following supplements, add them separately to your daily intake.

• RNA/DNA complex
Stimulates formation of new cells; helps improve texture of skin.
• Superoxide dismutase (SOD) and wild yam, 300 mg.
Aids in growth and repair of tissues and helps to maintain soft, pliant skin.
• Beta-carotene, 10,000 IU
Helps protect skin from free radical damage.
• Vitamin C with bioflavonoids, 500 mg.
Aids in preventing breakage of capillaries; promotes healing of wounds, bruises, and scar tissue.
• Vitamin E, 400–800 IU
Improves circulation in tiny face capillaries. Aids in replacing cells on the skin's outer layer.
• Vitamin B complex with pantothenic acid, 50 mg.

Helps in cell building and aids in wound healing.
- MSM (Methylsulfonylmethane), 1,000 mg.
    Promotes the formation of collagen, which helps produce new skin.
- Essential Fatty Acids, 1,000 mg.
    Flaxseed oil is a fine source of moisture replenishing omega-3 fatty acids.
- L-Cysteine, 1 g. daily. (Taken between meals with juice or water)
    Helps maintain supple, young-looking skin.
- Zinc, 15–50 mg.
    Aids in growth and repair of badly blemished skin.

315. Vitamins for Healthy Hair

Shampoos and conditioners are not enough. To make sure that you're giving your crowning glory its due, you have to be aware that nutrition plays a very important role in having terrific, shiny hair. Unlike the skin, hair cannot repair itself; but you *can* get new, healthier hair to grow.

The first thing to do is examine your diet. Does it include fish, wheat germ, yeast, and soybeans? It should. The vitamins and minerals that these foods supply are what your hair needs, along with frequent scalp massage, a good pH-balanced, protein-enriched shampoo, and supplements.

SUPPLEMENTS
(Take with meals unless otherwise indicated.)

- An all-natural, high-potency multiple vitamin and amino acid–chelated mineral complex (see section 314 above for optimal supplement contents)—1 twice daily, A.M. and P.M.
    Essential for general health of hair.
- A broad-spectrum antioxidant formula (see section 314 above for optimal supplement contents)—1 twice daily, A.M. and P.M.
    Aids in replenishing antioxidants and protecting hair from oxidative damage.

If your multivitamin-mineral complex and antioxidant formula do not contain the following supplements, add them separately to your daily intake.

• Essential fatty acids (flaxseed or any omega-3 fatty acid), 1,000 mg.
  Prevents dry, brittle hair; improves texture.
• Silica, 500 mg., 1–3 daily
  Aids in forestalling hair loss; helps keep hair shiny.
• Biotin and inositol, 50–100 mg.
  Helps prevent hair loss; vital for hair growth.
• Coenzyme-Q10, 60 mg.
  Helps improve scalp circulation.
• L-Cysteine, 1 g. (Take between meals with juice or water.)
  Cysteine is the chief protein constituent of hair, and can help keep tresses looking lustrous.
• MSM (Methylsulfonylmethane), 1,000 mg.
  Helps promote thicker and shinier hair.
• B complex, 50–100 mg. with pantothenic acid, folic acid, and PABA
  Essential for hair growth; can help hair retain natural color.
• Beta-carotene, 10,000 IU
  Works with the B vitamins to keep hair shiny.

Keep in mind that it is normal to lose 50–100 hairs a day.

316. Vitamins for Hands and Feet

Your hands take lots of abuse. Detergents strip away natural oils, and water and weather alone can cause chapping. Rubber gloves are a good idea, but if you already have splits in your skin or some sort of dermatitis, they should *not* be put directly on your hands. (A pair of cotton gloves beneath the rubber ones will absorb perspiration and prevent reinfection.) Also, do not use cornstarch in the gloves; it can promote the growth of microorganisms. If you want to use something to absorb the moisture, try plain unscented talcum powder.

As for toenails and fingernails, the best remedy for problems is diet. Gelatin is commonly accepted as the cure for weak nails, but this is a misconception. The nails do need protein, but gelatin is a poor supplier. Not only are two essential amino acids missing, but another amino acid, glycine, is supplied in amounts you do not need. Foods rich in sulfur (see section 67), should be part of your diet, and an easily absorbed form of organic sulfur, MSM (methylsulfonylmethane), 1,000 mg. with a vitamin C complex should be taken as a supplement twice daily with meals.

SUPPLEMENTS
(Take with meals unless otherwise indicated.)

- An all-natural, high-potency multiple vitamin and amino acid-chelated mineral complex (see section 314 for optimal supplement contents)—1 twice daily, A.M. and P.M.
  Promotes health, growth, and strength of nails.
- A broad-spectrum antioxidant formula (see section 314 for optimal supplement contents)—1 twice daily, A.M. and P.M.
  Helps protect against free radical damage to tissues.

If your multivitamin-mineral complex and antioxidant formula do not contain the following supplements, add them separately to your daily intake.

- RNA/DNA complex
  Stimulates formation of new cells; helps improve skin texture and nail strength.
- B complex, 50–100 mg., with pantothenic acid
  Helps build resistance to fungus infections; vital to nail growth.
- Beta-carotene, 10,000 IU
  Aids in preventing splitting nails.
- Silica, 500 mg., 1–3 times daily
  Helps prevent white spots and peeling nails.
- Vitamin E, 400 IU
  Necessary for proper utilization of vitamin A.

• Zinc, 15–50 mg.
    Aids in strengthening brittle nails and eliminating white spots.

317. Natural Cosmetics—What's in Them?

Many cosmetics nowadays are advertised as "natural," but looking at the ingredients can cause you to wonder. To be sure of what you're getting, read the label carefully. The following explanation of cosmetic ingredients should make things clearer.

Amyl Dimethyl PABA—a sunscreening agent from PABA, a B-complex factor

Annatto—a vegetable color obtained from the seeds of a tropical plant

Avocado oil—a vegetable oil obtained from avocados

Caprylic/Capric triglyceride—an emollient obtained from coconut oil

Carrageenan—a natural thickening agent from dried Irish moss

Castor oil—an emollient oil collected from the pressing of castor bean seeds

Cetyl alcohol—a component of vegetable oils

Cetyl palmitate—a component of palm and coconut oils

Citric acid—a natural organic acid found widely in citrus plants

Cocamide DEA—a thickener obtained from coconut oil

Coconut oil—obtained by pressing the kernels of the seeds of the coconut palm

Decyl oleate—obtained from tallow or coconut oil

Disodium monolaneth-5-sulfosuccinate—obtained from lanolin and used to improve the texture of hair

Fragrance—oils obtained from flowers, grasses, roots, and stems that give off a pleasant or agreeable odor

Goat milk whey—protein-rich whey obtained from goat's milk

Glyceryl stearate—an organic emulsifier obtained from glycerin

Hydrogenated castor oil—a waxy material obtained from castor oil

Imidzaolidinyl urea—a preservative derived naturally as a product of protein metabolism (hydrolysis)

Lanolin alcohol—a constituent of lanolin that performs as an emollient and emulsifier

Laureth-3—an organic material obtained from coconut and palm oils

Methyl glucoside sesquistearate—an organic emulsifier obtained from a natural simple sugar

Mineral oil—an organic emollient and lubricant

Olive oil—a natural oil obtained from olives

Peanut oil—a vegetable oil obtained from peanuts

Pectin—derived from citrus fruits and apple peel

PEG lanolin—an emollient and emulsifier obtained from lanolin

Petrolatum—petroleum jelly

P.O.E. (20) methyl glucoside sesquistearate—an organic emulsifier from a simple natural sugar

Potassium sorbate—obtained from sorbic acid found in the berries of mountain ash

Safflower oil-hybrid—a natural emollient obtained from a strain of specially cultivated plants

Sesame oil—oil of pressed sesame seeds

Sodium cetyl sulfate—a detergent and emulsifier obtained from coconut oil

Sodium laureth sulfate—a detergent obtained from coconut oil

Sodium lauryl sulfate—a detergent obtained from coconut oil

Sodium PCA—a naturally occurring humectant found in the skin, where it acts as the natural moisturizer

Sorbic acid—a natural preservative derived from berries of mountain ash

Tocopherol—a natural vitamin E

Undecylenamide DEA—a natural preservative derived from castor oil

Water—the universal solvent, and the major constituent of all living material.

318. Not So Pretty Drugs

Medications are necessary for certain conditions, but doctors often fail to mention their possible side effects. It is a rare physician who puts his patient on the pill and tells her that her face might break out, or that she might suffer hair loss; but many women on oral contraceptives find this out soon enough. In fact, many drugs can be the cause of skin and other cosmetic problems. The following is a list of just a few:

Alfenta®	Skin rash, flushing
Codeine	Skin rash, itching, sweating
Coumadin™	Skin rash, itching, hives
Darvon™	Skin rash, flaking skin, itching
Demerol®	Skin rash, flushing, water retention
Doxycycline	Rashes, open sores, teeth discoloration
Fentanyl	Flushing, sweating, allergic reactions
Miltown™	Welts, flaking skin, itching
Nembutal™	Skin rash
Phenobarbital	Rash, itchy skin, swollen eyelids
Quaalude™	Pimples, welts
Talwin™	Rash, facial swelling, skin peeling
Tetracycline	Taken during pregnancy and in infancy may cause permanent discoloration of child's teeth
Thorazine®	Peeling skin, jaundice, welts, swelling
Tofranil®	Rash, itchy skin, jaundice
Tuinal™	Can aggravate existing skin condition
Valium™	Jaundice, rash, swollen patches

319. Any Questions About Chapter XX?

What do you think of jojoba oil as a beauty aid?

Personally, I think it's one of the best. It's available in a variety of forms—an oil, a cream, a soap, a shampoo—and it works wonders naturally!

For example: As a moisturizer, use a few drops under your makeup. Massage gently into your skin, particularly around the eyes where lines occur. (Be careful to avoid direct contact with the eyes and if any irritation results, discontinue use.) At night, use the oil to soften your skin as you sleep. Just apply a light layer over your face and neck—after they've had a good cleansing, of course.

The oil can also be used to soften skin after showers (all you need is a few drops) and as a luxuriant bath oil (again, just a few drops). For dry, chapped, or recently shaved skin, it should be applied directly.

After shampooing your hair, try rubbing a few drops of the oil into your hair and scalp. (Don't rinse.) Daily use will help even the driest hair return to its natural luster.

My nails just won't grow. I've tried all sorts of vitamins, but they don't work. Where do I go from here?

It's possible that you might have a thyroid problem, so you might want to check with a nutritionally oriented physician. (See section 342.)

In the meanwhile, you could try silica, an organic herb that's also known as horsetail and *Equisetum arvense,* which is changed by the body into readily available calcium—which nourishes nails, skin, hair, bones, and the body's connective tissue.

XXI

Staying Young, Energetic, and Sexy

320. Retarding the Aging Process

Aging is caused by the degeneration of cells. Our bodies are made up of millions of these cells, each with a life of somewhere around two years or less. But before a cell dies, it reproduces itself. Why, then, you might wonder, shouldn't we look the same now as we did ten years ago? The reason for this is that with each successive reproduction, the cell goes through some alteration—basically, deterioration. So as our cells change, deteriorate, we grow old.

> You can look and feel six
> to twelve years younger.

The good news is that deteriorating cells can be rejuvenated if provided with substances that directly nourish them—substances such as nucleic acids.

DNA (deoxyribonucleic acid) and RNA (ribonucleic acid) are our nucleic acids. DNA is essentially a chemical boilerplate for new cells. It sends out RNA molecules like a team of well-trained workers to form them. When DNA stops giving the orders to RNA, new cell construction ceases—as does life. But by helping the body stay well supplied with nucleic acids, you can look and feel 6–12 years younger than you actually are.

We need 1–1½ g. of nucleic acid daily. Though the body can produce its own nucleic acids, they are broken down too quickly into less useful compounds and need to be supplied from external sources if the aging process is to be retarded.

Foods rich in nucleic acids are wheat germ, bran, spinach, asparagus, mushrooms, fish (especially sardines, salmon, and anchovies), chicken liver, oatmeal, onions, and certain types of nutritional yeast which clearly say on the label "rich in RNA and DNA."

Soon after I started eating a diet high in nucleic acids and taking RNA-DNA supplements many years ago, I noticed a dramatic difference in how I looked and felt. I had more energy and my skin looked healthier and more youthful. Many clients and friends experienced similar results. Though a high–nucleic acid diet and RNA-DNA supplementation might not reverse the aging process, I believe it can slow it down.

CAUTION: Gout and certain forms of arthritis may be aggravated by a diet rich in nucleic acids. If you have these conditions, check with your physician before eating these foods or taking any supplements.

OTHER ANTIAGING SUPPLEMENTS

SOD (superoxide dismutase) is one of the most popular arrivals in the battle to combat aging. (See section 116.) This enzyme fortifies the body against the ravages of free radicals, destructive molecules which speed the aging process by destroying healthy cells as well as attacking collagen ("cement" that holds cells together).

As we age, our bodies produce less SOD, so supplementation—along with a natural diet that restricts free radical formation—can help increase our energetic and productive years. It's important to note, though, that SOD can become inactive very quickly if essential minerals, such as zinc, copper, and manganese, are not supplied.

Grapeseed Extract is also being touted as a potent free-radical fighter and antiaging supplement. It contains *proanthocyanidins,* bioflavonoids which greatly enhance the activity of vitamin C. By helping vitamin C enter cells, grapeseed extract aids in strengthening the cell membranes and protecting the cells from oxidative damage. It can improve circulation, strengthen capillaries, and help protect collagen fibers—necessary for the growth and repair of cells—from damage caused over the years by free radicals. (Proanthocyanidins are also in grape skins, bilberry, cranberry, blackcurrant, and green and black tea.)

As an antiaging supplement, I suggest taking 1–2 grapeseed extract capsules (30–100 mg.) daily.

Coenzyme-Q10, a substance that can be synthesized by the body (although it is also obtained from food) is used by our cells during the process of respiration, and deficiencies are common in the course of normal aging. In fact, studies have shown that reduced levels of coenzyme-Q10, which shares many of vitamin E's antioxidant properties, may directly contribute to aging and that increasing levels can retard the process as well as:

• reduce the risk of heart attack (aid respiration of the heart muscle; help provide a protective effect against viral-caused heart inflammations; help prevent cardiac arrhythmias; minimize myocardial injury caused by heart bypass surgery; reduce frequency of angina attacks)
• stimulate the immune system
• aid in the treatment of periodontal disease
• help lower blood pressure
• aid in the prevention of toxicity from drugs used to treat many diseases associated with aging.

As a supplement, I recommend one 30 mg. capsule twice daily with food.

DHEA (dehydroepiandrosterone), a natural hormone that is produced by the adrenal glands and the most abundant steroid hormone in the body, decreases as we age. (Steroids are a class of compounds that help balance emotions and increase the body's ability to handle stress, among other functions.) About the age of forty-five, we produce only *half* of the DHEA we produced at age twenty. By age seventy production falls to almost nothing. Leading researchers link the decline in hormones such as DHEA with the physical and mental decline of normal aging. Boosting DHEA back to youthful levels may prevent and even reverse many age-related problems. Older people given DHEA have an increased sense of well-being, more energy, an increase in lean body mass, and produce more sex hormone.

DHEA has been found to strengthen the immune system; slow down the production of fats that contribute to obesity; offer postmenopausal women protection against heart disease; reduce fatigue; increase cognitive function; and enhance mood and stress responses.

New research indicates that DHEA may be a promising treatment for osteoporosis and depression, as well as in reducing the symptoms of lupus, an autoimmune disorder for which, at this time, there is no cure. (Anyone with lupus should certainly talk to his or her physician about trying DHEA.)

If you are over forty, have your DHEA level checked by a physician. The usual dose is one 25 mg. tablet daily for women over age forty; one 50 mg. tablet for men over forty. As a supplement, look for "pharmaceutical grade" on the DHEA label—it ensures as pure a product as possible.

CAUTION: DHEA is a hormone and can theoretically stimulate the growth of hormone-dependent cancers. If you have a history of prostate or breast cancer, I advise that you *not* use DHEA.

Pregnenolone, produced in the brain and adrenal cortex from cholesterol, functions as a parent hormone, converting into DHEA, estrogen, testosterone, progesterone, and other hormones.

Touted as a general antiaging supplement for men and women, pregnenolone levels peak in our thirties and then decline. Recent studies suggest that supplements may improve concentration and memory, act as an antidepressant, reduce stress, and help relieve symptoms of rheumatoid arthritis, lupus, and multiple sclerosis.

The usual supplement dose is 5–10 mg. daily.

CAUTION: Pregnenolone can elevate levels of sex hormones and interact adversely with other medications. It should not be taken by pregnant women. Before taking this hormone, I recommend that you consult with a knowledgeable physician.

321. Basic Keep Yourself Young Program

Along with proper diet, a good supplement regimen is important to the success of looking, feeling, and keeping yourself young. MVP (see section 172)

If you are over forty years of age add:

Vitamin E, 400 IU A.M. and P.M.
Vitamin C, 500 mg. with bioflavonoids A.M. and P.M.
Coenzyme-Q10 complex, 1 daily
RNA-DNA, 100 mg. tablets, 1 daily
SOD, 125 mcg. daily
Ginkgo biloba, 60 mg. 1–3 standardized capsules daily
Cayenne pepper, 500 mg. 1–3 capsules daily
For women: Soy isolate complex with 1,000 mg. calcium and 500 mg. magnesium, 1 daily
For men: Soy isolate complex with 500 mg. calcium and 150 mg. magnesium, 1 daily
St. John's wort polyphenol complex, 1 daily as needed.

322. High-Pep Energy Regimen

Whether you want to feel good, or just look good, exercise, diet, and the right supplements are the tickets to high energy.

If you're not into jogging, can't afford the sneakers, don't play tennis, find yourself reluctant to swim in twenty-below weather, and hate calisthenics, I have the perfect exercise for you—jumping rope.

A jump rope is inexpensive, convenient (you can take it everywhere), and lots of fun to use. And it works! In terms of calories burned, jumping rope can outdo bicycling, tennis, and swimming. An average person of about 150 pounds uses up 720 calories an hour jumping rope (120–140 turns per minute). When you realize that an hour of tennis uses up only 420 calories, you have a better idea of just how good jumping rope can be for you.

For keeping energy high, remember to eat a combination of 2 protein foods (or a protein drink) at each meal; drink at least 6 glasses of water daily (a half hour before or after meals); avoid refined sugar, flour, tobacco, alcohol, tea, coffee, soft drinks, processed and fried foods.

A good pep-up protein drink:

1 tbsp. soy-food powder
1 tbsp. lecithin granules
1 tbsp. whey
2 tbsp. acidophilus (non-dairy) liquid
Blend with low- or nonfat soy milk, water, or juice, with 3–4 ice cubes, for 1 minute. (Add fresh or frozen fruit if desired. A peeled frozen banana tastes great!)

323. High-Pep Supplements

With breakfast:

MVP (see section 172)
Vitamin E (dry form), 400 IU
Coenzyme-Q10 complex

Women: Soy isolate complex with 1,000 mg. calcium and
 500 mg. magnesium
Men: Soy isolate complex with 500 mg. calcium and 250
 mg. magnesium

With dinner:

MVP (see section 172)
Coenzyme-Q10 complex
Women: Soy isolate complex with 1,000 mg. calcium and
 500 mg. magnesium
Men (over 45): Saw palmetto, pygeum, zinc, pumpkin seed
 oil complex, 2 with meals

324. Vitamins and Sex

The important thing to remember is that if you're not feeling up to par, your sex drive is going to suffer along with the
rest of you.

There have been many claims for vitamin E in relation to
sex. Studies have indeed shown that it increases the fertility
in males and females and helps restore male potency. That it
strongly influences the sex drive in men and women has yet
to be proven, though I have met many vitamin-E takers who
are happily convinced that it does.

The largest percentage of zinc
in a man's body is found in
the prostate.

Another noteworthy sex nutrient is zinc. The largest percentage of zinc in a man's body is found in the prostate, and
a lack of the mineral can produce testicular atrophy and
prostate trouble.

Remember, vitamins that keep up your energy levels (see
section 322) will also do a lot for your sexual performance.

325. Foods, Herbs, and Super New Supplements for Enhancing Sex

If you want to boost your libido or just add spice to your nightly love life, incorporate some of the following into your daily diet:

Asparagus	Ginseng
Avena sativa	Kava Kava
Avocados	Oysters
Barley	Pine nuts
Brewer's yeast	Quince
Cardamom	Sarsaparilla
Carrots	Shiitake mushrooms
Cinnamon	Soy foods
Coriander	Wheat germ
Fertilized chicken eggs	Whole grains
Ginkgo biloba	Yohimbe (see section 156)

Supplement Regimen

MVP (see section 172)
Vitamin E (dry form), 400 IU, 1–3 times daily
Zinc, 15–50 mg. (chelated) daily
Ginkgo biloba complex, 60 mg. twice daily
Women over 40: DHEA 25 mg. daily
Men over 50: DHEA 50 mg. daily
Men: Arginine, 3–6 g. 45 minutes before sex

326. Any Questions About Chapter XXI?

I understand that octacosanol can improve a male's sexual performance enormously. What do you feel about this?

I feel that a lot is still going to depend on the male involved. It is true, though, that octacosanol (which is a natural food substance present in very small amounts in many vegetable oils, the levels of alfalfa and wheat, wheat germ, and other foods) has an energy-releasing function, increasing strength and stamina, and in laboratory experiments it seems to improve reproductive disturbances.

If you try it, don't be impatient, it often takes 4–6 weeks for beneficial effects from octacosanol to be noticed.

Always keep in mind, too, that an energizing diet of raw or lightly cooked foods, rich in B vitamins and amino acids, will contribute to a good sex life.

I'm an active, happily married forty-five-year-old woman, but my sex drive seems to have stalled. What natural love-life enhancers would you recommend?

Along with following my MVP vitamin regimen (see section 172), I'd suggest you increase your diet of soy foods. Soybeans are rich in plant estrogens called isoflavones. They can alleviate some of the symptoms of perimenopause that often interfere with sexual desire. You might also want to have your DHEA levels checked. If they're low, 25 mg. of supplemental DHEA daily could elevate your libido. Additionally, I'd suggest you try the herb damiana, which has the reputation of being a sexual stimulant. Take one capsule 1–3 times daily before meals. Add a little candlelight to the evening and you may be pleasantly surprised with the results.

What is Spanishfly and is it really a natural aphrodisiac?

Far from it! Spanish fly is actually cantharides made from the outer skeletons of beetles. It causes itching, but not necessarily for sex. In fact, it's a poisonous substance that can be anything *but* a turn-on. It has been linked to convulsions and kidney disorders, and has been reported to make urination virtually impossible, to say nothing of causing men to experience extremely painful erections.

What's legally marketed in this country as Spanish fly is generally nothing more than dried herbs that are no more potent than parsley. I'd advise saving your money for a romantic dinner. As old-fashioned as it sounds, I feel that a candlelight dinner will beat a beetle skeleton as an aphrodisiac every time.

I've been told that there's something called DMG that is an aphrodisiac. Have you heard of it and does it work?

I've heard of it, but I can't vouch for its effectiveness. DMG is dimethyglycine, a derivative of the amino acid glycine, found mostly in seeds and grains. It aids in increasing the supply of oxygen to the bloodstream and body tissues. Those touting it as an aphrodisiac say that the increased oxygen in the tissues enhances your sexual response. (Maybe eating those Wheaties™ does work.) Anyway, it is available as a supplement, so you might want to give it a try. It might not be your ticket to ecstasy—but it won't hurt.

My grandmother used to say that sweet potatoes and carrots were women's fertility foods. She ate them frequently and had nine children. Was this just coincidence?

Maybe yes and maybe no. Carrots and sweet potatoes (yams) have been found to have chemical structures similar to estrogen—a necessary female fertility hormone. In fact, pregnenolone supplements are made from wild yam.

A friend of mine told me about a supplement that could boost my energy level, help reverse formation of liver spots, and improve my memory—but I've forgotten what it was. Any ideas?

My guess would be DMAE (dimethylaminoethanol). It is a safe, natural substance that can boost acetylcholene, which enhances memory and mental function. It can cross the blood-brain barrier and get right to the brain cells where it's needed. It is also a very efficient antioxidant. I take a combination formula of DMAE, ginkgo biloba, phosphatidylserine, inositol, and choline daily—and can recommend it highly.

XXII

Pets Need Good Nutrition Too

327. Vitamins for Your Dog

Dogs need vitamins as much as people do. Their requirements, of course, are not the same as ours, but they too need all the nutrients. (There are no RDAs for dogs. If you want to know exactly what they need for basic nutrition, write for the National Research Council's *Nutrient Requirements for Dogs,* National Academy of Sciences, Washington, D.C.)

An adult dog needs 4.4 g. protein daily, along with 1.3 g. fat, 0.4 g. linoleic or arachidonic acid, and 15.4 g. carbohydrate. Puppies need twice that amount.

Proteins are essential for a dog's growth and body repair. Those with high biological value, such as eggs, muscle meat, fish meat, soybeans, milk, and yeast, are the best. If you want to give your dog eggs, be sure that they're cooked. Raw egg white contains avidin, which prevents biotin from being absorbed. Milk, though good for dogs, often causes diarrhea, so yogurt and cottage cheese are recommended.

Carbohydrates are used by dogs for energy, but it is suggested that no more than 50–60 percent of their food include them.

Fats, the most concentrated energy source, supply the essential fatty acid for healthy skin and hair. A deficiency can retard puppies' growth and lead to coarse hair and flaking skin. One teaspoon of safflower or corn oil added to the dog's dry food can help.

> Imbalanced supplements can
> harm your dog.

Calcium and phosphorus, in a ratio of 1.2:1, should be included in the dog's diet. If the ratio is incorrect, abnormal mineralization can occur in the bones of growing puppies as well as adult dogs. There must also be sufficient vitamin D for proper absorption of these two minerals. Because the balance is so important, *be certain that the vitamin supplements you give are balanced.* Too much bonemeal or cod liver oil can result in problems as severe as those you're trying to combat.

Cod liver oil is not advised as a routine supplement; it can lead to vitamin-D overload. (With enough calcium and phosphorus in the diet, your dog has a very low requirement for vitamin D. Vitamin D can be toxic to dogs with as little as ten times the daily requirement.)

All-meat diets are not good for your pet because the calcium-phosphorus ratio is wrong, and there are inadequate amounts of vitamins A, D, and E.

> Stop fleas with brewer's
> yeast and garlic.

Brewer's yeast and garlic, mixed in with your dog's food, will help prevent fleas. (It works for cats, too.) Fleas despise the odor it gives off after your dog ingests it.

Do not give your dog supplemental vitamins A, D, or niacin unless you know there is a deficiency or your veterinarian recommends it. They can have an adverse effect on your pet. (See section 334 for "Cautions.")

328. Arthritis and Dysplasia Regimen For Dogs

Dogs, unlike humans, manufacture their own vitamin C, but research has shown that supplemental C can be effective in the treatment of arthritis and dysplasia. I recommend, though, that you consult your vet before starting any supplement program. Ask him or her about this regimen:

Vitamin C, 500–1,000 mg. (sodium ascorbate or some other form of buffered vitamin C; plain ascorbic acid may cause stomach upset.)
4–5 alfalfa tablets (helps reduce inflammation)
Vitamin E, 100–200 IU (liquid or powder)
Selenium, 25–50 mcg. (depending on size of dog)
Glucosamine, 500 mg.
Ev.Ext-33, 1 capsule daily (2 capsules daily for dogs over 100 pounds)
Mix with food daily.

329. Cancer Prevention Regimen for Dogs

One in four dogs develops cancer, and approximately 50 percent of dogs over ten years old die from cancer. A dog with a healthy immune system is the least likely to get the disease. The following is a daily supplement prevention program that can help. [Note: The dosages given are for medium size dogs. Cut in half for small dogs and double for large and giant dogs. If your dog is already taking a multi-vitamin-mineral, be sure that you are not double-dosing.]

Vitamin C, 1,000–2,000 mg.
Vitamin E, 200 IU
Beta-carotene, 15 IU (all size dogs)
Selenium, 25 mcg. (double for all dogs over 20 pounds)

330. Antioxidants for a Healthier Pet

Dogs and cats need antioxidants as much—if not more—than people do. Think about it: they are exposed to chemicals more intensively than most humans because they are shorter and breathe in greater concentrations of floor and lawn chemicals. Their self-grooming behavior also increases their risk of toxic exposure, to say nothing of their chemically treated flea collars and the unhealthy "snacks" they often pick up in the park or on the street.

VITAMIN C

Just because dogs and cats manufacture their own vitamin C, it is not, however, in amounts needed for disease prevention or supplying significant health benefits. Supplementing your pet's diet with this powerful antioxidant can reduce cancer risk, boost the immune system, stimulate wound repair, reduce the risk of cataracts, alleviate allergies, aid in preventing and curing cystitis. Vitamin C is also important for proper bone formation and helpful in preventing heart disease.

Supplemental dosage:

- For adult dogs: Vitamin C, 500–1,000 mg.
- For adult cats: Vitamin C, 50–300 mg.

(Sodium ascorbate or some other form of buffered vitamin C is recommended to avoid stomach upset. Specially formulated supplements for dogs and cats are available at pet stores or can be obtained from your veterinarian.)

[NOTE: Loose stools or diarrhea is usually a sign of too much vitamin C, so reduce dosage.]

VITAMIN A

Though dogs and cats metabolize it differently, vitamin A provides both with protection against free radicals, increases immunity, promotes growth, skin and coat health, fertility, improves vision, and aids in the prevention of bladder, respiratory, and other infections.

Cats, unlike dogs and humans, cannot convert beta-carotene to vitamin A and must obtain it from retinol (an animal source). Make sure vitamin A is listed on the label of whatever food you're feeding—and make sure sodium nitrite isn't. (It can deplete vitamin A.) Unless you suspect a serious deficiency, a little liver goes a long way in the way of supplementing your pet's diet. (It should not make up more than 25 percent of the cat's usual meal—and should not be given more than 3 or 4 times a week.)

The way dogs process vitamin A allows them to tolerate higher doses than humans (only 30 percent of excess accumulates in the liver, the rest is excreted through the kidneys), nonetheless, toxic levels are deemed the same as for humans and an oversupply can cause serious problems. Supplements have, however, helped prevent progressive retinal atrophy (PRA), a genetic retinal eye disease, and many skin problems. (To test for a vitamin A deficiency in your dog, pull out one of the animal's hairs. If it has a sticky, goopy substance on the end, your pet might need more vitamin A. Check with your vet.)

VITAMIN E

This antioxidant vitamin has a strong influence on the immune system, and offers pets protection against environmental pollutants and toxins. (This is especially important for animals living in cities.) Dogs under stress or larger breeds that are more susceptible to heart disease would benefit from vitamin E supplements. Vitamin E can help protect cats from steatitis, a condition caused by all-fish diets, which deplete this important vitamin. (If your cat is eating a diet high in polyunsaturated fats, found in canned tuna fish, she probably needs more vitamin E.)

Supplemental dosage:

• For adult dogs: Vitamin E, 100–400 IU (depending on size)
• For adult cats: Vitamin E, 10–15 IU (for aging, pregnant or lactating cats, dosage may be increased to 15–30 IU daily; divided in two doses each day with meals).

SELENIUM

Selenium works with vitamin E to help boost your pet's immune system and help prevent heart disease and cancer. It also works with iodine for proper thyroid function. Most dogs and cats get adequate amounts in their diets from fish, red meat, organ meat, eggs, and chicken. As a supplement, only micrograms are necessary and the amount should be determined by your veterinarian according to your pet's weight and special nutritional needs.

ZINC

This top-notch mineral, which works best with adequate amounts of calcium, phosphorus, and vitamin A, is crucial for the production of enzymes. Zinc supports the immune system, aids in wound healing and removing toxins from the body, helps protect against cancer, and is necessary for your pet's healthy coat, skin, and nails. Dogs and cats get dietary zinc in lamb, pork, beef, liver, brewer's yeast, and beans. If your cat's diet is high in soy meal (check labels), more zinc might be called for in your animal's diet.

Recommended daily doses are:

• For adult dogs: Zinc, 10–30 mg. (depending on size)
• For adult cats: Zinc, 0.25–0.5 mg.

331. Vitamins for Your Cat

Cats need vitamins, just as people and dogs do, but nutritional requirements for them have not been as well established. (For the most recent available information, you can write for the National Research Council's *Nutrient Requirements of Laboratory Animals,* National Academy of Sciences, Washington, D.C.)

> Cow's milk is insufficient
> for a growing kitten.

Protein requirements for cats are high, considerably higher than those of dogs or people. Adult cats need 3 grams per pound of body weight daily. Kittens need 8.6 grams per pound of body weight daily. And *cats cannot store excess protein and must replenish their supply every day through food!* Muscle meats, organ meat, poultry, fish, cheese, eggs, and milk are all good sources. (Eggs should be cooked or, if given raw, only the yolk should be used.) If you are giving a kitten milk, use a dry powdered milk at double the concentration given a human baby; cow's milk isn't nutritious enough for an infant cat.

Carbohydrates are not actually required in a cat's diet, but they are used as energy. If there are adequate levels of fats and protein, 33 percent of the diet can be made up of carbohydrates.

> Give your cat the fats
> you shouldn't eat.

Fats are a cat's most concentrated source of energy. Unlike people, cats can have diets of up to 64 percent fat and show no signs of vascular problems. Only because fats are more costly than carbohydrates do most cat foods have low percentages. In fact, you can give your cat the fats you need to cut down on—butter, animal fat, vegetable. Where cats are concerned, polyunsaturates are not the good guys. Too much polyunsaturated fatty acid is antagonistic to vitamin E, and fat deposits in the cat's body can be seriously affected.

Although levels of all the essential vitamins haven't been established for cats, the importance of certain vitamins in a cat's diet should be noted. For example, cats are dependent on their diet for fully formed vitamin A. (Their requirement is much higher than that of dogs because unlike dogs they cannot manufacture vitamin A in the body from carotene.) On the other hand, too much vitamin A can result in bone deformities. Liver as a supplement (not a total diet) is recommended, as is a *balanced* vitamin-mineral preparation. Fish, butter, milk, and cheese are also high in vitamin A.

The B vitamins are also important for a cat's nerve stability, outer coat, and inner tissues. B6 (pyridoxine) helps prevent urinary calculi, a serious problem for altered male cats. (A diet low in ash is recommended.) In general, cats require twice the amount of B vitamins needed by dogs (their requirement for B6 in particular is four times that of a dog!). Feeding dog food to a cat for an extended period of time can result in a B-complex deficiency. It should also be noted that B1 (thiamine) can be destroyed by an antagonist in raw fish. (For foods high in B vitamins, see sections 29 through 42.)

All-fish diets are not
healthy for cats.

Vitamin-E deficiency can occur from feeding excessive amounts of red meat tuna. (It can also occur because of any all-fish diet.) Lack of appetite, fever, pain, and a reluctance to move are characteristic symptoms of pansteatitis, which results from vitamin-E deficiency. If this occurs, see your vet, don't feed tuna unless it is supplemented with vitamin E, and don't use fish oils as supplements.

The calcium-phosphorus ratio in a cat's diet should be about one to one, with adequate amounts of vitamin D. Since manufacturers of canned cat foods usually add irradiated yeast, a source of vitamin D, supplements of D are unnecessary—and can be dangerous. (See section 334 for "Cautions.")

A multiple vitamin with iron—prepared especially for cats—is often given for feline anemia. The disease is rare in cats on a balanced diet that includes cooked and raw muscle meat, organ meats, cooked meats, cooked or canned chicken, and fish, vitamin-rich cereals, and vegetables.

Keep in mind that pregnant or lactating cats, who often eat 10–15 ounces of food a day, have double or triple the vitamin requirements of an average 5–7-pound cat.

332. Cats and Alternative Remedies That *Don't* Mix

Cats have very different reactions to drugs and herbs because of their species bioindividuality. (Morphine, for example, a sedative, painkilling drug causes excitation in cats.) And many commonly used alternative compounds that work wonders for people can harm your pet.

Any compounds with benzene, benzyl alcohol, or phenol-containing essential oils such as thyme, cinnamon, and tea tree can be toxic to cats. They should not be given orally or used on the skin, as the cat will lick it off.

Other herbs that should not be used for cats are those high in salicin (white willow), coumarins (red clover), and licorice (glycyrrhiza globra). Garlic (*Allium sativum*) is a close relative of the onion (*Allium cepa*) and may cause anemia if used long-term to control fleas. Consult an experienced practitioner before trying new alternatives on your pet. (See section 343.)

333. Any Questions About Chapter XXII?

I take coenzyme-Q10. Is it okay to give it to my dog, who's getting on in years (she's ten)?

It's not only okay, I recommend it. Coenzyme-Q10 is a safe, nontoxic nutrient that's vital to life. Without it, your dog's cells would not work properly. As dogs age they produce less Co-Q10, so now would be a very good time to supplement. It can strengthen her heart, her immune system, and her ability to cope with stress. It is available as a powder in a capsule or in a gel capsule. (The gel capsule is more potent.) For small and medium dogs I suggest 10 mg. daily. If she is one of the large or giant breeds, you can give her 30 mg. daily, mixed with food.

Every time we take our Siamese cat with us to our country home, he sneezes, scratches, and loses hair. Could this be an allergy—and if so, what can we give him?

It sounds as if your pet is having an allergic reaction to something (dust, mold, airborne spores) in your country home. I suggest you try supplementing his diet with 100 mg. of vitamin C, a natural antihistamine, for at least a month before you plan to leave, and then continue the supplementation while you're there. You'll all have a better time of it. (Feline vitamin C supplements are available at pet stores or from your vet. I know that owners often want to share their vitamins with their pets, but a pill that's easy for you to take might be too large for your cat—and if it's ascorbic acid, it could burn your pet's esophagus.)

XXIII

Vitamin "Yeses" and "Nos" You Should Know

334. Cautions

Though we all know that vitamins are good for us, there are times, situations, and metabolic conditions where caution and special adjustments are advised. I recommend you look over the following list carefully for your own well-being and in order to get the most from your vitamins.

• Chronic hypervitaminosis A can occur in patients receiving megadoses as treatment for dermatological conditions. Use beta-carotene instead.
• A deficiency of vitamin A can lead to loss of vitamin C.
• Large doses of vitamin A may cause birth defects, particularly if taken in the first trimester, and should be avoided by pregnant women. Use beta-carotene instead.
• An oversupply of vitamin B1 (thiamine) can affect thyroid and insulin production and might cause B6 deficiency, as well as loss of other B vitamins.
• Prolonged ingestion of any B vitamin can result in significant depletion of the others.
• Pregnant women should check with their doctors before taking sustained doses of over 50 mg. of vitamin B6 (pyridoxine).
• B6 should not be taken by anyone under L-dopa treatment for Parkinson's disease.

• Large doses of vitamin B2 (riboflavin), especially if taken without antioxidant supplements, may cause a sensitivity to sunlight.

• Because vitamin D promotes absorption of calcium, a large excess of stored vitamin D can cause too much calcium in the blood (hypercalcemia).

• Don't eat raw egg whites. They deactivate the body's biotin.

• It is possible that large amounts of vitamin C might reverse the anticoagulant activity of the blood thinner warfarin, commonly prescribed as the drug Coumadin™.

• Diabetes and heart patients should check with their doctors, because vitamin C might necessitate a lower dosage of pills.

• High doses of vitamin C wash out B12 and folic acid, so be sure you are taking at least the daily requirement of both.

• Excessive doses of choline, taken over a long period of time, may produce a deficiency of vitamin B6.

• If you have a heart disorder, check with your physician for the proper vitamin-D dosage to take.

• Vitamin E should be used cautiously by anyone with an overactive thyroid, diabetes, high blood pressure, or rheumatic heart disease. (If you have any of these conditions, start at a very low dosage and build up gradually by 100 IU daily each month to between 400 and 800 IU.)

• Rheumatic heart fever sufferers should know that they have an imbalance between the two sides of their hearts and large vitamin-E doses can increase the imbalance and worsen the condition. (Before using supplements, consult your physician.)

• Vitamin E can elevate blood pressure in hypertensives, but if supplementation is started with a low dosage and increased slowly, the end result will be an eventual lowering of the pressure through the vitamin's diuretic properties.

• Diabetics have been able to reduce their insulin levels with E. Check with your physician.

• Decreases in vitamin E should be gradual, too.

• An excessive intake of folic acid can mask symptoms of pernicious anemia.

• High doses of folic acid for extended periods of time are not recommended for anyone with a medical history of convulsive disorders or hormone-related cancer.

• High doses of vitamin K can build up and cause a red cell breakdown and anemia.

• Folic acid supplements are contraindicated for anyone taking the anticonvulsant phenotoin.

• Patients on the blood thinner dicumarol should be aware that synthetic K could counteract the effectiveness of the drug. Conversely, the drug inhibits the absorption of natural vitamin K.

• Sweats and flushes can occur from too much vitamin K.

• Niacin should be used cautiously by anyone with severe diabetes, glaucoma, peptic ulcers, impaired liver function, or gout.

• Do not give niacin to your dog or cat; it causes flushing and sweating and greatly discomforts the animal. Do not supplement a pet's diet with vitamins A or D unless your vet specifically advises it.

• Excessive amounts of PABA (para-aminobenzoic acid) in certain individuals can have a negative effect on the liver, kidneys, and heart.

• Iron should not be taken by anyone with sickle-cell anemia, hemochromatosis, or thalassemia.

• If your iron supplement is ferrous sulfate, you're losing vitamin E.

• Large quantities of caffeine can inhibit iron absorption.

• Anyone with kidney malfunction should not take more than 3,000 mg. of magnesium on a daily basis.

• Too much manganese will reduce utilization of the body's iron.

• High doses of manganese can cause motor difficulties and weakness in certain individuals.

• Diets high in fat increase phosphorus absorption and lower your calcium levels.

• If you take cortisone drugs, such as Aldactone™ and prednisone, you lose potassium and retain sodium. Check with your physician for proper supplements.

• Excessive perspiration can cause a depletion of sodium.

• Too much sodium can cause a potassium loss.

• Excessive zinc intakes can result in iron and copper losses.

• If you add zinc to your diet, be sure you're getting enough vitamin A.

• Anyone suffering from Wilson's disease is susceptible to copper toxicity.

• Too much cobalt may cause an unwanted enlargement of the thyroid gland.

• Anyone taking thyroid medication should be aware that kelp also affects that gland. If you have been using both, a consultation with your doctor and retesting are advised. You might need *less* prescription medicine than you think.

• Large amounts of raw cabbage can cause an iodine deficiency and throw off thyroid production in individuals with existing low-iodine intakes.

• Oyster shells, dolomite, and bonemeal, although good sources of calcium, may contain lead or other toxic substances.

• Milk that contains synthetic vitamin D can deplete the body of magnesium.

• Heavy coffee and tea drinkers—cola drinkers, too—should be aware that large caffeine ingestion creates an inositol shortage.

• Inform your doctor if you're taking large amounts of vitamin C. C can change results of lab tests for sugar in the blood and urine and give false negative results in test for blood in stool specimens.

• Don't engage in strenuous physical activity within four hours after taking vitamin A if you want optimum absorption.

• Copper has a tendency to accumulate in the blood and deplete the brain's zinc supplies.

• RNA-DNA supplements increase serum uric acid levels and should *not* be taken by anyone with gout.

• Tyrosine and phenylalanine may increase blood pressure and should *not* be taken with MAO inhibitors or other anti-depressant drugs. These amino acids are also contraindicated for anyone with pigmented malignant melanomas.

• PABA is contraindicated with *methotrexate* (Mexate™), a cancer-fighting drug.

• Drinking grapefruit juice with allergy medication such as Seldane, which contains terfenadine, can cause irregular heartbeat and increase your risk of heart attack.

• People taking MAO inhibitors should avoid aged foods high in tyramine (cheese, wine, etc.) and be aware that the tyramine content of foods generally *increases* with age.

• Folacin (folic acid) decreases the anticonvulsant action of *phenytoin* (Dilantin™).

• Antibiotics are reduced in their effectiveness when taken with supplements. (Take supplements at least an hour before or two hours after prescription antibiotics.)

• Calcium can interfere with the effectiveness of tetracycline.

• High doses of vitamin D or calcium ascorbate are contraindicated if you are taking the heart medication *digoxin* (Lanoxin™).

• Broad-spectrum antibiotics should not be taken with high doses of vitamin A.

• Vitamin A should not be taken in conjunction with the acne drug Accutane™ (*isotretinoin*).

• Choline is not recommended during the depressive phase of manic-depressive conditions, since it can deepen this particular sort of depression.

• Papaya, as well as raw pineapple, is not recommended for anyone with an ulcer.

• The herbs bilberry, burdock, damiana, juniper, peppermint, sage, willow, and yarrow can interfere with iron absorption.

335. Any Questions About Chapter XXIII?

Is it true that licorice candy can be dangerous to people taking antihypertensive medication?

Surprisingly, yes. In fact, just two or more candy twists made with natural licorice can interfere with many antihypertensive (and diuretic) medicines by increasing sodium reabsorption, potassium excretion, and water retention.

I've been told to stay away from foods containing MSG, so I read labels carefully and generally avoid Chinese food. But are all foods that contain MSG labeled?

The FDA requires products containing MSG to list it on their labels. (Look for monosodium glutamate or glutamate, which mean MSG.) But recent studies have shown that there are foods—tomatoes and cheese, for instance—that contain monosodium glutamate (MSG) naturally! In other words, an Italian meal may contain as much MSG as an Asian one. (You might be interested to know that Asian foods frequently contain natural chemicals such as salicylates and amines that can also cause allergic reactions.)

XXIV

Fast Facts at a Glance

336. Supplements Simplified

So many supplements these days are referred to by letters that nutrition can often seem like an alphabet soup of confusion. I hope this list of commonly used abbreviations simplifies sorting out supplements that might be right for you.

AHAs (alpha-hydroxy acids)—skin exfoliants used to "unglue" old cells and stimulate new cell growth.

AKG (alkyglycerol)—disease-fighting compound in shark liver oil.

BHAs (beta-hydroxy acids)—skin exfoliants used to "unglue" old cells and stimulate new cell growth.

CLA (conjugated linoleic acid)—helps reduce body fat, promote weight loss, enhance muscle tone; protects against many types of cancer.

Co-Q10 (coenzyme-Q10)—helps strengthen the heart, reverse gum disease, lower blood pressure.

DGL (deglycyrrhizinated licorice)—provides a natural buffer against stomach acid; relieves pain due to excess gas or ulcers; helps reduce pain from arthritis.

DHA (docosahexaenoic acid)—essential fatty acid that may prevent depression, memory loss, and enhance vision.

DHEA (dehydroepiandrosterone)—a natural hormone that strengthens the immune system; may help in treating symptoms of lupus, rheumatoid arthritis, other autoimmune diseases.

DMAE (dimethylaminoethanol)—enhances mental function; acts as a natural alternative to Ritalin™ in helping children with attention deficit disorder.

DNA (deoxyribonucleic acid) and **RNA** (ribonucleic acid)—present in every cell in the body, essential for cell repair and growth; nucleic acids that may retard and even reverse the aging process.

Ev.Ext-33—a patented extract of a unique subspecies of ginger that can reduce pain and inflammation.

FOS (fructo-oligosaccharide)—a complex plant sugar; enhances immune function; normalizes blood sugar levels; increases good bacteria in the gut; helps protect against gastrointestinal cancers.

GLA (gamma-linolenic acid)—a fatty acid in borage oil used for the treatment of arthritis.

HCA (hydrocitric acid)—a natural appetite suppressant.

HMB (beta-hydroxy beta-methylbutyrate)—sports supplement; builds muscle, decreases fat.

5-HTP (5-hydroxytryptophan)—similar to tryptophan; a natural alternative to Prozac™; suppresses appetite; helps alleviate depression and promote restful sleep.

IHN (inositol hexanicotinate)—a "no-flush" niacin; helps prevent heart disease by lowering blood triglyceride levels and raising HDL (good cholesterol) levels; may enhance memory.

MCP (modified citrus pectin)—a carbohydrate found in plant cell walls; can slow down the spread of cancer.

MCTs (medium-chain triglycerides)—saturated fats that are burned rapidly by the body and do not promote weight gain or raise blood cholesterol levels; improve athletic endurance; may help dieters shed pounds.

MSM (methylsulfonylmethane)—an organic sulfur; helps reduce allergic symptoms; promotes wound healing; relieves pain and inflammation from arthritis.

NAC (n-acetyl cysteine)—increases levels of the body's most abundant antioxidant, glutathione; helps treat ear infections, speed recovery after exercise; protect against cancer-causing chemicals in cigarette smoke.

NADH (nicotinamide adenine dinucleotide)—protects against brain aging; helps memory; relieves some symptoms of Alzheimer's and Parkinson's diseases; enhances ability to work out.

PC (phosphatidylcholine)—supports liver function; helps to reverse liver damage.

PCOs (proanthocyanidins)—antioxidants found in the bark, stems, leaves, and skins of some plants; help protect collagen from free-radical damage; promote good circulation; may prevent skin from aging.

PS (phosphatidylserine)—helps enhance memory and ability to concentrate.

PSK (coriolus versicolor extract)—derived from an edible mushroom; boosts and normalizes immune function; improves effect of cancer therapies.

SAMe (s-adenosyl-L-methione)—works as a natural antidepressant and anti-inflammatory; may alleviate pain associated with osteoarthritis.

SOD (superoxide dismutase)—a potent antioxidant that can help retard the aging process.

TMG (trimethylglycine)—also known as betain; converts harmful homocysteine into a beneficial amino acid; reduces risk of heart disease; helps prevent certain cancers; helps protect against Alzheimer's disease.

337. Finding Good Fats Fast

There's a lot of confusion about good fats and bad fats, which I hope I've cleared up in Chapter VI. (See sections 87 through 94.) But if you need to know which are the good-for-you fats fast, here's a healthy short list:

Borage Oil—contains GLA (gamma-linolenic acid); helpful in reducing inflammation and pain of arthritis; can strengthen adrenal glands; may help regulate menstrual cycles and reduce PMS.

Canola Oil—excellent source of monounsaturated fat which can raise levels of good cholesterol and lower risk of heart disease.

Evening Primrose Oil—another essential fatty acid containing GLA; converts into hormonelike compounds helpful in treating PMS symptoms, maintaining healthy skin, reducing cholesterol, and controlling high blood pressure.

Flaxseed Oil—one of the best sources of omega-3 fatty acids; may block growth of cancerous tumors; reduces inflammation; helps normalize hormone levels.

Olive Oil—high in monounsaturated fat that can raise levels of good cholesterol; lowers risk of heart disease. (Go for the extra-virgin cold-pressed if you're using it in food.)

Pumpkin Seed Oil—high in omega-3 and omega-6 essential fatty acids; helps digestion, circulation, good for pregnant and lactating women.

338. Quick Amino Acid Reference

These building blocks of protein are vital to our health, but they, too, can be confusing when it comes to remembering which is which and what does what. (For an in-depth look at individual amino acids, see Chapter V, sections 72 through 86.) For faster reference the following list should help:

ALANINE: Enhances immune system; lowers risk of kidney stones; aids in alleviating hypoglycemia.

ARGININE: Increases sperm count; accelerates wound healing; enhances sexual performance in men; tones muscle tissue.

ASPARAGINE: Promotes balance in the central nervous system.

ASPARTIC ACID: Enhances immune system; increases stamina and endurance; expels harmful ammonia from the body.

BRANCHED CHAIN AMINO ACIDS (LEUCINE, ISOLEUCINE, VALINE): (See aspartic acid.)

CYSTEINE: Helps prevent baldness; alleviates psoriasis; improves condition of hair, skin, and nails; promotes fat burning and muscle building. (Converts into cystine as needed.)

CYSTINE: Aids in preventing side effects from chemotherapy and radiation therapy; reduces accumulation of age spots. (Converts into cysteine as needed.)

GLUTAMIC ACID: Helps improve brain function; aids in metabolism of sugars and fats; useful in treatment of children's behavioral disorders, epilepsy, and muscular dystrophy. (Converts into glutamine as needed.)

GLUTAMINE: Helps improve brain function; alleviate fatigue; aid in ulcer healing time; build and maintain muscle; elevate mood; reduce craving for sugar and alcohol. (Converts to glutamic acid in brain.)

GLYCINE: Necessary for central nervous system function; aids in healing; helps treat stomach hyperacidity; prevent seizures. (Can be converted into serine in the body when needed.)

HISTIDINE: Helps alleviate rheumatoid arthritis; alleviates stress; aids in improving libido.

LYSINE: Helps improve concentration; enhances fertility; aids in preventing herpes simplex infection.

METHIONINE: Aids in lowering cholesterol; helps in treatment of schizophrenia and Parkinson's disease; may protect against tumors.

ORNITHINE: Works as a muscle-building hormone; increases potency of arginine.

PHENYLALANINE: Acts as an antidepressant; helps suppress appetite; can function in some forms as a natural painkiller.

PROLINE: Aids in wound healing; helps increase learning ability.

SERINE: Helps alleviate pain; can act as a natural antipsychotic.

TAURINE: Helps strengthen heart function; may prevent macular degeneration; aids in digestion of fats and absorption of fat-soluble vitamins.

THREONINE: Necessary for utilization of protein in diet; may provide symptomatic improvement in some patients with Lou Gehrig's disease, amytrophic lateral sclerosis (ALS).

TRYPTOPHAN: Aids in reducing anxiety; helps induce sleep; may help in control of alcoholism.

TYROSINE: Improves sex drive; helps alleviate stress; can act as an appetite suppressant and mood elevator.

339. Herbal Sources of Primary Antioxidant Vitamins and Minerals

Vitamin A and Carotenoids: alfalfa, borage leaves, burdock root, cayenne, capsicum, eyebright, fennel seed, hops, horsetail, kelp, lemongrass, nettle, paprika, parsley, peppermint, raspberry leaf, red clover, rose hips, sage, uva ursi, watercress, yellow dock.

Vitamin C: alfalfa, burdock root, cayenne, chickweed, eyebright, fennel seed, fenugreek, hops, horsetail, kelp, peppermint, mullein, nettle, oat straw, paprika, parsley, plantain, raspberry leaf, red clover, rose hips, skullcap, yarrow, yellow dock.

Vitamin E: alfalfa, dandelion, dong quai, flaxseed, nettle, oat straw, raspberry leaf, rose hips.

Selenium: alfalfa, burdock root, catnip, cayenne, chamomile, chickweed, fennel seed, fenugreek, garlic, ginseng, hawthorn berry, hops, horsetail, lemongrass, milk thistle, nettle, oat straw, parsley, peppermint, raspberry leaf, rose hips, sarsaparilla, uva ursi, yarrow, yellow dock.

Zinc: alfalfa, burdock root, cayenne, chamomile, chickweed, dandelion, eyebright, fennel seed, hops, milk thistle, mullein, nettle, parsley, rose hips, sage, sarsaparilla, skullcap, wild yam.

340. Big-Time Immune System Boosters

Because the immune system is the most powerful weapon you have for keeping healthy, being able to quickly recall major nutrients, herbs, and supplements that can strengthen it will not only simplify your life—it can help extend it!

Acidophilus
Astragalus
Bayberry
Beta-1, 3 Glucan
Bioflavonoids
Bovine trachel cartilage
Cat's claw (una de gato)
Chlorella
Coenzyme-Q10
DHEA (dehydroepiandrosterone)
Echinacea
Essential fatty acids
Feverfew (American)
Garlic
Germanium
Ginseng
Glutathione
Goldenseal
Grapeseed extract
Gugul
Kelp
L-arnine and L-ornithine
Maitake, shiitake,
    and raishi mushroom
Manganese
Melatonin
Propolis
PSK (coriolus versicolor
    extract)
Quercetin
Selenium
Shark cartilage/liver oil
Suma
Vitamin A
Vitamin B complex
Vitamin C
Vitamin E
Whey
Zinc

341. Quick Reference Cancer Defense Guide

Along with antioxidant vitamins and minerals (see section 101), there are many naturally occurring substances in foods that appear to have even more powerful anticancer properties. Among them: beta-carotene, quercetin, indoles and isothiocyanatos (in cruciferous vegetables), and omega-3 fatty acids.

Since your best defense against cancer is a strong nutritional offense—be sure you put the following winning foods in your diet.

CANCER-FIGHTING FOODS TO INCREASE IN DIET

Food	Comments
Carrots	Highest in beta-carotene; more easily absorbed when cooked.
Cantaloupe	Great vitamin A, beta-carotene, and vitamin C source; low calorie and high fiber; aids in combatting excess sodium.
Cabbage	A cruciferous vegetable; can lower risk of colorectal cancer; just 2 tablespoons cooked daily has been found to help prevent stomach cancer.
Squash	Same as carrots above.
Sweet potatoes	Same as carrots above.
Papaya	Same as cantaloupe.
Spinach	Same as cantaloupe. (See "Cautions" in section 334.)
Broccoli	A cruciferous vegetable that contains indoles and isothiocyanates (substances that help reduce and prevent certain cancerous tumors); rich in carotenoids.
Brussels sprouts	Same as broccoli and other crucifers.
Bok choy	Same as broccoli and other crucifers.
Cauliflower	Same as broccoli and other crucifers.
Kale	Same as broccoli and other crucifers.

Radish	Same as broccoli and other crucifers.
Horseradish	Same as broccoli and other crucifers.
Rutabaga	Same as broccoli and other crucifers.
Kohlrabi	Same as broccoli and other crucifers.
Celery	Same as broccoli and other crucifers.
Onions	High in quercetin (not destroyed by cooking); can suppress malignant cells before they become tumors.
Tuna	Rich in omega-3 fatty acids; helps immune system to prevent and inhibit spreading cancers. (May help halt metastasis once tumor occurs.)
Salmon	Same as tuna.
Sardines	Same as tuna.
Mackerel	Same as tuna.
Bluefish	Same as tuna.
Wheat bran	Dietary fiber content helps prevent colon cancer. (The National Cancer Institute suggests 35 grams of fiber daily.)
Corn bran	Provides protection against carcinogens.
Rice bran	Same as corn and wheat bran.
Oat bran	Same as corn and wheat bran.
Fruits and vegetables high in vitamins A, C, E, and selenium	(See sections 28, 43, 45, and 65)
Soybeans and soy-based foods	High in many cancer-fighting phytochemicals (See section 129.)

HIGH-RISK CANCER FOODS TO DECREASE IN DIET

Food	Comments
Bacon	Contains nitrite, an additive that can interact with natural chemicals in our foods and bodies to form nitrosamines, potent cancer-causing substances.
Luncheon meats	Same as bacon above.
Frankfurters	Same as bacon above.
Knockwurst	Same as bacon above.
Smoked fish	Same as bacon above.
Butter, margarine, mayonnaise, oils	It's recommended that no more than 20–30 percent of the calories in your diet come from fat. (Individuals whose diets contain over 40 percent fat, saturated as well as unsaturated, are more likely to develop colon, breast, and prostate cancers.) In these foods, 100 percent of the calories are fat.
Coffee (regular or decaffeinated)	Implicated in bladder and pancreatic cancers.
Liver and high-fat meat	Contaminants accumulate in an animal's liver and fat cells.
Tobacco	Cigarettes, cigars, pipes, chewing tobacco, and snuff have been implicated in the development of cancer of the mouth, throat, esophagus, pancreas, and bladder as well as the lung. (Smoking—as well as secondhand smoke—

	also increases the risk of cervical cancer for women.)
Alcohol	Found to cause liver cancer and to contribute to cancers of the mouth, larynx, and esophagus, particularly among smokers.
Food additives, particularly BHA, BHT, Food Dyes Red No. 3, Blue No. 2, Green No. 3, and Citrus Red No. 2; propyl gallate and sodium nitrite	Highly suspect carcinogens.

XXV

Locating a Nutritionally Oriented Doctor

342. How to Go About It

If you want to consult a nutritionally oriented physician—or other alternative health practitioner—but don't know any in your area, the following organizations can help you find one. If you're seeking a Board-certified physician, you should specify that, as not all nutritional health professionals are M.D.s

Organizations that have home pages on the World Wide Web, and most do, can provide you with immediate information about licensing, certification, and the fastest way to access a local practitioner. (If you are not on-line, you can probably find a library in your area that is.)

It should be understood that no endorsement or other opinion of any practitioner contacted through these services (or such practitioner's diagnoses, treatments, or credentials) is implied or should be inferred.

(If you contact an organization by mail, as a courtesy please be sure to enclose a self-addressed, stamped envelope with all queries.)

ADDRESS

American Academy of Medical Acupuncture (AAMA)
5820 Wilshire Blvd., Suite 500
Los Angeles, CA 90036

(213) 937-5514 or 1-800-521-2262
Web site: www.medicalacupuncture.org

American Academy of Osteopathy (AAO)
3500 DePauw Blvd., Suite 1080
Indianapolis, IN 46268
(317) 879-1881
Web site: www.aao.medguide.net

American Association of Naturopathic Physicians
601 Valley, Suite 105
Seattle, WA 98109
(206) 298-0126 or (206) 298-0125 (referral line)
Web site: www.naturopathic.org

American Chiropractic Association (ACA)
1701 Clarendon Blvd., Suite 200
Arlington, VA 22209
(703) 276-8800 or 1-800-986-4636
Web site: www.amerchiro.org

American Holistic Medical Association
6728 Old McLean Village Drive
McLean, VA 22101
(703) 556-9728
Web site: www.ahma.holistic.com

American Holistic Nurses Association
P.O. Box 2130
Flagstaff, AZ 86003-2130
1-800-278-2462 or 1-800-278-AHNA
Web site: www.ahna.org

American Massage Therapy Association
820 Davis St., Suite 100
Evanston, IL 60201
(847) 864-0123
Web site: www.amtamassage.org

Council for Homeopathic Certification
1199 Sanchez Street
San Francisco, CA 94114
(415) 789-7677

Council for Responsible Nutrition
1300 19th St. NW
Washington, DC 20036
(202) 872-1488
Web site: www.crnusa.org

HEAL (Human Ecology Action League)
P.O. Box 29629
Atlanta, GA 30359
(404) 248-1898
Web site: http://members.aol.com/HEALNatnl/index.html

Herb Research Foundation
1007 Pearl Street, Suite 200
Boulder, CO 80302
(303) 449-2265
Web site: www.herbs.org

Homeopathic Academy of Naturopathic Physicians
(HANP)
1232 South East Foster Place
Portland, OR 97266
(503) 761-3298 Fax: (503) 761-3298
Web site: www.healthy.net/hanp
E-mail: hanp@igc.apc.org

International Academy of Holistic Health & Medicine
218 Avenue B
Redondo Beach, CA 90277
(310) 540-0564

International Foundation for Homeopathy
P.O. Box 7

Edmonds, WA 98020-0007
(206) 776-4147 Fax: (206) 776-1499
E-mail: ish@nwlink.com

National Center for Homeopathy
801 N. Fairfax, #306
Alexandria, VA 22314
(703) 548-7790 Fax: (703) 548-7792
Web site: www.homeopathic.org

National Health Federation
P.O. Box 688
Monrovia, CA 91017
(626) 357-2181
Web site: www.healthfreedom.com

Nutrition Consultants of Tulsa
2021 South Lewis, Suite 710
Tulsa, OK 74105-5713
(918) 749-9077

Office of Alternative Medicine (OAM) at the National
Institutes of Health (NIH)
OAM Clearinghouse
P.O. Box 8218
Silver Spring, MD 20907-8218
1-888-644-6226
Fax: (301) 495-4957
Web site: www.altmed.od.nih.gov

Prevention Magazine Readers' Service
Emmaus, PA 18049
1-800-813-8070
Web site: www.healthyideas.com

343. Finding Specialized Nutritional Help

(Enclose a self-addressed, stamped envelope with all mail queries.)

For AIDS	The American Foundation for AIDS Research (AMFAR) 733 Third Avenue, 12th floor New York, NY 10017 (212) 682-7740 Web site: www.thebody.com/amfar/amfar/.html
For alcoholism	Alcoholics Anonymous World Services 475 Riverside Drive New York, NY 10115 (212) 870-3400 Web site: www.alcoholics-anonymous.org
For allergies	Asthma & Allergy Foundation of America 1125 15th Street NW, Suite 502 Washington, DC 20005 1-800-7ASTHMA; (202) 466-7643 Web site: www.housecall.com/sponsors/nhc/1996vha/aafa.html
For Alzheimer illnesses	Alzheimer's Disease Education and Referral Center (ADEAR) P.O. Box 8250 Silver Spring, MD 20907-8250 (301) 495-3311 or 1-800-438-4380 Web site: www.alzheimers.org
For arthritis	Arthritis Consulting Services 4620 North State Road 7, Suite 206 Ft. Lauderdale, FL 33319 1-800-327-3027 Web site: www.stoparthritis.com

Arthritis Foundation
1330 W. Peachtree Street
Atlanta, GA 30309
1-800-282-7800 or (404) 872-7100
Web site: www.arthritis.org

For breast-feeding   La Leche League, Int., Inc.
1400 N. Meacham Road
Schaumburg, IL 60173
(847) 519-7730
Web site: www.lalecheleague.org

For cancer   American Cancer Society
1599 Clifton Road NE
Atlanta, GA 30329-4251
1-800-ACS-2345 or (404) 320-3333
Web site: www.cancer.org

Cancer Information Service, National
Cancer Institute
32 Center Drive, MSC2580
Building 31, Room 10A07
Bethesda, MD 20892
1-800-332-8615 or 1-800-4-CANCER
Web site: www.nci.nih.gov/hpage/
cis.htm

National Cancer Institute
9000 Rockville Pike
Bethesda, MD 20892
(301) 496-4000 or 1-800-422-6237
Web site: www.nih.gov/science/
campus

For cardiovascular   American Heart Association
disorders   P.O. Box 3049
Syracuse, NY 13220-3049
1-800-242-8721
Web site: www.amhrt.org

National Stroke Association
96 Inverness Drive East, Suite 1
Englewood, CO 80112
1-800-787-6537 or (303) 649-9299
Web site: www.stroke.org

For chronic fatigue syndrome

Chronic Fatigue and Immune Dysfunction Syndrome Association of America, Inc.
P.O. Box 220398
Charlotte, NC 28222-0398
1-800-44-CFIDS or 1-800-442-3437
Web site: www.cfids.org

For communicative disorders

American Tinnitus Association
P.O. Box 5
Portland, OR 97207
(503) 248-9985
Web site: www.ata.org

National Center for Stutterers
200 East 33rd Street
New York, NY 10016
1-800-221-2483
Web site: www.stuttering.org

For depression

National Depressive and Manic-Depressive Association
730 N. Franklin, Suite 501
Chicago, IL 60610
1-800-826-3632 or (312) 642-0049
Web site: www.ndma.org

For diabetes

American Diabetes Association
1600 Duke Street
Alexandria, VA 22314
1-800-232-3472 or (703) 549-1500
Web site: www.diabetes.org

International Juvenile Diabetes Foundation

120 Wall Street, 19th floor
New York, NY 10005
1-800-533-3873 or 1-800-JDS-CURE
Web site: www.jdscure.org

For eating disorders   Anorexia Nervosa and Related Eating
Disorders, Inc. (ANRED)
P.O. Box 5102
Eugene, OR 97405
(541) 344-1144
Web site: www.anred.com

For epilepsy   Epilepsy Foundation of America
4351 Garden City Drive
Landover, MD 20785
(301) 459-3700
Web site: www.efa.org

For infertility   Resolve
1310 Broadway
Somerville, MA 02144
(617) 623-0744 or (617) 643-2424
Web site: www.resolve.org

For osteoporosis and   The Osteoporosis and Related Bone
related bone   Diseases National Resource Center
diseases   1150 17th Street NW Suite 500
Washington, DC 20036-4603
(202) 223-0344 or 1-800-624-BONE
Web site: www.osteo.org

For pets   The American Holistic Veterinary
Medical Association
2214 Old Emmerton Road
Bel Air, MD 21015
(410) 569-0795
Web site: www.altvetmed.com

For sleep disorders   San Diego Sleep Disorder Center
1842 Third Ave.
San Diego, CA 92101

(619) 235-0248

For women   National Organization for Women
                       (NOW)
                       1000 16th Street NW, Suite 700
                       Washington, DC 20036
                       (202) 331-0066
                       Web site: www.now.org

                       National Women's Health Network
                       514 10th Street NW, Suite 400
                       Washington, DC 20004
                       (202) 628-7814 Fax: (202) 347-1168

344. Free Calls for Fast Answers

The National Health Information Center, sponsored by the
Department of Health and Human Services, can direct you
to numerous free health information services. Just call:
1-800-336-4797.

Among the many toll-free health hotlines available are:

• Acne Help Line: 1-800-222-SKIN; in California, 1-800-
221-SKIN
• Alzheimer's Disease and Related Disorders Association:
1-800-621-0379; in Illinois, 1-800-572-6037
• American Council for the Blind: 1-800-424-8666
• American Society for Dermatologic Surgery: 1-800-441-
ASDS
• Arthritis Medical Center: 1-800-327-3027
• Bulimia and Anorexia Self-Help: 1-800-762-3334
• Cancer Information Service: 1-800-4-CANCER
• CDC National AIDS/HIV HotLine: 1-800-342-AIDS
• Dial-a-Hearing Screening Test: 1-800-222-EARS
• Epilepsy Foundation of America: 1-800-EFA-1000
• Food Allergy Network: 1-800-929-4040
• Heartlife: 1-800-241-6993

- Herbs: Penn Herb, 1-800-523-9971; Herbal Pathways, 1-800-631-3575; Green Mountain Herbs, 1-800-525-2696; Foodscience Corporation, 1-800-451-5190
- Juvenile Diabetes Foundation International: 1-800-JDF-CURE
- National AIDS HotLine: 1-800-342-AIDS
- National Center for Stuttering: 1-800-221-2483
- National Drug Abuse Treatment Referral and Information Service: 1-800-COCAINE
- National Institute on Drug Abuse: 1-800-662-4357
- National Psoriasis HotLine: 1-888-551-6700
- Second Surgical Opinion HotLine: 1-800-638-6833
- Sexually Transmitted Disease HotLine: 1-800-227-8922
- Sudden Infant Death Syndrome HotLine: 1-800-221-7437
- Temporomandibular joint disorders (TMJ) tooth & jaw problems: 1-800-822-6637
- Vegetarian Information Service (Morningstar Farms—A division of Miles Laboratories): 1-800-243-4143
- Vegetarian Awareness Network: 1-800-872-8343
- Y-Me Breast Cancer Support Program: 1-800-221-2141

Afterword

As more and more people have become aware of the importance of nutrients and supplements in their daily lives—and increasingly dissatisfied with HMOs' mismanaged care and the high cost and alarming side effects of drugs—the need for clear, practical information needed for self-health has grown enormously. Conventional scientific research has finally validated what I and other nutritionists have known all along—that optimal nutrition *can* pave the way to optimal well-being. And with more and more people living longer—and determined to do so staying youthful, sexy, and healthy—a guide to the nutritional pathways available, and pitfalls to avoid, has become a necessity. It is my hope that this extensively revised millennium edition has fulfilled that need.

Whether you have read the book cover to cover or simply thumbed through to personally relevant points, I believe you'll find its reference value will increase as new life situations arise. My intention has always been to provide an omnibus guide that could answer not only your present vitamin and supplement questions, but future ones as well. In this edition, I have tried in all ways to highlight the health concerns of the new century based on the scientific information available at this writing. As time goes by you'll probably find that certain sections, such as those on retarding the aging process, will bear rereading, as will those offering regimens for whatever your new particular health or lifestyle circumstance happens to be. In other words, the information I have set down is meant to be pursued, and is intended not just for today, but for many, many happy and healthy tomorrows.

DR. EARL L. MINDELL, R.PH., PH.D.
Beverly Hills, California
July 31, 1998

Glossary

Absorption: the process by which nutrients are passed into the bloodstream.

Acetate: a derivative of acetic acid.

Acetic acid: used as a synthetic flavoring agent, one of the first food additives (vinegar is approximately 4–6 percent acetic acid); it is found naturally in cheese, coffee, grapes, peaches, raspberries, and strawberries; Generally Recognized As Safe (GRAS) when used only in packaging.

Acetone: a colorless solvent for fat, oils, and waxes, which is obtained by fermentation (inhalation can irritate lungs, and large amounts have a narcotic effect).

Acid: a water-soluble substance with sour taste.

Adrenals: the glands, located above each kidney, that manufacture adrenaline.

Alkali: an acid-neutralizing substance (sodium bicarbonate is an alkali used for excess acidity in foods).

Allergen: a substance that causes an allergy.

Alzheimer's disease: a progressively degenerative disease, involved with loss of memory, which new research indicates might be helped with extra choline.

Amino acid chelates: chelated minerals that have been produced by many of the same processes nature uses to chelate minerals in the body; in the digestive tract, nature surrounds the elemental minerals with amino acid, permitting them to be absorbed into the bloodstream.

Amino acids: the organic compounds from which proteins are constructed; there are twenty-three known amino acids, but only nine are indispensable nutrients for man—histidine, isoleucine, leucine, lysine, total S-containing amino acids, total aromatic amino acids, threonine, tryptophan, and valine.

Anorexia: loss of appetite.

Antibiotic: any of various substances that are effective in inhibiting or destroying bacteria.

Anticoagulant: something that delays or prevents blood clotting.

Antigen: any substance not normally present in the body that stimulates the body to produce antibodies.

Antihistamine: a drug used to reduce effects associated with histamine production in allergies and colds.

Antioxidant: a substance that can protect another substance from oxidation; added to foods to keep oxygen from changing the food's color.

Antitoxin: an antibody formed in response to, and capable of neutralizing, a poison of biologic origin.

Assimilation: the process whereby nutrients are used by the body and changed into living tissue.

Ataxia: loss of coordinated movement caused by disease of the nervous system.

ATP: a molecule called adenozine triphosphate, the fuel of life, a nucleotide—building block of nucleic acid—that produces biological energy with B1, B2, B3, and pantothenic acid.

Avidin: a protein in egg white capable of inactivating biotin.

Bacteriophage: a virus that infects bacteria.

Bariatrician: a weight-control doctor.

B cells: white blood cells, made in the bone marrow, which produce antibodies upon instructions from T cells, white blood cells manufactured in the thymus.

BHA: butylated hydroxyanisole; a preservative and antioxidant used in many products; insoluble in water; can be toxic to the kidneys.

BHT: butylated hydroxytoluene; a solid, white crystalline antioxidant used to retard spoilage of many foods; can be more toxic to the kidney than its nearly identical chemical cousin BHA.

Bioflavonoids: usually from orange and lemon rinds, these citrus-flavored compounds needed to maintain healthy blood-vessel walls are widely available in plants, citrus fruits, and rose hips; known as vitamin P complex.

Buffered: an antacid has been added to protect the stomach; helps pill dissolve faster.

Calciferol: a colorless, odorless crystalline material, insoluble in water; soluble in fats; a synthetic form of vitamin D made by irradiating ergosterol with ultraviolet light.

Calcium gluconate: an organic form of calcium.

Capillary: a minute blood vessel, one of many that connect the arteries and veins.

Carcinogen: a cancer-causing substance.

Carotene: an orange-yellow pigment occurring in many plants and capable of being converted into vitamin A in the body.

Casein: the protein in milk that has become the standard by which protein quality is measured.

Catabolism: the metabolic change of nutrients or complex substances into simpler compounds, accompanied by a release of energy.

Catalyst: a substance that modifies, especially increases, the rate of chemical reaction without being consumed or changed in the process.

Chelation: a process by which mineral substances are changed into easily digestible form.

Chronic: of long duration; continuing; constant.

CNS: central nervous system.

Coenzyme: the major, though nonprotein, part of an enzyme; usually a B vitamin.

Collagen: the primary organic constituent of bone, cartilage, and connective tissue (becomes gelatin through boiling).

Congenital: condition existing at birth, not hereditary.

Dehydration: a condition resulting from an excessive loss of water from the body.

Dermatitis: an inflammation of the skin; a rash.

Desiccated: dried; preserved by removing moisture.

Dicalcium phosphate: a filler used in pills, which is derived from purified mineral rocks and is an excellent source of calcium and phosphorus.

Diluents: fillers; inert material added to tablets to increase their bulk in order to make them a practical size for compression.

Diuretic: tending to increase the flow of urine from the body.

DHA: docosahexaenoic acid; a member of omega-3 family of essential fatty acids; made in the body from alpha-linolenic acid; found mainly in cold-water fish.

DNA: deoxyribonucleic acid; the nucleic acid in chromosomes that is part of the chemical basis for hereditary characteristics.

DV: the Percent Daily Value; used on food labels as recommendations for nutrients regardless of age or gender.

Endogenous: being produced from within the body.

Enteric coated: a tablet coated so that it dissolves in the intestine, not in the stomach (which is acid).

Enuresis: bed-wetting.

Enzyme: a protein substance found in living cells that brings about chemical changes; necessary for digestion of food.

Excipient: any inert substance used as a dilutant or vehicle for a drug.

Exogenous: being derived or developed from external causes.

FDA: Food and Drug Administration.

Fibrin: a insoluble protein that forms the necessary fibrous network in the coagulation of blood.

Free radicals: highly reactive chemical fragments that can produce an irritation of artery walls, start the arteriosclerotic process if vitamin E is not present; generally harmful.

Fructose: a natural sugar occurring in fruits and honey; called fruit sugar; often used as a preservative for foodstuffs and an intravenous nutrient.

Galactosemia: a hereditary disorder in which milk becomes toxic as food.

Gamma oryszanol: a by-product of rice bran which helps increase lean body mass while decreasing fatty tissue.

GLA: gamma-linolenic acid; member of omega-6 family; made in the body from linoleic acid.

Glucose: blood sugar; a product of the body's assimilation of carbohydrates and a major source of energy.

Glutamic acid: an amino acid present in all complete proteins; usually manufactured from vegetable protein; used as a salt substitute and a flavor-intensifying agent.

Glutamine: an amino acid that constitutes, with glucose, the major nourishment used by the nervous system.

Gluten: a mixture of two proteins—gliadin and glutenin—present in wheat, rye, oats, and barley.

Glycogen: the body's chief storage carbohydrate, primarily in the liver.

GRAS: Generally Recommended As Safe; a list established by Congress to cover substances added to food.

HDL: high-density lipoprotein; carries fats and cholesterol through bloodstream; considered the "good" cholesterol.

Hesperidin: part of the C complex.

Holistic treatment: treatment of the whole person.

Homeostasis: the body's physiological equilibrium.

Hormone: a substance formed in endocrine organs and transported by body fluids to activate other specifically receptive organs.

Humectant: a substance that is used to preserve the moisture content of materials.

Hydrochloric acid: a normally acidic part of the body's gastric juice.

Hydrogenation: a commercial process that solidifies oils (margarines and shortenings) by a chemical process; transfatty acids created by this process can raise cholesterol levels.

Hydrolyzed: put into water-soluble form.

Hydrolyzed protein chelate: water-soluble and chelated for easy assimilation.

Hypervitaminosis: a condition caused by an excessive ingestion of vitamins.

Hypoglycemia: a condition caused by abnormally low blood sugar.

Hypovitaminosis: a deficiency disease owning to an absence of vitamins in the diet.

Ichthyosis: a condition characterized by a scaliness on the outer layer of skin.

Idiopathic: a condition whose causes are not yet known.

Immune: protected against disease.

Insulin: the hormone, secreted by the pancreas, concerned with the metabolism of sugar in the body.

IU: International Units.

Lactating: producing milk.

Laxative: a substance that stimulates evacuation of the bowels.

LDL: low-density lipoprotein; the "bad" substance that deposits cholesterol along the artery walls when oxidized.

Linoleic acid: one of the polyunsaturated fats, a constituent of lecithin; known as vitamin F; primary member of the omega-6 family; indispensable for life, and must be obtained from foods.

Lipid: a fat or fatty substance.

Lipofuscin: age pigment in cells.

Lipoprotein: a carrier of fatty substances (fats, oil, cholesterol); transporter of lipids between intestine, liver, and body cells; characterized by weight (i.e. low-density, high-density, etc.).

Lipotropic: preventing abnormal or excessive accumulation of fat in the liver.

Megavitamin therapy: treatment of illness with massive amounts of vitamins.

Metabolize: to undergo change by physical and chemical processes.

Mucopolysaccharide: thick gelatinous material that is found many places in the body; it glues cells together and lubricates joints.

MUFA: monounsaturated fatty acid.

Nitrites: used as fixatives in cured meats; can combine with natural stomach and food chemicals to cause dangerous cancer-causing agents called nitrosamines.

Omega-3: a family of essential fatty acids generally supplied inadequately in the modern diet; the primary omega-3 is alpha-linolenic acid.

Omega-6: a family of essential fatty acids abundant in the modern diet; the primary omega-6 is linolenic acid.

Orthomolecular: the right molecule used for the right treatment; doctors who practice preventive medicine and use vitamin therapies are known as orthomolecular physicians.

OSHA: Occupational Safety and Health Administration.

Oxalates: organic chemicals found in certain foods, especially spinach, which can combine with calcium to form calcium oxalate, an insoluble chemical the body cannot use.

PABA: para-aminobenzoic acid; a member of the B complex.

Palmitate: water-solubilized vitamin A.

Phospholipids: a class of fatty compounds found in cell membranes; lecithin is best known.

PKU (phenylketonuria): a hereditary disease caused by the lack of an enzyme needed to convert an essential amino acid (phenylalanine) into a form usable by the body; can cause mental retardation unless detected early.

Polyunsaturated fats: highly nonsaturated fats from vegetable sources; tend to lower blood cholesterol.

Predigested protein: protein that has been processed for fast assimilation and can go directly into the bloodstream.

Proprioception: the mind's ability to know what the body is doing.

Prostaglandins: hormonelike substances that aid in regulation of the immune system.

Provitamin: a vitamin precursor; a chemical substance necessary to produce a vitamin.

PUFA: polyunsaturated fatty acid.

RDA: Recommended Dietary Allowances as established by the Food and Nutrition Board, National Academy of Sciences, National Research Council.

RDI: Reference Daily Intake; based on Recommended Dietary Allowances; recommends nutrient levels regardless of age or sex; used on labels as the Percent Daily Value (DV).

RNA: the abbreviation used for ribonucleic acid.

Rose hips: a rich source of vitamin C; the nodule underneath the bud of a rose called a hip, in which the plant produces the vitamin C we extract.

Rutin: a substance extracted from buckwheat; part of the C complex.

Saturated fatty acids: usually solid at room temperature; higher proportions found in foods from animal sources; tend to raise blood cholesterol levels.

Sequestrant: a substance that absorbs ions and prevents changes that would affect flavor, texture, and color of food; used for water softening.

Syncope: brief loss of consciousness; fainting.

Synergistic: the action of two or more substances to produce an effect that neither alone could accomplish.

Synthetic: produced artificially.

Systemic: capable of spreading through the entire body.

T Cells: white blood cells, manufactured in the thymus, which protect the body from bacteria, viruses, and cancer-causing agents, while controlling the production of B cells, which produce antibodies, and unwanted production of potentially harmful T cells.

Teratological: monstrous or abnormal formations in animals or plants.

Tocopherols: the group of compounds (alpha, beta, delta, episilon, eta, gamma, and zeta) that make vitamin E; obtained through vacuum distillation of edible vegetable oils.

Toxicity: the quality or condition of being poisonous, harmful, or destructive.

Toxin: an organic poison produced in living or dead organisms.

Trans-fatty acids: artificial fatty acids produced by hydrogenation; although unsaturated, act like saturated fats and are unhealthy.

Triglycerides: fatty substances in the blood.

Unsaturated fatty acids: most often liquid at room temperature; primarily found in vegetable fats.

USAN: United States Adopted Names Council; cosponsored by the American Pharmaceutical Association (APhA), the American Medical Association (AMA), and the United States Pharmacopeia (USP) for the specific purpose of coining suitable, acceptable, nonproprietary names in the drug field.

USRDA: United States Recommended Daily Allowance.

Xerosis: a condition of dryness.

Zein: protein from corn.

Zyme: a fermenting substance.

Bibliography and Recommended Reading

I owe a great debt of thanks to the many scientists, doctors, nutritionists, professors, and researchers whose painstaking and all too often unrewarding work in the field of vitamins and nutrition has made this book possible.

The following list is given to show my sincere appreciation and make known the foundation upon which I have built my knowledge. Many of the books are highly technical and confusing for the layman, meant as they are for professionals in the field. But others, which I have marked with an asterisk, I heartily commend to you for further reading and a healthier future.

*Abrahamson, E. M., and Pezet, A. W. *Body, Mind and Sugar.* New York: Avon Books, 1977.

*Abravanel, Elliot D., M.D., and King, Elizabeth A. *Anti-Craving Weight Loss Diet.* New York: Bantam Books, 1990.

*Adams, Ruth. *The Complete Home Guide to All the Vitamins.* New York: Larchmont Books, 1972.

*Adams, Ruth, and Murray, Frank. *Minerals: Kill or Cure.* New York: Larchmont Books, 1976.

*Aguilar, Nona. *Totally Natural Beauty.* New York: Rawson Associates Publishers, 1977.

*Airola, Paavo. *Are You Confused?* Phoenix, AZ: Health Plus, 1972.

*————. *How to Get Well.* Phoenix, AZ: Health Plus, 1975.

*————. *Hypoglycemia, A Better Approach.* Phoenix, AZ: Health Plus, 1977.

Amberson, Rosanne. *Raising Your Cat.* New York: Bonanza Books, 1969.

Arnot, Robert, M.D. "Carbo Unloading." *Men's Health* (June 1997).

*Atkins, Robert C. *Dr. Atkins' Diet Revolution.* New York: David McKay, 1972.

*———. *Dr. Atkins' Nutrition Breakthrough.* New York: William Morrow and Company, Inc., 1981.

*———. *Dr. Atkins' New Diet Revolution.* New York: Avon Books, 1997.

*Bailey, Hubert. *Vitamin E: Your Key to a Healthy Heart.* New York: ARC Books, 1964, 1966.

*Balch, James F., and Balch, Phyllis A. *Prescription for Nutritional Healing: Second Edition.* Garden City, N.Y.: Avery, 1997.

*Bicks, Jane R., D.V.M. *Dr. Jane's 30 Days to a Healthier, Happier Cat: The Complete Guide to Nutrition and Health.* New York: Perigee, 1997.

Bieri, John G. "Fat-soluble vitamins in the eighth revision of the Recommended Dietary Allowances." *Journal of the American Dietetic Association* 64 (February 1974).

Blood: The River of Life. American National Red Cross, 1976.

*Bolles, Edmund Blair. *Learning to Live with Chronic Fatigue Syndrome.* New York: Dell Medical Library, 1990.

*Borek, Carmia. *Maximize Your Health-Span with Antioxidants: The Baby Boomer's Guide.* New Canaan, CT: Keats Publishing Co., 1995.

*———. "Aging Gracefully with Antioxidants." *Nutrition Science News* (March 1998).

*Borsaak, Henry. *Vitamins: What They Are and How They Can Benefit You.* New York: Pyramid Books, 1971.

"Bread: You Can't Judge a Loaf by Its Color." *Consumer Reports* 41 (May 1976).

*Bricklin, Mark. *Practical Encyclopedia of Natural Healing.* Emmaus, PA: Rodale Press, 1976.

*———. *Prevention Magazine's Nutrition Advisor.* Emmaus, PA: Rodale Press, 1993.

Brody, Jane E. "Cancer-blocking Agents Found in Foods." *New York Times* (March 6 1979).

*———. *The New York Times Guide to Personal Health.* New York: Times Books, 1982.

———. "In Vitamin Mania, Millions Take a Gamble on Health." *New York Times* (October 26, 1997).

*Burack, Richard, with Fox, Fred J. *New Handbook of Prescription Drugs.* New York: Pantheon Books, 1967.

Burton, Benjamin. *Human Nutrition.* 3rd ed. New York: McGraw-Hill, 1976.

"Buying Beef." *Consumer Reports* 39 (September 1974).

*Carper, Jean. *Miracle Cures.* New York: HarperCollins, 1997.

*Carr, William H. A. *The Basic Book of the Cat.* New York: Gramercy Publishing Co., 1963.

*Chapman, Esther. *How To Use the 12 Tissue Salts.* New York: Pyramid Books, 1977.

*"Chronic Fatigue Syndrome: A Modern Medical Mystery." *Newsweek* (November 12, 1990).

Cichoke, Anthony J. "Nutritional Libido Boosters." *Health Foods Business* (June 1998).

*Clark, Linda. *The Best of Linda Clark.* New Canaan, CT: Keats Publishing Co., 1976.

*———. *Know Your Nutrition.* New Canaan, CT: Keats Publishing Co., 1973.

*———. *Secrets of Health and Beauty.* New York: Jove Publications, 1977.

*Consumer Reports, Editors of. *The Medicine Show.* Mount Vernon, N.Y.: Consumers Union, 1981.

Cooper, Barber, Mitchell, Rynberge, Green. *Nutrition in Health and Disease.* New York: Lippincott, 1963.

Cooper, Kenneth H., M.D. *Overcoming Hypertension.* New York: Bantam Books, 1990.

Cowley, Geoffrey, and Underwood, Anne. "Memory." *Newsweek* (June 15, 1998).

Cumulative Index for Journal of Applied Nutrition. La Habra, CA: International College of Applied Nutrition, 1947–76, 1976.

*Davis, Adelle. *Let's Eat Right to Keep Fit.* New York: Harcourt, Brace and World, 1954.

*————. *Let's Get Well.* New York: Harcourt, Brace and World, 1965.

*————. *Let's Have Healthy Children.* 2nd ed. New York: Harcourt, Brace and World, 1959.

*Dufty, William. *Sugar Blues.* Pennsylvania: Chilton Book Co., 1975.

*Ebon, Martin. *Which Vitamins Do You Need?* New York: Bantam Books, 1974.

Farrar, Jill. "Health & Fitness." *Vogue Australia* (December 1990).

Flynn, Margaret A. "The Cholesterol Controversy." *Journal of the American Pharmacy* NS18 (May 1978).

"Food Facts Talk Back." *Journal of the American Dietetic Association,* 1977.

*Frank, Benjamin S. *No-Aging Diet.* New York: Dial, 1976.

*Fredericks, Carlton. *Eating Right for You.* New York: Grosset and Dunlap, 1972.

*————. *Look Younger/Feel Healthier.* New York: Grosset and Dunlap, 1977.

*————. *Psycho Nutrients.* New York: Grosset and Dunlap, 1975.

*Gomez, Joan, and Gerch, Marvin J. *Dictionary of Symptoms.* New York: Stein and Day, 1963.

Goodhart, Robert S., and Shills, Maurice E. *Modern Nutrition in Health and Disease.* 5th ed. Philadelphia: Lea and Febiger, 1973.

*Graedon, Joel. *The People's Pharmacy.* New York: St. Martin's Press, 1976.

*Graedon, Joel and Teresa, Ph.D. *The People's Guide to Deadly Drug Interactions.* New York: St. Martin's Press, 1995.

Guidelines for the Eradication of Iron Deficiency Anemia. New York: International Nutritional Anemia Consultative Group (INACG), 1976.

Guidelines for the Eradication of Vitamin-A Deficiency and Xerophthalmia. International Vitamin-A Consultative Group (IVACG).

Harper, Alfred E. "Recommended Dietary Allowances: Are They What We Think They Are?" *Journal of the American Dietetic Association* 64 (February 1974).

Head, Anthony. "Diet Watch: Resolutions for the Happy—and Healthy—New Year." *Health News & Views* (January 1998).

Hermann, Mindy. "A Call for Calcium." *Modern Maturity* (March/April 1998).

Holvey, David, ed. *The Merck Manual.* 12th ed. Rahway, NJ: Merck and Co., 1972.

Howe, Phyllis S. *Basic Nutrition in Health and Disease.* 6th ed. Philadelphia: W.B. Saunders Co., 1976.

"How Nutritious Are Fast-Food Meals?" *Consumer Reports* (May 1975).

*Hunter, B. T. *The Natural Foods Primer.* New York: Simon and Schuster, 1972.

Index of Nutrition Education Materials. Washington, DC: Nutrition Foundation, 1977.

Jones, Cindy, Ph.D. "Rosemary's Whole Plant Properties Counter Cancer." *Nutrition Science News* (March 1998).

Journal of Applied Nutrition. International College of Applied Nutrition, La Habra, CA, 1974–76.

*Karelitz, Samuel. *When Your Child Is Ill.* New York: Random House, 1969.

Katz, Marcella. *Vitamins, Food, and Your Health.* Public Affairs Committee, 1971, 1975.

Knowlton, Leslie. "Vitamins: Why They're Vital." *Los Angeles Times* (April 3, 1998).

*Kordel, L. *Health Through Nutrition.* New York: MacFadden-Bartell, 1971.

*Kowalsi, Robert E. *The 8-Week Cholesterol Cure.* New York: Harper and Row, 1987.

Lewin, Renate. "Chronic Fatigue Syndrome: It's Not All in Your Head." *Let's Live,* February 1991.

Lin, Judith and Goldstein, Laura. "The New Cholesterol Busters." *Prevention,* May 1998.

*Linde, Shirley. *The Whole Health Catalog.* New York: Rawson Associates Publishers, 1977.

"The Losing Formula." *Newsweek* (April 30, 1990).

*Lucas, Richard. *Nature's Medicines.* New York: Prentice-Hall, 1965.

"Marijuana: The Health Questions." *Consumer Reports* 40 (March 1975).

*Martin, Clement, G. *Low Blood Sugar: The Hidden Menace of Hypoglycemia.* New York: Arco Publishing Co., 1976.

Martin, Marvin. *Great Vitamin Mystery.* Rosemont, IL: National Dairy Council, 1978.

*Mayer, Jean. *A Diet for Living.* New York: David McKay, 1975.

McCord, Holly, RD. "Ins and 'Oats' of Soluble Fiber." *Prevention* (July 1997).

———. "Revealed: How Tofu Helps Your Ticker." *Prevention* (January 1997).

*McGinnis, Terri. *The Well Cat Book.* New York: Random House-Bookworks, 1975.

*———. *The Well Dog Book.* New York: Random House-Bookworks, 1974.

The Merck Manual of Medical Information: Home Edition. Whitehouse Station, NJ: Merck & Co., Inc., 1997.

Miller, Sue. "A Natural Mood Booster." *Newsweek* (May 5, 1997).

*Mindell, Earl. *Earl Mindell's Anti-Aging Bible.* New York: Fireside, 1996.

*———. *Earl Mindell's Herb Bible.* New York: Fireside, 1992.

*———. *Earl Mindell's Nutrition & Health for Dogs.* Rocklin, CA: Prima Publishing, 1998.

*———. *Earl Mindell's Secret Remedies.* New York: Fireside, 1997.

*———. *Earl Mindell's Soy Miracle.* New York: Fireside, 1995.

*———. *Earl Mindell's Supplement Bible.* New York: Fireside, 1998.

*———, and Hopkins, Virginia. *Prescription Alternatives.* New Canaan, CT: Keats, 1998.

Mitchell, Helen S. "Recommended Dietary Allowances Up to Date." *Journal of the American Dietetic Association* 64 (February 1974).

National Health Federation Bulletin. November 1973.

National Research Council. *Recommended Dietary Allowances.* 8th ed., revised. Washington, DC: National Academy of Sciences, 1974.

National Research Council. *Recommended Dietary Allowances.* 10th ed. Washington, DC: National Academy Press, 1989.

*Newbold, H. L. *Dr. Newbold's Revolutionary New Discovery About Weight Loss.* New York: Rawson Associates Publishers, 1977.

*————. *Mega-Nutrients for Your Nerves.* New York: Peter H. Wyden, Publisher, 1973.

*Null, Gary. *The Natural Organic Beauty Book.* New York: Dell, 1972.

*Null, Gary and Steve. *The Complete Book of Nutrition.* New York: Dell, 1972.

**Nutrition Almanac.* New York: McGraw-Hill, 1973.

Nutrition—Applied Personally. La Habra, CA: International College of Applied Nutrition, 1978.

Nutrition Information Resources for the Whole Family. National Nutrition Education Clearing House, 1978.

Nutrition Labeling: How It Can Work for You. National Nutrition Consortium, American Dietetic Association, 1975.

Nutrition Source Book. Rosemont, IL: National Dairy Council, 1978.

"Organic Chemicals in Water: A Major Health Concern." *Consumer Reports* 69 (February 1983).

*Passwater, Richard A. *Super Nutrition.* New York: Dial, 1975.

————. *The New Supernutrition.* New York: Pocket Books, 1991.

*Pauling, Linus. *Vitamin C and the Common Cold.* New York: Bantam Books, 1971.

*Pearson, Durk, and Shaw, Sandy. *Life Extension.* New York: Warner Books, 1983.

Pelton, Ross, R.Ph., Ph.D. "Drug-Induced Nutritional Deficiencies." *Natural Pharmacy* (June 1998).

Pennington, Jean A. T., Ph.D. et al. *Bowes and Church's Food Values of Portions Commonly Used.* 17th ed. New York: Lippincott, 1997.

Piltz, Albert. *How Your Body Uses Food.* Rosemont, IL: National Dairy Council, 1960.

*Pommery, Jean. *What to Do till the Veterinarian Comes.* Radnor, PA: Chilton Book Company, 1976.

"Present Knowledge in Nutrition." *Nutrition Reviews.* Nutrition Foundation, Inc., 1976.

*Pritikin, Nathan. *The Pritikin Permanent Weight-Loss Manual.* New York: Grosset & Dunlap, 1981.

*Rodale, J. I. *The Complete Book of Minerals for Health.* 4th ed. Emmaus, PA: Rodale Books, 1976.

*———. *The Encyclopedia of Common Diseases.* Emmaus, PA: Rodale Press, 1976.

Roman, Mark. "Your Sexual Appetite." *Men's Health* (September 1997).

*Rosenberg, Harold, and Feldzaman, A.N. *Doctor's Book of Vitamin Therapy: Megavitamins for Health.* New York: Putnam's, 1974.

*Schiffman, Susan S., and Scobey, Joan. *The Nutri/System Flavor Set-Point Weight-Loss Cookbook.* Boston: Little Brown and Company, 1990.

*Seaman, Barbara, Gideon. *Women and the Crisis in Sex Hormones.* New York: Rawson Associates Publishers, 1977.

*Sears, Barry, Ph.D. *Mastering the Zone.* New York: Reagan Books/HarperCollins, 1997.

Shapiro, Laura. "Fat, Fatter: But Who's Counting?" *Newsweek* (June 15, 1998).

*Shute, Wilfrid E., and Taub, Harold J. *Vitamin E for Ailing and Healthy Hearts.* New York: Pyramid Books, 1969.

*Sinopoulus, Artemis P., M.D., and Robinson, Jo. *The Omega Plan.* New York: HarperCollins, 1998.

*Smith, Lendon, M.D. *Feed Yourself Right.* New York: McGraw-Hill, 1983.

*Spock, Benjamin. *Baby and Child Care.* New York: Simon and Schuster, 1976.

Starr, Sara. "Ten Supplements That Promise a Younger Future." *Health Foods Business* (October 1997).

*Steinman, David. *Diet for a Poisoned Planet.* New York: Harmony Brooks, Crown Publishers, 1990.

*Stoff, Jesse A., M.D. *Chronic Fatigue Syndrome: The Hidden Epidemic.* New York: Harper and Row, 1988.

Thompson, Trisha. "Eat Your Heart Out?" *Fame* (February 1990).

"Too Much Sugar." *Consumer Reports* 43 (March 1973).

Underwood, Eric J. *Trace Elements in Human and Animal Nutrition.* 4th ed. New York: Academic Press, 1977.

United Nations, Food and Agriculture Organization. *Calorie Requirements,* 1957, 1972.

U.S. Department of Agriculture. *Amino Acid Content of Food,* by M. L. Orr and B. K. Watt. 1957; rev. 1968.

U.S. Department of Agriculture. Consumer and Food Economics Institute, Agricultural Research Service. *Composition of Foods: Raw, Processed, Prepared,* by Bernice K. Watt and Annabel L. Merrill, 1975.

U.S. Department of Agriculture. *Energy Value of Foods: Basis and Derivation,* by Annabel L. Merrill and Bernice K. Watt, 1973.

U.S. Department of Agriculture. *Nutritive Value of American Foods,* by Catherine F. Adams, 1975.

U.S. Department of Health, Education and Welfare. *Consumer Health Education: A Directory,* 1975.

U.S. Department of Health, Education and Welfare. *Ten-State Nutrition Survey.* Washington, D.C.: U.S. Government Printing Office, 1968–70.

"The U.S. Food and Drug Administration: On Food and Drugs." *Consumer Reports* 38 (March 1973).

U.S. President's Council on Physical Fitness and Sports. *Exercise and Weight Control,* by Robert E. Johnson. Urbana, IL: University of Illinois Press, 1967.

U.S. Senate. Select Committee on Nutrition and Human Needs. *Diet and Killer Diseases with Press Reaction and Additional Information.* Washington, DC: U.S. Government Printing Office, 1977.

U.S. Senate. Select Committee on Nutrition and Human Needs. *National Nutrition Policy: Nutrition and the Consumer II.* Washington, DC: U.S. Government Printing Office, 1974.

"Vitamin-Mineral Safety, Toxicity and Misuse." *Journal of the American Dietetic Association,* 1978.

*Wade, Carlson. *Magic Minerals.* West Nyack, NY: Parker Publishing Co., 1967.

*———. *Miracle Protein.* West Nyack, NY: Parker Publishing Co., 1975.

*———. *Vitamin E: The Rejuvenation Vitamin.* New York: Award Books, 1970.

Walker, Morton, D.P.M. "New Information on Calcium." *Health Foods Business* (December 1997).

"Weigh too much? How to figure it out." *USA Today* (February 2, 1998).

*Whelan, Elizabeth, M., Ph.D,. and Stare, Fredrick, J., M.D. *The 100% Natural, Purely Organic, Cholesterol-Free, Megavitamin, Low-Carbohydrate Nutrition Hoax.* New York: Atheneum, 1983.

"Which Cereals Are Most Nutritious?" *Consumer Reports* 40 (February 1975).

Williams, Roger J. *Nutrition Against Disease.* New York: Pitman Publishers, 1971.

*Winter, Ruth. *A Consumer's Dictionary of Food Additives.* New York: Crown, 1973.

*Young, Klein, Beyer. *Recreational Drugs.* New York: Macmillan, 1977.

*Yudkin, John. *Sweet and Dangerous.* New York: Peter H. Wyden, 1972.

Zimmerman, Marcia, C.N. "Is DHEA an Antidote to Aging?" *Nutrition Science News* (October, 1996).

Index